DEAR WRITER...
DEAR ACTRESS...

Dear Writer...
Dear Actress...

THE LOVE LETTERS OF
OLGA KNIPPER AND ANTON CHEKHOV

Selected, translated and edited by

Jean Benedetti

METHUEN

First published in Great Britain in 1996
by Methuen Drama
First published in paperback in 1998
Reissued in this edition in 2007 by Methuen

1

Methuen Publishing Ltd
11–12 Buckingham Gate
London SW1E 6LB

www.methuen.co.uk

A CIP catalogue record for this book is available from the
British Library

ISBN 10: 0-413-77637-9
ISBN 13: 9780-413-77637-2

Printed and bound in Great Britain by
Bookmarque Limited, Croydon, Surrey

To the Happy Few
of Les Fontenelles

CONTENTS

INTRODUCTION

The friendship, liaison and marriage of Olga Knipper and Anton Chekhov is one of the most extraordinary love stories in the history of the theatre. She was thirty when they met, he thirty-eight, and already in the advanced stages of tuberculosis. Their relationship lasted five years, from April 1899 to July 1904 when he died.

Olga Leonardovna Knipper was born in the small provincial town of Glazov in 1868, of German parents. Her father became a Russian citizen and she was given a normal middle-class upbringing. Chekhov first saw her in the autumn of 1898 when she was an unknown. He attended a rehearsal of *The Seagull* which the newly formed Moscow Art Theatre was intending to stage. He later attended a rehearsal of *Tsar Fyodor Ioannovich*, the opening production of the season. He was much taken with her performance, and with her, and felt, when the play opened, she did not receive the critical attention she deserved. Her performance as Arkadina in *The Seagull*, a role for which she was, in fact, too young, established her as a leading actress and a firm favourite with Moscow audiences. She went on to play Elena in *Uncle Vanya* in the second season, 1899–1900. Then followed the two great roles Chekhov wrote specially for her, Masha in *Three Sisters* and Ranevskaya in *The Cherry Orchard*. Although she continued to act for some fifty years after Chekhov's death, nothing, except perhaps Natalya Petrovna in *A Month in the Country*, could match these roles. They became a part of her. Late in life she attended a gala evening at the Moscow Art Theatre, in which the parting of Masha and Vershinin in *Three Sisters* was performed. At the climactic moment, a strong deep voice rang out from one of the boxes. It was the eighty-year-old Knipper, unable to restrain herself from speaking the line before the unfortunate young actress on stage could get it out. It was 'her' line.

It is one of the ironies of their story that circumstances kept them apart at the very moment when their love was beginning to blossom. Knipper's increasing commitments to the Art Theatre kept her in Moscow, while he was obliged to live in Yalta, his 'hot Siberia' as he called it, in order to stay alive. Few dramatists can have been so cruelly fated as Chekhov. His doctors' insistence that he live in Yalta during the cold winter months meant that he could not attend the opening nights of his plays. He did not see *The Seagull* until a special performance was put on for him in May 1899. He never saw Knipper in *Uncle Vanya*; he had to wait months before seeing *Three Sisters*; and while he attended the first night of *The Cherry Orchard,* it is not certain that he saw the whole show.[1] He had to rely on letters, not all of which were reliable, for news of his plays. Knipper was his lifeline, since she could keep him informed as to what was happening in rehearsal and performance from the inside.

The months of separation they had to endure made them, at times, desperate. Their misfortune, however, is our gain, since we are able to follow their story through the many hundreds of letters they exchanged.

Neither could ever have imagined that their private correspondence would be made public. It reveals them too glaringly, at times too unflatteringly; it bears all the marks, all the inconsequence, of spontaneity, moving from expressions of frustration and anger or of undying devotion to home remedies for baldness within a few lines. That is their value and their fascination.

These letters also reveal the living material out of which Chekhov's plays were fashioned. His habitual untidiness, his unkempt state, to which allusion is often made, his passion for fishing, reveal him as the model for Trigorin in *The Seagull*, even down to note-taking. His passion for gardening, for planting flowers and shrubs, links him to Astrov (a doctor) in *Uncle Vanya*. Knipper's writing often takes on the colour of the character she is playing. During the rehearsals and performances of *Three Sisters*, her style becomes Masha-like.

Temperamentally, no two people could have been more different. Knipper was impetuous: the creature, not to say the victim, of her impulses and emotions, both as a person and an artist. She was, on the whole, a hit-or-miss artist, relying on instinct to get her to the heart of a role. Sometimes she could be quite wrong in her judgements, as in *Uncle Vanya* and *Three Sisters* and had to be steered by Stanislavski, Nemirovich-Danchenko and even Chekhov himself somewhat unwillingly in the right direction. Stanislavski thought her lazy and told her so. She lacked a basic working method which would get her out of trouble when instinct failed. How good an actress she actually was is

1. See Viktor Borovsky, *Discord in the Cherry Orchard,* in *Encounter,* January/February 1990.

difficult to judge. She became an icon of Soviet art. No breath of criticism was allowed to touch her, nothing could be said to tarnish her reputation. However, when Nemirovich staged *Three Sisters* again in later years with another actress playing Masha, he is reported to have said, 'Maybe this time I'll be able to get it right.' But, it would seem that when she was good, she was very, very good and her passionate energy and spontaneity carried audiences away.

Chekhov was reserved, guarded, shying away from all direct expression of feeling, taking refuge in irony or banter. Hyper-sensitive and vulnerable, he had built up such an efficient defence system he found it almost impossible to let it go; he was trapped in it. Knipper often found this inability ever to express any emotion seriously both disturbing and annoying. Even after they had become lovers, she was worried by his refusal to call her by her proper name, Olga. But then Chekhov rarely called himself by his real name, preferring Antoine, Antonino, Antonius academicus and, as their relationship developed into marriage and he began to feel their separation more and more acutely, he found a series of pet names – doggie, baboon, granny, cricket, sperm whale and, not surprisingly, little German – for her. The more he missed her, the more outlandish the names became. Only occasionally does real emotion show through and then the pain is all too evident.

Knipper was not Chekhov's first lover, but she was the only one he ever thought of marrying. It is questionable whether he would have taken this ultimate step had Knipper not insisted. She felt, and rightly, that their situation ought to be regularized. Russian society in 1900 did not tolerate open cohabitation easily. Gorki created a scandal by his blatant affair with another Art Theatre actress, Andreeva. Most people in the Art Theatre assumed that Knipper and Chekhov had secretly married long before the actual event took place. But mainly Knipper felt embarrassed faced with Chekhov's mother and sister, Masha, staying as their guest and having to pretend that she and Anton were 'just good friends'.

As they circled round the question of marriage, many games were played. They teased each other with rumours of fictitious marriages. He encouraged rumours that he had married the simple, uneducated daughter of a local priest in Yalta – and there were other candidates. She retaliated with constant references to his lifelong friend, Vishnievski, a fellow actor in the Art Theatre company. It was a shrewd riposte. Chekhov's jealousy pierces through the banter at moments.

Perhaps part of the reason for Chekhov's reluctance to marry was his sister, Masha. She had dedicated her life to him. A schoolmistress by profession, she never married, but acted as his housekeeper, nurse, agent and business manager, negotiating on his behalf, collecting his royalties. She was deeply shocked by Chekhov's announcement that he was going to marry Knipper, which, typically, he sprung on her without warning. Chekhov, however, was careful to give her all sorts of assurances. In a letter of June 2 1901, he promised her that neither his life, nor the lives of those closest to him, would be changed by his marriage and that he would, of course, continue to live in Yalta. On June 4 he wrote again, reiterating his assurances and pointing out that Knipper had her own income, so that there would be no financial implications. It was a marriage and no marriage.

Chekhov's assurances to his sister echo sentiments he had expressed three years before he even met Knipper. Writing to his friend Suvorin in 1895, he stated:

> All right, I'll get married if that is what you want. But my conditions are: everything must be as it was, i.e. she must live in Moscow and I in the country and I'll go and visit her. I can't bear happiness that continues either from day to day or from morning to morning. I promise to be a good husband, but find me the kind of wife who, like the moon, doesn't appear in my sky every day.

After the marriage, Masha wrote an extraordinary letter to Knipper more or less marking out the frontiers. She attempted a light tone, but her resentment is clear. She expresses the fear that marriage will put a strain on Anton, who is a sick man. Why marriage should be more of a strain than a regular affair is not clear. After all, as Mrs Patrick Campbell assures us, marriage provides the 'deep, deep peace of the double bed after the hurly-burly of the *chaise longue*'. Masha goes on to warn Knipper that if she behaves like Natasha in *Three Sisters*, she will strangle her with her bare hands. The comparison with Natasha, a vulgar, tasteless and insensitive creature, is unflattering but apt. Natasha marries the brother, moves in, takes over and destroys the harmony of the household.

Chekhov lived in fact, in a *ménage à trois*. Though married to him, Knipper continued essentially to function as a mistress, providing physical and emotional pleasure and diversion for short periods while Masha retained her position as the centre of the household. Sometimes, Olga felt that Chekhov reserved his serious discussions for his sister, while treating her merely as 'someone nice to have around', someone to be shielded from important issues, a 'doll'. Once she pointedly asked him whether he did not have 'stereotyped ideas about women being silly'. When staying in Yalta, she was careful never to encroach on Masha's position, to behave as a 'visitor'. Even when she tried to set up a home in Moscow, looking for an apartment in which Anton could live for a greater part of the year and so get away from his Yalta 'prison', it was not a home for her and Anton alone. She always had to provide 'Masha's room'.

Masha cast a long shadow on the marriage. Both she and Olga realized, however, the necessity to reach an accommodation and both managed it well. Only once, in the summer of 1902, did the latent hostility break into the open.

Chekhov and Olga's relationship settled into a fixed pattern very early. Knipper was committed to the Art Theatre in Moscow from September to March and the season was usually followed by a tour in Petersburg. After that, from mid-April to the end of August, she was free to be a wife. Their winter separations were a great ordeal and desperate attempts were made to enable Chekhov to spend more time in Moscow, if the right apartment could be found and if the weather was right.

The weather is a constant topic in their correspondence. Warmth and sunshine, or dry frost were the condition of Chekhov's well-being. A few extra warm days in Moscow meant the possibility of a visit. They pleaded with the Art Theatre to release Olga for a few days so that she could go to Yalta, but she was playing a series of leading roles. The train journey to Yalta took two or three days and so a forty-eight-hour visit required a week's absence. What infuriated Chekhov was the fact that the weather in Yalta was by no means as good as it was reputed to be, and often worse than in Moscow.

Knipper and Chekhov promised to write to each other every day and, by and large, kept their promise. They were, however, the victims of distance and the postal service. Letters were late and crossed, so that both were regularly in the dark about each other's current activities and, more importantly, state of health. The result was often the cry 'Why no letters?' and a flurry of telegrams.

They kept each other informed of their daily routine. Knipper was kept busy at the Art Theatre both rehearsing and performing and kept Chekhov abreast of events. She was used by both Stanislavski and Nemirovich-Danchenko as a go-between to put pressure on her husband for a new play.

She was also quite open about her taste for good living. She liked nothing better than to stay up half the night eating, drinking and talking to friends. Chekhov accepted this, and only once raised an objection. He disapproved of her going to Aumont's theatre. Charles Aumont was a Frenchman of dubious reputation, who ran a theatre known for presenting low farce. It was only frequented by women of a certain type, certainly not the respectable wives of well-known authors. Knipper attempted to laugh this off as she did her other excesses, signing herself on occasion, 'your dissolute wife'.

Chekhov on his side gave accounts of his life in Yalta, his gardening, his visits to Tolstoi and Gorki, his attempts to write, frequently complaining of the constant flow of unwanted visitors. This is a typical Chekhovian paradox. Chekhov needed human presence. He wrote to Gorki that when he talked of 'boredom' it was not in the sense of *'ennui'* or *'Weltschmerz'*; he simply meant there was nobody around.

Only in the last months of Chekhov's life were he and Olga truly together and, as Chekhov's health declined, Knipper's sense of remorse and self-reproach at not being a 'proper wife' grew. This emerges clearly in her posthumous diary, in which all her guilt surfaces, as does a frank admission of the tensions between her and Masha which she had carefully concealed. If only she had given up the theatre...

Dear Writer ... Dear Actress does not pretend to be a biographical study either of Chekhov or Knipper, that is a matter for specialists. The aim is to feel, not interpret, their lives. It offers a selection of their most intimate letters, to reveal the way in which they experienced themselves, not the way others saw, or see, them. It can be read as a kind of novel.

A NOTE ON THE EDITING

The text of the letters is to be found in the two volumes of the Chekhov-Knipper correspondence published in Moscow in 1934 and 1936 and completed in Volume I of the two-volume edition of Knipper's letters, published in Moscow in 1972. Many of the original letters contained matter which was cut by the authorities as unsuitable – disparaging remarks about, for example, Stanislavski, another Soviet untouchable. In Chekhov's case, it is possible to restore these cuts from the thirteen-volume edition of his correspondence. In Knipper's case, we shall have to wait until a new Russian edition of her letters appears, although some material can be found in the Notes to the Chekhov edition. Some letters have, therefore, been pieced together from these sources.

While many of Chekhov's letters have been published, either in whole or in part, Knipper's correspondence remains widely unknown. This book is therefore biased towards her point of view.

In selecting and editing these letters, I have tried to chart the course of their relationship, omitting material which refers to friends and acquaintances that would require a plethora of footnotes and not aid the reader's understanding. I have also omitted details of rehearsals of plays, except for Chekhov's own, which do not illuminate their own inner lives. I have tried not to duplicate material to be found in *The Moscow Art Theatre Letters*, although some overlap has been unavoidable.

Where possible, the original (not always grammatical) punctuation has been preserved, as it indicates the informal and often rushed nature of their correspondence. Similarly, the use of numerals and abbreviations has been preserved. Some names have been changed, surnames being substituted for patronymics. Both Knipper and Chekhov refer to Alekseev, Stanislavski's real name, but Stanislavski has been substituted throughout as being more familiar to readers. The same holds for other members of the Art Theatre company who had stage names – for example, Sanin (real name Schoenberg). The letters also sometimes contain words or sentences in Roman script. These have been indicated by italics.

A Note on the Editing

One important language feature that has been impossible to reproduce is the use of the formal second person plural *vy* (French *vous*) and the intimate *ty* (French *tu*). In the section 'Friend', both Knipper and Chekhov use *vy* whereas in 'Lover' they have changed to the intimate *ty*, marking a new stage in their relationship.

I have added as little commentary of my own as possible. The linking passages are edited extracts from Knipper's own *Memoir* published in the 1934 Volume I of the *Correspondence*.

I am indebted to Harvey Pincher's invaluable book *Chekhov's Leading Lady* (John Murray, 1979) and Ernest J. Simmons standard biography of Chekhov (University of Chicago Press, 1962) for biographical details.

Friend

1899

Knipper, *Memoirs*

There are moments in life that seem like a glorious celebration. Such was 1898 for me, the year I finished drama school, the year the Moscow Art Theatre opened, the year I met Anton Chekhov. So were the years that followed, years of creative joy, of work, of the fullness of love, of confidence, of high emotion and deep faith. My path to the stage was a difficult one. I was born into a family which did not tolerate poverty. My father was a scientist and an engineer and for a short while managed a factory in Glazov, where I was born. My parents came to Moscow when I was two and I have lived here ever since. My mother was a highly gifted musician, she had a fine voice and was a good pianist but at my father's insistence, and for the sake of the family, did not play professionally or even go to the *conservatoire*. After my father's death, when her life of comparative ease came to an end, she became a teacher and professor of singing at the Philharmonic School. She sometimes took part in concerts but found it difficult to come to terms with her failure to have a career. After finishing my education at a private school, I led the life then considered suitable for a 'young lady'. I passed my time in languages, music and drawing. My father had hopes I might become an artist or a translator – I translated stories from my earliest years and enjoyed it. I was the only girl in the family and I was pampered and kept well away from real life. In our childhood and early youth, we put on shows every year. We turned the hall at home into a theatre and put on amateur shows for our friends and acted at their homes, too and in charity evenings. But when I was twenty and we were seriously thinking of starting an amateur dramatic circle, my father, seeing how keen I was, gently but quite categorically put an end to such thoughts and I went on living in a kind of prison, doing this and that, but not seeing the point of it all. After my father's death, our financial difficulties brought about radical change. We had to think about earning a crust of bread because all we had left was a large, rented, private apartment, five servants and debts. We transformed the apartment, got rid of the servants and set to work with incredible energy, as though inspired. We created a 'commune' with my mother's brothers (one, Karl, was a doctor, the other, Sasha, an army officer[1]) and worked long and hard. My mother gave singing lessons and I taught music. My younger brother was a student and became a répétiteur, my older brother was already working as an engineer in the Caucasus. It was a time of great personal change, I turned from a 'young lady' into a free individual, earning my own living and, at first, finding it all very colourful. But my long-standing dreams of going into the theatre grew ever stronger. Little by little the stage became a dream I had to fulfil. I could think of no other life than that of an actress. Unbeknown to my mother, I prepared my entry to the Maly Theatre drama school, I was received very kindly and spent several months there when, suddenly, a 'test' was announced, after which it was suggested to me that I should leave the school, but stated clearly that I would not be allowed to proceed to the following year. That was pure mockery. It later transpired that I was the only one out of four students who did not have a protector and that they had to take someone who had – a powerful protector. The school could not refuse. It was a terrible blow because the theatre meant everything to me even then – to be or not to be – sun or darkness. My mother, seeing how downcast I was, and despite the fact that she had been opposed all along to my going on the stage, arranged with her colleagues at the Philharmonic School for me to enter the Drama Department, although entry had already been closed for a month. I spent three years studying with Nemirovich-Danchenko and A.A. Fedotov, rushing through classes so I could earn my living and pay for my tuition. In the winter of 1897–8 I finished my course. We had already heard vague rumours a new, 'special' kind of theatre was to be created in Moscow. The picturesque figure of Stanislavski, with his silver hair and black moustache had already appeared in the school with Sanin's[2] characteristic form at his side; they saw a rehearsal of *La Locandiera*[3] and our hearts thumped with excitement. In midwinter, Nemirovich-Danchenko told Savitskaya, Meyerhold and me that we were to be members of the theatre and

1. Known in the family as the 'Cut-throat' because of his wild drinking and fits of depression.
2. Sanin, Aleksandr Akimovich (real name Schoenberg, 1869–1956), friend of Stanislavski, actor and director at the Art Theatre.
3. By Carlo Goldoni.

we kept that a tight secret. Nemirovich-Danchenko spoke of *The Seagull* with passion and wanted to produce it for our final examination. This took place on the stage of the Maly Theatre. I had finally reached my goal, my dream had come true, I was an actress and in a new, special kind of theatre. Chekhov and I met for the first time on September 9 1898: a special, a memorable day ... I'll never forget how overcome with fright I had been the previous day when I read the notice Nemirovich-Danchenko had put up telling us Chekhov would be at the rehearsal of *The Seagull* on the 9th, or the unusual mood I was in when I went to the Hunting Club where we were rehearsing. We were all captivated by the extraordinarily subtle charm of his personality, his simplicity, his inability to 'teach' or 'demonstrate'. We didn't know what to say ... And he looked at us, first smiling, then suddenly extraordinarily serious. When we asked Chekhov anything, his answers were rather unexpected, somehow tangential, generalized. We didn't know whether to take his remarks seriously or as a joke. But that was only in the first few minutes; then we could feel these offhand, seemingly casual remarks sinking in, and the essence of the man began to emerge from one subtle hint. Chekhov put in a second appearance at rehearsals for *Tsar Fyodor*[4] in our new theatre, the Hermitage where we proposed to play the season. We were rehearsing in the evening in the grey, cold, unfinished premises. Without a floor, with candle-ends in bottles instead of lights, muffled up in our overcoats ... And it was a joy to think that out there in the dark empty stalls there was a 'soul' we all loved, listening to us. Then, on a grey, rainy day he left for the south, for Yalta, for which he had no liking. In the spring, Chekhov came to Moscow. Of course we wanted him to see *The Seagull* but we didn't have our own theatre. We rehearsed where we could, taking private theatres. One evening we decided to take the Paradiz, a touring theatre. It was unheated, the sets weren't ours, the whole place was depressing after 'our' new theatre. That spring I got to know Chekhov and his sweet family better. I had met his sister, Masha, during the winter, and we took to each other most at once. I remember Vishnievski[5] brought her to my dressing-room during a performance of *The Seagull*. I remember joyous, sunny days, the first day of Easter, the joyful ringing of the bells, filling the spring air

---

4. *Tsar Fyodor Ioannovich* by Aleksei Tolstoi, the inaugural production of the Moscow Art Theatre.
5. Aleksandr Leonidovich Vishnievski (1861–1943), actor, founder member of the Moscow Art Theatre.

with a kind of pleasure, full of expectation. And, on that first Easter day, suddenly Chekhov called on us, Chekhov who never paid calls on anyone. On such a happy, sunny day, I went with him to an exhibition, to see his friend, Levitan.[6] [In May] I spent three wonderful days at Melikhovo, a small property Chekhov owned.[7] Everything breathed comfort, a simple healthy life, you could feel the presence of a loving family. His mother was a charming, quiet Russian woman, I loved her dearly. He was so joyful, so happy. He showed me his 'domain': a pond with carp, of which he was very proud – he was a passionate fisherman – the kitchen garden, the flowers. He loved gardening, he loved all earth's gifts. I found everything there enchanting: the house, the little cottage where he wrote *The Seagull*, the garden, the pond, the flowering fruit trees, the calves, the ducks, and the village schoolmistress, running along the road with her pupils. They were three days full of wonderful intimations of the future, full of joy and sun. When the season was over, I went on holiday to the Caucasus, where my brother was living with his family in a dacha near Mtskhet. While still in Moscow I had promised to travel from the Caucasus to the Crimea where Chekhov had purchased a plot of land[8] and was building a house.

Chekhov

June 16
Melikhovo

What is happening? Where are you? You seem quite determined not to give us any news, so that we've been reduced to idle speculation – perhaps you've forgotten us, or have married someone in the Caucasus. If so, who is he? Will you give up the theatre?

The writer has been forgotten, how awful, how cruel, how heartless!

Everyone sends their greetings. No news. No flies, either, practically. Nothing. Even the calves don't bite.[9]

I wanted to take you to the station but, fortunately, the rain prevented me.

6. Isaac Ilyich Levitan (1861–1900), one of the Itinerants, leading Russian landscape painter of his time.
7. Some 2½ hours by train from Moscow.
8. In 1898.
9. A family joke.

I've been to Petersburg and had two photographs taken. I almost froze to death. I shan't be going to Yalta before the beginning of July.

I take your hand in mine, if you will allow me, and wish you all that's best.

Your A.C.

Knipper

June 22–23
Mtshket

Please don't think this is just a reply to your letter. I would have written to you long since but I have been in such a foul mood I couldn't have written a line. I've only been getting back into sorts for the last two days and am starting to feel and understand nature. Today, I got up at 6 and went for a walk in the mountains, taking a copy of *Uncle Vanya* with me for the first time. But mostly I just sat with the book in my lap, enjoying the wonders of the morning and the ravishing view of the mountains. [...] I felt cheerful, healthy and happy. Then I went down to the post for the papers and books, got your little letter, which I enjoyed enormously, I even laughed out loud. And there was I thinking the writer, Chekhov, had forgotten the actress, Knipper. So you do remember me from time to time? Thank you, kind sir. Are you doing anything interesting at Melikhovo? Is it cold? I am so happy to be warming myself in the southern sun. May was so cold. And Marya Pavlovna, your sister, is she sketching or just being idle? Give her my best love and tell her I will write. Why aren't the calves biting? Are [your dogs] Bromide and Quinine still alive? Do you often sit on the little bench next to the gate? Beautiful as it is here, I often think of the vast, open spaces of the dear north. Mountains are oppressive. I couldn't stay here long. But it is beautiful, with wonderful walks, many old ruins and at Mtshket there's an interesting, old Georgian church. Not far from our dacha, in the park in fact, there is a poetically sheltered little chapel to Saint Nina, the patron saint of Georgia. It has been restored, of course, and two women who love peace and solitude live there. What if you were to come down here, it is really beautiful and we could go to Batumi and Yalta together, what do you say? My brother, Karl, and his wife, Elena, are very nice people, you would be happy here. Think about it. Not long ago we made an excursion to Aleksandropol by the new railway (it hasn't got as far as Kars yet), it was so beautiful. We had the last carriage all to ourselves, so that we had the full benefit of the view from the back platform. I never thought to see anything so splendid. You can't describe it in a few words. Once you start writing, you go on for ever. It is better to tell it in person.

I didn't manage to finish my letter yesterday. Last evening we walked about eight miles, we explored an interesting little valley. There was no road and we had to walk on pebbles: I was exhausted and didn't have the energy to write. I got up at 6 again this morning, had a short walk, worked and bathed for the first time – there is a superb pond in our park, fed by the famous Mtshket spring, with a temperature of 11 or 12C. I would have bathed long since had I not been so off-colour after my journey here. I felt bad for almost two weeks.

We spent an eternity on the road to the Caucasus. Travel is never easy there. We waited two days at Kazbek and there was no carriage so we had to travel on the platform of an omnibus with the luggage to boot! But it was all very cheerful, the eleven of us who had been let down by the carriage formed a happy little band. I spent a whole day at Kazbek half-dead with a pounding headache. What is all this I am telling you, are you bored? If you are, forgive me, I won't do it again. [...] Give my compliments to your mother, your sister [...] I take your hand in mine.

                                        Olga Knipper

Will you write to me again? Perhaps there will be flies in Melikhovo?

Chekhov

                                        July 1
                                        Moscow

You are quite right: the writer, Chekhov, hasn't forgotten the actress, Knipper.

And, indeed, he finds your idea of going from Batumi to Yalta together a charming one. I will come, providing, first, that you wire the approximate date you expect to leave Mtshket as soon as you receive this letter, without a moment's delay. Use this as a model: To Moscow, Chekhov, the twentieth. That means you are leaving Mtshket for Batumi on the 20th. Second, that I go direct to Batumi and that I meet you there without going via Tbilisi and, third, that you don't turn my head. Vishnievski thinks I am a level-headed person and I wouldn't like him to think I am as fallible as all the rest.

I'll write as soon as I get your telegram – everything will be wonderful. Meanwhile I send you all my good wishes and take your hand in mine. Thank you for your letter.

Your A. Chekhov.

We are going to sell Melikhovo. My property in the Crimea, or so I have heard, is wonderful now in the summer. You must spend some time there.

I went to Petersburg and had two photographs taken. They've come out quite well. I shall sell them at a rouble apiece. I have already sent five to Vishnievski cash on delivery.

As to our arrangements, the best thing would be for you to wire 'the fifteenth' but, in any event, no later than the 'twentieth'.

Knipper, *Memoirs*

We met on the steamboat in Novobrossisk around July 20 and travelled together to Yalta, where I stayed with Dr Sredin and his family, who were old friends of ours. Chekhov stayed in the hotel 'Marina' on the sea-front and went every day to attend to the building of his house in Autka. He didn't eat properly because he never thought about it, got very tired and though Dr Sredin and I, using one excuse or another, tried to get him to eat normally, we rarely succeeded. Chekhov didn't like 'visiting' and avoided eating except in his own home, although he liked the Sredins.

The place where Chekhov had chosen to build his house was far from the sea and the port and the town and was in the fullest sense of the word a wasteland with a few pear trees.

But because of his efforts, his love of everything the earth produces, this wasteland little by little became a wonderful, luxuriant, highly varied garden.

Chekhov supervised the construction of his house personally.

In August Chekhov and I left for Moscow, by coach as far as Bakhchisaraya, via Ai-Petri. We were pleasantly rocked on the soft springs, breathed the pine-scented air and chatted in the gentle, humorous way Chekhov did, and dozed when the June sun was hot and wore you out with its heat. It was fine going through the picturesque valley of Kokkoz, full of its own particular charms ...

Our route took us past a hospital situated some distance from the road. There was a group of people on the terrace, waving their hands in our direction, shouting something ... We continued on our way, deep in conversation and though we could see the people we never thought that they had anything to do with us, that they were lunatics ... It later transpired that they weren't lunatics but a group of doctors we knew from Yalta trying to get us to stop ...

Chekhov stayed in Moscow for a while and returned to Yalta at the end of August [26th] and our correspondence resumed.

Knipper began rehearsals for the 1899–1900 season which was to include The Death of Ivan the Terrible, *the second part of Aleksei Tolstoi's historical trilogy, Gerhardt Hauptmann's* Drayman Henschel *and* Lonely People, *Chekhov's* Uncle Vanya *and Shakespeare's* Twelfth Night.

Knipper

August 29
Moscow

You've only been gone four days and already I feel the need to write to you – is it too soon? Yesterday, I really wanted to talk to you – I was in such good spirits: Saturday evening, my favourite, I find the sound of the bells is so peaceful (oh, you sentimental German, I hear you say). I listened to the peals from the Strastnoe Monastery while I was at your house and thought of you. But I couldn't write to you yesterday evening: after rehearsal Nemirovich came round and stayed a long time.

Do you know, dear Mr Chekhov, dear friend, I have been cast as Anna in *Lonely People*!![10] You can imagine how pleased I am! [...] That's enough about the theatre for the moment, we'll come back to it some other time.

I was so downcast when you left, so heavy-hearted, I would have cried the whole way back had Vishnievski not been there to accompany me. Then I couldn't sleep, in my mind I was on the journey with you. Are you well? Didn't you feel the cold? And what were

10. The play was premièred on December 16, 1899.

your travelling companions like – a nuisance, passable or nice? I
kept mulling these questions over – will I get an answer? And was
that pretty little basket of provisions useful to you, and did you try
the sweets? I'm going to stop now. I'm being tedious.

You must have come alive again in the south, after the dampness
here, and the cold, the grey, lowering skies, one's heart lifts merely
to see the sweet southern sun and the shining sea. You are busy with
building work, you are going to visit Sinani, you will walk along the
waterfront and drink the local mineral water, as before, of course,
but without Knipper, the actress. The day after you left, the actress
was so melancholy she didn't go to your house as she promised your
sister she would, and on Friday was confined to bed, prostrate with a
headache; your sister was here yesterday. I hear her dear, gentle
voice, her laugh I love so much.

I went to your house before rehearsal, yesterday. [...] In your
study there is a sofa, a large picture of you on the wall, it is very
nice and I booked a season ticket on one end of the sofa, right opposite it, I shall come and sit there. There was no rehearsal of *Vanya*
yesterday. Nemirovich arrived, opened his ministerial office, there
were discussions, confessions and it was decided the rehearsal was
off. In the evening the whole company welcomed Stanislavski back.
He is much better, perky, stronger, steadier. Today there was a run
of *Terrible*. On the whole they seemed quite happy. Sanin was so
moved he almost gnawed his fingers off.

Today, your sister and I went to the Maly to see the public dress
rehearsal of *Egmont*. Fedotova[11] dragged us down to the second row
where [the management] Telyakovski, Nelidov *et compagnie* were
enthroned. I had a thorough view of [them] – quite a treat! We could
scarcely stop ourselves laughing when we heard their comments –
the soles of Yuzhin's boots were too white, the chair was ugly, or
they didn't like the belt on Yuzhin's mackintosh – not a word about
the acting.

And the looks on their faces! I remembered you and the way we
discussed *Uncle Vanya* and I was dying with laughter inside.
Fedotova, poor thing, was in tears, real tears, not pretend, because it
was 'historically true' and 'where, these days, can you still hear such
beautiful words as "to die for one's country" '? [...]

---

11. A leading actress at the Maly and one of Stanislavski's acting teachers.

You wouldn't have been able to contain yourself among our new companions, you would have run away. I met Kondratiev, he said he was a great admirer and tried hard to wheedle me into joining his company. In a word, I have seen what real connoisseurs of art are like.

I am boring you, Mr Writer, aren't I ? Write me a sweet little Epistle, if you feel like it, but if not, don't. [...] Do you have lunch every day? So, sleep sound, eat properly and keep in good health. I take your hand in mine.

Olga Knipper

Chekhov

September 3
Yalta

My dear actress, I shall answer all your questions. The journey was fine. My companions let me have the lower berth; later there were only two of us in the compartment, a young Armenian and myself. I drank tea several times a day, three glasses each time, slowly, at my leisure. I ate everything that was in the basket. But it seemed to me that running round the station with the basket trying to get boiling water could appear rather frivolous, and do the reputation of the Art Theatre no good at all. It was cold when we reached Kursk, then the weather turned warmer and it was quite hot in Sevastopol. I got to my house in Yalta and am living there with my faithful Mustapha to protect me. I don't have lunch every day because the town is too far away and cooking for oneself on an oil stove is bad for one's reputation. I eat cheese in the evening. [...] I've been to see Dr Sredin and his family twice: they took an affectionate look at your photograph and we ate sweets. He is now quite well. I don't drink the local mineral water. What else? I'm scarcely in the garden at all. I sit indoors, thinking of you. As we passed close to Bakhtshisarai, I thought of you and remembered our trip. My dear, my extraordinary actress, you remarkable woman, if only you knew the pleasure your letter gave me. I bow low before you, very, very low, so low, in fact, that my head touches the bottom of my well which is seventeen metres deep. I have grown used to you and now I am disconsolate, I cannot bear the thought of not seeing you before the spring, it drives me mad. [...]

The weather is fine in Yalta but it has been raining quite stupidly for two days, there's mud everywhere and you have to wear galoshes. Because of the damp, centipedes are climbing up the walls and frogs and baby crocodiles are playing in the garden. The green snake on the flower pot you gave me, and which I managed to get here without mishap, is sunning itself.

A naval squadron has arrived. I watch it through my binoculars.

They're giving an operetta at the theatre. Trained fleas continue to serve sacred art. I have no money. Guests turn up all the time. Most of the time it is boring and boredom is useless and absurd.

So, I take your hand in mine, I kiss it. Be healthy, be joyful, be happy, work, be lively, be passionate, sing and, if you can, spare a thought for this writer, ever at your service, your devoted admirer,

A. Chekhov

Knipper

beginning September
Moscow

Greetings, writer! How are you? I am angry and hurt that you don't want to write, you've forgotten the actress, but God bless you. I wish you good spirits all the same. The night is wonderful, moonlit, I want to be put of the city, in the open, will you come?...

Farewell, farewell writer, be in good health.

Olga Knipper

Chekhov

September 9
Yalta

[...]

Greetings dear, precious actress! Greetings my true companion on the road to Yalta! Greetings, my joy!

Masha tells me you didn't get my letter. How is that? I sent it ages ago, as soon as I got yours.

How are you? Working? How are rehearsals going? Is there really no news?

Masha and my mother have arrived. Being small, we fit into a large house, it's tolerable enough.

The telephone. It rings out of boredom on the hour. It's boring not being in Moscow, not being with you, dear actress. When shall we see each other again?

I've had a telegram from the Aleksandrinski [in Petersburg]. They're asking to do *Uncle Vanya*.

I'm going to run into town, to the bazaar. Be healthy, be lucky, be happy. Don't forget the writer, don't forget me, otherwise I shall drown or marry a cyclopendia.

I kiss your hand, hard, hard, hard!

Ever your Anton Chekhov

Knipper

September 10
Moscow

It was a year yesterday since we met, dear writer, do you remember, at the [Hunting] club, at a run-through of *Seagull*? How I trembled when I heard that the 'author' was going to be present that evening. Can you understand that? And now I am sitting here and writing to this 'author' without a trace of fear, indeed with lightness of heart. It's a wonderful day, today, warm, clear, if all goes well I shall go into town, take the air, admire the autumn weather and then enjoy Tverskoi Boulevard[12] on my way to the theatre, it really is very beautiful now. Oh, poor me, just a city dweller! There wasn't a second to write to you yesterday, and I wanted to so much! In the morning we rehearsed *Uncle Vanya*, at 5 *Terrible*[13] and then straight from the theatre to the [Philharmonic] School for a discussion about *Lonely People*. [...]

We looked at Acts 3 and 4 of *Vanya* today and tomorrow there is a dress rehearsal of *Terrible* and then we get down to proper work on *Uncle Vanya*. Lilina will be excellent as Sonya but what I will be like as Elena not even I can tell. I understand her perfectly but how I'll play her *Dieu sait*. Savva Morozov[14] is a regular visitor to the theatre, he attends rehearsals, stays till night-time and gets terribly

12. Tverskoi Boulevard was known during the Soviet period as Gorki Street, and runs from Pushkin Square down to Red Square.
13. *Terrible* premièred on September 29 1899.
14. Savva Morozov was a friend of Stanislavski, an industrialist, the major share-holder in the Art Theatre, which he also subsidized heavily. His presence was resented by Nemirovich-Danchenko.

worked up. We all, of course find it very funny ... I think he will soon be making his début here but I'm not sure as what. He's decided I won't be able to play Elena because I haven't got a nasty husband and so won't experience the part. I've decided to look for one. You wouldn't refuse to help me, dear writer, would you, particularly as it is for the success of your play? If I do that, I shall probably turn into a simply tremendous actress! [...]

Thank you for the photograph and the sweets. And thank you for writing to me, I was so impatient for a line, I was upset, I thought you didn't want to write to me. Don't you think I've grown used to you? Write everything, everything to me. [...]

I am very glad the ladies feed you because I knew the writer wasn't eating every day. It would be so difficult to go back and forth to town, wouldn't it? So, till the next letter; don't be bored, eat, sit in the garden, think of me. Have you started work yet?

My greetings to your sister and your mama, I hope everything will soon turn out all right.

I press your hand in mind and kiss your right temple. Don't be down.

Olga Knipper

Knipper

September 21
Moscow

It seems an absolute age since I wrote to you, dear writer and I feel you've stopped thinking about me. Why aren't you here? It's warm here now. It's really summer. I'd like to drink tea with you after rehearsal, play patience, chat about the Art Theatre. I'm busy the whole time right now – rehearsals every day, today's my only free moment. We open soon, it's terrible how nervous and jumpy everyone is. There isn't a single ticket left for the opening night, everything is sold out for *Henschel*,[15] too.

We do *Seagull* on the first Sunday. What pleasure it will be to play that stingy actress. They wanted to do a matinée of *Twelfth Night* but I absolutely refused. To play Viola in the day, in which I put on my disguise with dizzying speed [...] and which tires me and Arkadina in the evening, it doesn't bear thinking about! They'll

15. *Drayman Henschel* was premièred on October 5, 1899.

probably do a matinée of *Antigone*. We are rehearsing *Uncle Vanya* without Astrov [Stanislavski] who is tied up with *Terrible*. We are carried away by Act 3, we race ahead, the bit between our teeth, faces burning, eyes shining, hair flying back from our heads and with such feeling that no one can stop us. [...] Ah, writer Chekhov, if only you could be at the first night. What a treat that would be! But you have probably thought better of coming to Moscow, you've grown used to Yalta, your 'own home', and have put Moscow, our theatre and actresses out of your head [...]

Olga Knipper

Knipper

September 26
Moscow

Aren't you ashamed, you horrid writer, to say I'm 'biting as a snake'? You wicked writer! I don't write much? It's because I'm afraid my letters will be boring. If they aren't, we'll chat more often. [...]

The day the box office opened people had been waiting since the early hours of the morning, the queue was incredible, up to 2500 people. [...]

There isn't one ticket left for the opening of *Terrible*, and everything has practically gone for the three performances of *Terrible, Seagull, Fyodor*. We all jumped for joy, we were so excited. [...] I think you'll be interested to know that Chaliapin[16] was at last night's public dress rehearsal of *Terrible* and banged the wall with enthusiasm.

The staging of *Terrible* is fascinating.

I'm feeling all right today though I only got back from the dress rehearsal at midnight and had a meal, now I'm writing to you and have to dash off again to a dress rehearsal of *Fyodor* with a new Fyodor. The weather is vile, cold, wet, snow. We rehearsed *Twelfth Night* today with great style. We are beginning to get the measure of this world of beautiful women, pages, kisses, languid glances, peace, poetry, love, music mixed with scenes of senseless clowning and heavy English wit – I think it is an interesting show.

There are no rehearsals of *Uncle Vanya* this week.

16. Fyodor Chaliapin (1873–1938), famous Russian bass, friend of Stanislavski. His outstanding role was Boris Godunov in Mussorgski's opera.

[...]

Now I have to dash to the theatre. Farewell till my next letter, my dear writer, don't be angry with me, love me and think of me just a little. Send me your photo, signed, only a decent-sized one because I only have a small one of you with sad eyes, here in the middle of the table.

Give your mama and your sister my heartfelt greetings.

I press your hand in mine.

Olga Knipper

Chekhov

September 29
Yalta

I received your wise letter with a kiss on the right temple and another with a photograph. I thank you, dear actress, enormously. Your show opens today[17] and in thanks for your letter I send you my congratulations on the opening of the season, a million good wishes. I wanted to send a telegram to the two directors and congratulate everyone but as they don't write to me and haven't even sent the [annual] report (which, according to the press, came out some time ago) and as that Roksanova woman[18] is still playing in *Seagull*, I thought it better to give the impression I was offended – so, I only congratulate one person.

We had some rain but it has cleared up, the weather is cool. There was a fire last night, I got up and watched the conflagration from the terrace and felt terribly alone. We live indoors now, eat in the dining room, the piano is playing.

I have no money, not a penny, all I have is what I can hide from my creditors. That's how it will be until Marx[19] arrives in mid-December.

I would like to write something nice to you but I can't think of anything. You see, I haven't a season to open, I don't have anything new or interesting to relate, everything is as it was. I expect nothing, except a change in the weather, which is imminent.

They're doing *Ivanov* at the Aleksandrinski, *Uncle Vanya* too.

17. *The Death of Ivan the Terrible.*
18. Roksanova played Nina in *Seagull*. Chekhov disliked her performance and wanted her removed from the cast.
19. Chekhov's publisher.

So, be healthy, dear actress, wonderful woman, God keep you. I kiss both your hands and bow. Don't forget me.

Your A. Chekhov.

Knipper

September 29
Moscow

I can't sleep. We performed *Terrible* and everyone feels awful. Nothing is clear in my mind but I do realize that the opening of the Art Theatre's second season should not have gone the way it did. First, Stanislavski is ill. He had an announcement made to that effect before the show, although the whole company was against it, and it killed the audience. Everyone is enthusiastic about the actual production. [...] The reception was cool, the atmosphere backstage was very depressed. I am writing this, dear Mr Chekhov, to you *only to you*, no one else; but you, of course, will understand what I mean. I can't tell you how sick, how heavy-hearted I feel. At the moment there's total chaos and it will be worse tomorrow. [...] Nemirovich was right, we should have opened the season with *Uncle Vanya*. I can just imagine how the papers will tear us apart tomorrow – many of them have been waiting for an opportunity like this. [...]

So, you see how things stand. How painful, how hard it is to acknowledge the deficiencies the errors of our dear, beloved, young theatre. I tell myself that our forthcoming productions will wipe out this painful impression. You have completely forgotten your actress, you don't want to write – that is hurtful. Why are you silent?

Your downcast actress.

Chekhov

September 30
Yalta

[...]

It's suddenly turned cold in Yalta. [...] How I would like to be in Moscow, dear actress! I didn't send you my photograph because I haven't received yours, oh snake! I certainly didn't say you were 'biting as a snake', as you write. You are a big, a great big snake. Isn't that flattering?

I press your hand in mine, bow low, my head touches the ground, gracious lady. I will send you another present soon.

Your A. Chekhov.

Knipper

October 2
Moscow

Yesterday we performed our beloved *Seagull*. We played it with delight. The theatre was packed. [...] The acting was good, light. Stanislavski says my performance has never been better. The scene with Trigorin is better now. I'm not happy with Act 1 – I get tense, nervy, I play jerkily. You can calm down, dear writer, yesterday Roksanova, I'm told, was much better, she cut down on the pauses, didn't snivel and Meyerhold told me that the audience listened in quite a different way. The 3rd Act, as usual broke the audience's heart and Act 4 also evoked very audible approval.

Did you get my despondent letter after *Terrible*? The press was very favourable, good notices all round – it shows our theatre has put down roots and that makes me happy. Stanislavski is still unwell, although yesterday he played better than usual. General Trepov[20] has banned the scene in which Ivan comes out of the chapel, and won't allow the member of the Synod to read on his knees or let us have any icon lamps on stage. What do you say to that? What a glorious place Russia is! Also, the curtain has to come down before the crowd tears Kikin apart. I agree with that – it's too real and crude. I used to turn away in rehearsals – it was repulsive!

Terrible will make money, nonetheless. On Monday we shall really set to work on *Uncle Vanya*.

Why don't you write to me? Perhaps you don't feel the need? Or don't want to? I'm sorry, I won't ask any more questions. [...] Be healthy, go for walks, enjoy yourself, breathe the fine, southern air. I press your hand in mind.

A big kiss for Masha. My sincere good wishes to your mother. I will write soon.

Your Olga Knipper

20. The Chief of Police.

Chekhov

October 4
Yalta

Dear actress, you really did exaggerate in your gloomy letter, that's obvious, since the papers were very kind about the opening night. However that may be, one or two bad performances are no reason to feel down or lose any sleep over. Art, especially the theatre, is a realm you cannot enter without the odd stumble. There are still many more days of failure ahead, whole seasons of failure, things will go terribly wrong, you will have huge disappointments, but you have to be prepared for that, you have to expect it and be resolute and follow your own path.

And, of course, you're right [...]

I've been ill for 3 or 4 days and am staying at home.

An endless stream of visitors, idle, provincial tongues chatter away and I am bored, I get furious and envy the rat that lives under the floor in your theatre.

You wrote your last letter at 4 in the morning. If you feel *Uncle Vanya* doesn't have the success you would have wished, then you should go to bed and get a good night's sleep. Success has spoiled you and now the plain ordinary isn't enough.

[...]

How are you? Write more often. I've written to you almost every day. The writer writes to the actress so often, and that hurts my pride. I must treat the actress severely and not write to her. [...] Be healthy, little angel.

Your A. Chekhov

Chekhov

October 7
Yalta

Dear, celebrated, special actress, I am sending you a box to keep your gold and jewels in. Take it!

In your last letter you complain that I never write. I often send you letters, true, not every day, but more often than I receive them. [...]

Knipper

October 15
Moscow

It's so long since I wrote to you, dear, gentle writer! Are you angry
with me? No, no sulks, it really isn't my fault! I've been so crabby,
so down in the dumps, I haven't liked myself at all, I was tired, so I
haven't written. I could have scribbled a word or two, but that would
only have been to tell you I was still alive. I am playing every evening, except when *Henschel* is on: in the day there are rehearsals for
Uncle Vanya which go on till 5 and then at 6.30 I'm at the theatre
again. The mood in the company has been bad and even now it isn't
sparkling. *Henschel* is going very well, a total success but isn't
making money. [...] *Terrible* is making money but the reception is
frosty. This week Meyerhold stood out. We had a good rehearsal of
Uncle Vanya today, strong but as Astrov [Stanislavski] wasn't well
he didn't come to rehearsal. Tomorrow Stanislavski proposes to
spend the whole day on *Uncle Vanya*: rehearse all morning, go to the
Slavyanski Bazar[21] for lunch and then back to the theatre in the
evening. How do you like that, Mr Writer Chekhov? Lilina[22] has
refused, she is afraid of tiring herself out. In the morning we rehearse
Astrov's scenes and then, in the evening, have a run-through on
stage (or in the foyer) with props. The sets still aren't ready. And we
are supposed to open on the 14th. The fault lies entirely with *Terrible* and Stanislavski's illness. *Uncle Vanya* is supposed to be this
season what *Seagull* was last season. That will be essential. But think
of us, Mr Writer, be with us in spirit during rehearsals and wish us
luck. [...]

Oh, what a fine one I am! Here I am, writing away, and haven't
thanked you for the box you sent. But you are a bit of a joker, Mr
Chekhov! To give a poor actress of the Art Theatre a box for her
'gold and jewels'. Do we usually have any? I shall keep letters from
a dear, good man from Yalta in it. But when am I going to get a
photograph of you with your eyes open? Couldn't you have put it in
the box as a surprise? You're a hard man. I want to see you awfully.
Impossible before the spring? I so wish you were here, sitting comfortably on the sofa, drinking coffee (which I prepare scandalously

21. The famous restaurant in Moscow where artists met and where the Art Theatre
was created.
22. Stanislavski's wife.

strong) and I would chat to you about all sorts of things, about joy and sorrow. I would set out a game of patience with nice, torn cards. [...]

Why can't I get the idea out of my head of you standing on the terrace, staring into space, feeling lonely?...

Why do I sometimes want to tell you so many things but don't?

We played *The Seagull* again – well. [...]

It will soon be 3 o'clock, time for bed. Last evening I went to the Maly to see Boborikin's *Old Accounts*. Terrible play, detestable. – Tell your sister I kiss her warmly and miss her terribly, I live for her arrival. Give my greetings to your mama. How does life agree with her in the south? Dear Writer, I press your hand in mine, thank you for your letter, remember me.

Your Olga Knipper

Knipper

October 23
Moscow

Such air today! Gentle, balmy, the sun is really warm. Your little azalea and the laurel are turning a glorious green: only the writer Chekhov is sitting before me with crestfallen eyes – that is terrible! They're dragging me off somewhere, right out of Moscow, into the open to breathe real air and see myself with real eyes. Here I'm banging my head against a wall, I'm like a sardine in a tin. If only I could spend a moment or two with you, in the garden on the bench, absolutely quietly and rest properly.

I've been so tired recently that yesterday I just lay on the bed the whole day without the energy to move hand or foot; I didn't even go to the *Uncle Vanya* rehearsal and today I'm moving about as though I'd just got up from a serious illness. If there were the remotest chance I would run out of Moscow and see what is going on inside my head.

We had the first dress rehearsal of *Uncle Vanya,* the second is today, the third on the 25th in the daytime and we open on the 26th. I still haven't seen the set for Act 3, it's not finished. We are all very worried. The tickets are sold out. The posters will be interesting – the Act 1 décor, Uncle Vanya's accounts and a picture of Chekhov: I hear Simov has done a good job but haven't seen it yet. In Act 2 we'll hear the sound of real trees off-stage, wonderful thunder and lightning. I'm afraid to say anything about the acting before the first night. I have a feeling the audience will enjoy it. And you will be in a state, of course. So, be like the rest of us. I will go straight from the theatre and send you a telegram. I'm scared about the end of Act 2 – the writing is pure genius. After Act 3 our knees were shaking and our teeth chattering. I love the scenes with Astrov enormously. – So, now I have to run to the theatre, curtain up at 6, earlier than usual and tomorrow we have a matinée of *Seagull*. Farewell gentle, good, dear Mr Chekhov, my Mr Chekhov. I read you whenever I have a moment to spare. What I really want today is to remember our travels together. When shall we see each other again? I press your hand in mine. Write to me. Never forget

> Your little actress.

The first night of Uncle Vanya *took place on October 26.*

Knipper, *Memoir*

Uncle Vanya was not a happy experience. The opening night was almost a failure. What was the reason? We were, I think. Chekhov's plays are difficult to act, it is not enough to be a good actor with sufficient technique to play the role. You have to love Chekhov, be sensitive to him, steep yourself in the atmosphere of certain parts of society, you must love Man as Chekhov loves him and live the life of the people he creates. In *Uncle Vanya* we had not mastered the characters.

Both Knipper and Nemirovich-Danchenko tried to conceal the truth from Chekhov, assuring him that the play had gone well, but he quickly saw through the deception.

Knipper

> October 27–29
> Moscow

I hadn't intended writing to you today, dear Mr Chekhov, I feel so terribly low.

Last night we played *Uncle Vanya*. The play was a resounding success, the whole audience was enthusiastic, it goes without saying. I didn't close my eyes all night and today I just howl at the slightest thing. I acted so appallingly – why? Some of it I understand, some of it not. I have so many thoughts running through my head it's impossible to express myself clearly. I'm told I acted well at the final dress rehearsal but now I don't believe it. The problem to my mind is this: they wanted me to forget about my own interpretation of Elena because the director [Stanislavski] found it boring but I hadn't been able to follow my ideas right through. They imposed a different character on me, saying that it was essential for the play. I held out for a long time and was against it right to the end. At the final dress rehearsal I was calm, and perhaps for that reason played easily and evenly. On opening night I was infernally nervous and simply panicked, something that has never happened to me before, and so it was difficult to play a character that had been forced on me. If I'd been able to play the character as I wanted, the first night would probably not have worried me so. Everyone at home is appalled by my performance. [...] God, I feel so infernally low! Everything seems to have fallen apart. I don't know what to hold on to. One minute I'm banging my head against the wall, the next I just sit here like a block of stone. It's awful to think what the future will be like, the work that lies ahead, if I have to resist the director's tyranny again. That's why I can't settle down! I'm tearing my hair, I don't know what to do.

I didn't finish last night, I mean I couldn't. Today's a little better, but I still can't face people and am staying at home. I just went to your house, sat for two hours waiting for your sister and then went back home, while she, apparently, had come to my house in the meantime. Such a pity, such a nuisance! [...]

Strange, after *Seagull* I suffered physically, now, after *Uncle Vanya*, I am suffering psychologically. I can't tell you how depressed I am by the thought that I acted so badly, in your play of all plays! Nemirovich says I was too tense and played more aggressively, and was too loud, whereas the part needs half-tones – Perhaps, even then, I don't know, I only know that I didn't play simply, and that, for me, is awful. The papers and the public will damn me more than likely, but that is nothing in comparison to what I suffer at the thought of how I treated Elena Andreevna, i.e. you and myself, too. Please forgive me, don't be too harsh with me, tomorrow it will be all right. I just have to get my strength back.

This is what your actress's black days have been like. [...]

Write to me, even if it's only a few lines of consolation. Masha will be coming to the theatre tomorrow, I believe.

I press your hand in mine, hard, I bow my sick head, dear writer.

Your Olga Knipper

Chekhov

October 30
Yalta

Dear actress, you asked me if I would get into a state. But the fact is that *Uncle Vanya* was performed on the 26th and I only learned about it, naturally, on the 27th, when I received your letter. Telegrams started arriving that evening when I was already in bed. They were read to me over the telephone. I woke up each time and ran to the telephone in the dark, barefoot, very cold; then, hardly had I got back to sleep than it rang again. It was the first time in my life when my own fame wouldn't allow me to sleep. The next day, when I went to bed, I put slippers and a dressing-gown next to the bed, but no telegrams came.

All the telegrams talked about was curtain calls and dazzling success but there was a nuance, a hint of something from which I concluded that your mood was not entirely positive. The papers, which came today, confirmed my suspicion. Yes, actress, all you Art Theatre actors had, for once, a middling success, there were one or two broadsides. You know, you are all spoiled by constant talk of success, of full or half-full houses, you've been poisoned by this drug and in two or three years nothing will ever satisfy you! Take a look at yourselves!

How are you in yourself? I am neither one thing nor the other: I work, I plant trees.

I had visitors, it was impossible to write. They stayed over an hour, wanted tea so we had to light the samovar. It's all so tedious!

Don't forget me, don't let your friendship die, then we can go together somewhere in the summer. Farewell! We probably won't see each other before April. What if you were all to come to Yalta in the spring, give some performances and rest? That would be wonderfully artistic.

One of the guests will take this letter and post it.

I press your hand in mine [...]

Write to me, actress, by all that's holy, I am so bored. I feel I am in prison and I get in such a rage.

Your A. Chekhov

Chekhov

November 1
Yalta

I understand your mood, dear actress, I really do, but all the same I wouldn't get myself into such a desperate lather. Neither the role of Anna[23] nor the play is worth tearing your nerves to shreds for. It's an old play, out of date and there are all sorts of faults in it. If over half the cast couldn't get into the mood then it's the play's fault – number one. Number two, once and for all you must stop worrying about success or failure. Your business is to work step by step, from day to day, steadily, and to be prepared for inevitable mistakes and failures, in a word, to follow your own path and leave competition to others. What is important for beginners, and so very useful, is to write or act and be aware that you are not doing well enough.

Number three, Nemirovich wired me that the second performance was wonderful and he was completely satisfied.

Chekhov

November 19
Yalta

Dear actress, Vishnievski wrote and told me that you would give 3 kopeks to be able to see me. That's what you told him. Thank you, you're very generous. But in a couple of months you won't even give 2 kopeks.

How people change!

I would give 75 roubles to see you. [...]

---

23. He means Elena in *Uncle Vanya*, not Anna in *Lonely People*.

Knipper

November 23
Moscow

So, you haven't given me up as lost, dear, gentle writer? I was so delighted when I recognized your hand! I had such a feeling of well-being and peace. I've been so very tired ...Why didn't I write to you, do you know? If you don't know, you can feel why, can't you? Do you really believe Vishnievski when he says I would give 3 kopeks to see you? It means men aren't without coquetry either. I don't know how much I would give to have you here and for you not to leave Moscow. Oh writer, writer, don't forget me, for the love of God, and love me a little, I need it. You just don't answer my letters, why? You only answered my last, despairing one and tried to understand.

Do you want another despairing letter only of a different kind? I won't, I won't—

Your sister tells me how you are getting on. I know you are working, finally. Your study is comfortable, pleasant and I am sure conducive to work. How are the blues? I suddenly have a picture of myself arriving at your house, I see your face, your smiling eyes, I can see us together, me telling you many things, talking. Would you be glad to see me?

How is the garden, did the perennial die – is everything taking root? How fine it will be in the spring!

What can I write to you about myself? I am alive, I am rehearsing *Lonely People* – there's a lot of work to do, the role is extremely taxing but I am being lazy and curse myself – where is my energy? [...] I love being with you, I love sitting and talking with your sister, she's a wonderful person. Today I am going to a literary evening at Morozov's, there will be a discussion about *Lonely People* – very interesting. I went to the Literary Club with your sister once, she wrote to you about it. I don't go anywhere else. Be healthy, I press your hand in mine. I will write soon.

Your Olga Knipper

My azalea is in bloom, I would terribly like to send you flowers from the cold north but only send petals.

My greetings to your mother.

I looked at your photo a long time and had a good cry. Sentimental German, do I hear you say? So be it.

Knipper

December 1
Moscow

Hurrah, hurrah! Now I have Writer Chekhov with eyes! I got it just a moment ago and can't go to rehearsal without writing you just a few lines. Thank you, thank you, sweet man, wonderful man! I press both your hands and kiss both temples.

What a wonderful photograph! And what a fine expression you have! The little actress is terribly lucky and will try to do well in rehearsal in consequence. Oh, I'm late, I must rush. But why no inscription? You'll put that right in the spring, won't you?

Be healthy, be calm, wait for the spring.

Everyone sends greetings: they all like your sister.

Give my compliments to your mother.

Once again I bow 'my poor bow'.

Your Olga Knipper

Chekhov

December 8
Yalta

We are cut off from the world: the telegraph has broken down, the post doesn't get here. It's been blowing a gale for three days, the like of which I've never seen.

Dear actress, fascinating woman, I haven't written to you because I sat myself down to work and wouldn't allow any distractions. [...]

Just write me the essentials: is the company coming to Yalta this spring? Has a decision been made or not?

You like to keep newspaper clippings so I am sending you two. The wind is raging. [...]

Knipper

December 12–26
Moscow

I haven't written to you, dear writer, because I'm tired, played out, exhausted. I live a stupid, absurd life, I don't like my life or myself and I haven't an ounce of energy and *Lonely People* is staring us in the face. I have performed almost every day since the opening of the season and apart from that there have been daily rehearsals for *Uncle Vanya* and *Lonely People* and they are draining my strength. I can't work at home and Stanislavski is huffy with me because of it, he can't understand what's wrong. The play is terribly unwieldy and heavy cuts were made after the first public dress rehearsal and so there were a lot of tears – the audience is cool.

18th. I wrote all that a few days ago and, as you see, put the letter aside, the actress just collapsed and today for the first time feels fit for anything. *Lonely People* had an unexpectedly glittering success, whereas we were prepared, if not for a flop, for just a middling success and suddenly they were cheering! [...]

26th. I want to wish you a happy New Year and everything a dear man's heart desires.

Knipper

December 22–26
Moscow

[...]

Thank you for the clipping – I laughed a lot! [...] You ask if we shall be coming to play in Yalta in the spring – who knows, dear writer? You know how our director [Nemirovich] shrouds himself in mystery. I hear that we are going [on tour] to Petersburg – it's been decided; but I don't really believe it. [...]

Whatever day I write to you I can't finish my letter, and write nonsense, as usual, of course.

26th. We are definitely going to Petersburg. Nemirovich came back from there with the news. I'm terribly happy we are going, it's something to look forward to. I don't know what we shall be doing in the spring.

1900

Chekhov

> January 2
> Yalta

Greetings, dear actress! Are you angry with me for not writing to you? I write often but you didn't receive my letters because someone we know is intercepting them at the post office.

I send you New Year greetings and wishes for all good fortune. [...] Be lucky, be rich, be healthy, be happy.

We live tolerably well, eat a lot, gossip a lot, talk about you a lot. Masha will tell you how we spent Christmas when she comes to Moscow.

I won't congratulate you on the success of *Lonely People*. I still have faint hopes of your all coming down to Yalta and of seeing the play staged and will congratulate you properly then. [...]

My sister tells me you played Anna marvellously. Ah, if only the Art Theatre would come to Yalta!

> Your A. Chekhov

When are you going to send your photograph? How uncivilized!

Knipper

> January 13
> Moscow

[...] Do you know what kind of New Year we had at the theatre? Of course we performed *Uncle Vanya* and did it well. After Act 4, in the middle of thunderous applause, we heard a voice, calling for the director. Vishnievski was the first to realize what was happening and told us not to bring down the curtain. When the audience quietened down, an emotional voice rang out from the first circle, thanking us profoundly on behalf of Moscow audiences for everything they had experienced in the theatre: that this had only happened previously at the Maly. Then a voice rang out from one of the boxes in the grand tier – 'here's better, here's better!'.

How do you like that?

We are going to Petersburg and will play in the *conservatoire*, they say it's wonderful. What awaits us there I wonder!? [...]

In January 1900 Chekhov was elected to the Russian Academy of Language and Literature, an honour which, like all others, he treated with ironic humour and mild contempt.

Knipper

January 19–28
Moscow

I've just got back from rehearsal and in an hour have to go back again to do Seagull – but I wanted to chat with you for a while, dear writer. I have tired myself out this winter, I am exhausted, I can't pull my thoughts together – not that I have that many. I can't wait till we're together again...

We've just got back from your sister's. She tells me you're going to marry the priest's daughter. Congratulations, dear writer. So, you couldn't resist? God grant you love and happiness. You have bought a piece of the sea for her, of course? Perhaps, when I come down, I shall be able to admire your conjugal happiness and possibly disturb it a little. Because we did agree, didn't we ... remember the hill at Kokkoz?...

Knipper

February 5
Moscow

What does this mean, dear writer? Yesterday I heard from your sister that you're going abroad for the whole summer. You can't, you hear! That's just something you wrote and now you've forgotten all about it, right? It really is cruel to write such things. Tell me instantly it isn't true, and that we shall spend the summer together. Won't we, won't we, won't we? I still talk like that, remember the way I talk?

For the first time in my life I have toothache. I went to the dentist's and she gave me a filling which touched the nerve and caused a lot of pain. I simply howled, I yelled, I wept, it was so awful. [...] It's infernally cold in the street. I want warmth. [...]

I still haven't congratulated you on being elected to the Academy. Are you happy or don't you care? [...] My tooth hurts like the devil. I can't finish. I'll write every day. Have you really given me up for lost? You can't have. I don't want you to. For the love of God write, I'm waiting, I'm waiting.

> Your Olga Knipper, little
> actress

I write appallingly, like a schoolgirl.

Chekhov

> February 10
> Yalta

Dear actress, the winter is long, I've not been well and no one has written to me for a month. I had decided all I could do was go abroad where one is rather less bored. But now the weather is warmer, more pleasant, and I've decided not to go abroad before the end of the summer for the [Paris] Exposition.

Why are you in such low spirits? Why? You're alive, you're working, you have hopes, you drink, you're amused when your uncle reads to you, what more do you want? With me, it's quite different. I've been uprooted from my native soil, I don't have a life, I don't drink, though I like to, I like noise and there isn't any, I'm like a transplanted tree with a problem to solve: do I put down roots or wither away and die? If I complain of boredom from time to time in my letters, I have good cause, but you? Meyerhold, too, is complaining about his life. By the way, he has to spend the whole summer in the Crimea, for his health. The whole summer, it's imperative.

I'm in good health right now. I'm doing nothing except prepare for work. I wander round the garden.

You write that for little people like you, the future is a mystery. Not long ago, I had a letter from your director, Nemirovich. He writes that the company will be in Sevastopol and then in Yalta at the beginning of May. Only 'valuable' members of the company will stay behind to rehearse, the others can take a rest wherever they like.

I hope that you are 'valuable'. Valuable for the director and invaluable for the writer. There's a pun for openers! I won't write again until have sent the picture. I kiss your little hand.

Your Antonio academicus.

The company will also be in Kharkov in the spring. I will come and see you, only not a word to anyone. [...]

I thank you for your good wishes on my marriage. When I told my fiancée, just to tease her, that you intended coming to Yalta, she replied that when 'that wicked woman' came, she would keep tight hold of me. I answered that such prolonged proximity was not very hygienic in hot weather. She got angry and went very quiet as though she was trying to fathom out where I could have picked up that *façon de parler* and, a little later, said the theatre was wicked and my intention not to write any more plays was a good thing and then asked me to kiss her. I replied that at present, with my title of academician, it wasn't seemly to kiss too often. She burst into tears and I left.

Chekhov

February 14
Yalta

Dear actress, the photographs are very, very good, particularly the one in which you look sad, with your elbows on the back of the chair. Your expression is one of modest melancholy with an imp lurking behind it. The other is also wonderful but there you look a little Jewish, like someone musical, who's attending the *conservatoire* but also studying the mysteries of dentistry whenever she can. [...]

In the garden, of the seventy roses I planted in the autumn only three haven't taken. The lilies, the irises, the tulips, the tuberoses, the hyacinths are all coming through. The willow is burgeoning; the grass round the bench is lush. The almond tree is in flower. I've put benches everywhere, not fancy ones with cast-iron legs but wooden ones which I paint green. I've made three bridges across the stream. I am planting palms. There are so many new things you wouldn't recognize, the house, the garden or the street. [...] I've heard no music or singing since autumn, I haven't seen one decent-looking woman – wouldn't you be down in the dumps?

I had decided not to write to you but as you sent the photographs and I think I am in your bad books, I am writing, as you can see. [...] I was joking when I said you looked Jewish. Don't be angry, my precious. I hereby kiss your hand and remain your

A. Chekhov

Knipper

February 16
Moscow

If you knew what pleasure your letter gave me, dear writer! I've missed your letters. I'm glad you're no longer down in the mouth and are making plans to go abroad and that you are idling in the garden – lucky man!

You know your azalea is flowering. I never thought it would; it flowered so well in the autumn. The laurel is now glorious, I love to look at it. [...]

I hear we shall be in Yalta at Easter time. That means we shall see each other soon. Are you happy? Can you imagine our meeting?

Olga Knipper

Knipper

February 18
Moscow

Yesterday I had news and need to write to you. I've heard we shall be playing at Korsh's[24] theatre over Easter and will be rehearsing all through Lent. I'm terribly annoyed we aren't coming to see you at Easter – I'd grown used to the idea, I was beginning to dream and suddenly it's all gone up in smoke! I'm sick to death of these eternal plans and discussions which never come to anything. [...] If the weather is warm and fine, you will come won't you, dear writer? We shall be performing at Easter. You can see our plays. We can celebrate the anniversary of our first meeting. We shall drink white wine

24. Korsh was the proprietor of one of the most successful commercial theatres in Moscow.

No. 24 – that's your favourite, isn't it? I'll cook delicious meals for you and make terribly strong coffee, we'll wander round town together. [...]

I'm free today and tomorrow as on Sunday I have a matinée of *Lonely People* and an evening performance of *Uncle Vanya* (!). [...]

Tolstoi came to see *Lonely People*. He liked it very much and said the women were better than the men.

Be healthy, dear writer. I press your hand in mine. [...]

Your actress Olga Knipper

Knipper

March 22
Moscow

Every day I wait for just the tiniest little letter from you, when I leave the house the first thing my eyes goes to is the table with the letters – and nothing! If you were to write something about the weather, your garden, whether the road is finished, whether, finally, you're glad the Art Theatre isn't resentful and is coming to see you. [...] You ask why I don't write to you. It's because I feel so dreadful the whole time and hate myself. There are three unfinished letters to you here. I shall see you soon. Do you know, I saw us meeting in a dream, but I'm sure it won't be like that in reality. It's dull without your letters. Answer this one, it would be easier for me to come to you. Does that seem ridiculous to you? But I never thought you would grow out of me and that I would become a stranger. The weather is nasty, filthy, grey, depressing. I'm free today, no rehearsal. [...] Soon I'll start packing. I'm sure that my bad mood will pass as soon as I breathe southern air. [...]

You know I'm coming earlier than the rest, with your sister? So, for the moment, farewell. Be healthy, be happy, be lucky. People are talking about your new play. I know nothing, I've heard nothing. No one believes me when I shrug my shoulders quite sincerely and say I am in the dark. If that is what you want. Oh, how tedious it is to live and even more tedious to know the tedium is your own.

Forgive me,
Mr Academician,
Olga Knipper

Chekhov

March 26
Yalta

Your letter, dear actress, exudes black melancholy; you're gloomy, you're strangely unlucky but tell yourself it won't last long and that soon, very soon, you'll be on the train, tucking in with enormous appetite. It's good you are coming earlier than the rest, with Masha, we shall be able to talk, walk, visit and eat. [...]

I have no new play, the papers are lying. The papers never tell the truth about me. If I were writing a new play, you, of course, would be the first to know.

The wind is blowing, spring still hasn't come. But we have taken off our galoshes and go out only in hats. The garden is fine, but not really decorative, it's a jumble, an amateur's garden.

Gorki is here. He's full of praise for you and your theatre. I'll introduce you.

Damn! Someone's come. A guest. Farewell, actress!

Your A. Chekhov

Knipper, *Memoir*

At the end of March the Art Theatre decided to go down to the Crimea with *The Seagull, Uncle Vanya, Lonely People* and *Hedda Gabler.* I had already travelled down with Masha during Holy Week. How pleasant and warm it was in a new house that had scarcely been built the previous summer and was now so comfortable. Everything was fascinating, every little detail. Chekhov liked to walk around and tell you about what still needed doing and what would happen in time. But most of all, he was busy with his garden, his orchard. Chekhov drew up a plan for his garden with his sister's help, showing where every tree would be, every bench. He ordered trees, craftware and fruit trees from the far corners of Russia, he planted pear trees, apple trees with trellises and the result was really excellent peaches, apricots, cherries, apples and pears. He lovingly planted a silver birch tree, to remind him of our northern countryside, tended his roses in which he took great pride, and a eucalyptus near his favourite seat, which did not last long, any more than the birch. There were storms, the wind bent the fragile white tree which could not, of course, take strong root in foreign soil. The acacias grew along the path with incredible speed; long and supple, they seemed to quiver deliberately in the wind, bend and stretch in the slightest breeze and there was something fantastic on those movements, something unsettling and melancholy ... Chekhov always watched them through the Venetian window in his study ... There were Japanese trees, too, spreading plums with red leaves, there were almond trees and Lombardy poplars which all took and grew with amazing speed thanks to his loving eyes. Only one thing wrong, the lack of water because Autku was still not connected to Yalta and there was no possibility of building an aqueduct. Chekhov usually spent the mornings in the garden with his eternal lieutenants, two mongrel dogs who had turned up out of nowhere and settled in thanks to the kindness Chekhov showed them, and also two cranes with clipped wings which were always close to people but wouldn't be picked up. These cranes were very attached to Arseni (both servant and gardener) and were very sad when he was not there. The whole house knew when Arseni was coming back from town from the cries of these grey birds made and the strange movements with which they expressed their pleasure – something like a waltz. Holy Week, a week of rest, passed quietly, comfortably, quickly then I had to go to Sevastopol where the company of the Art Theatre were to be found ... We started to rehearse our shows and then Chekhov arrived and life was one long whirl. It was like a spring festival ... We went to Yalta and the mood was even more festive, we were literally strewn with flowers ... The festivities ended on the roof of Tatarinova's dacha, a very hospitable woman. The actors often went to see Chekhov, lunched, wandered round the garden, sat in his comfortable study and he loved it all, he liked a life full of activity and effervescence, and at that time we were all hope, liveliness and joy ... It was a pity to leave the south and the sun and Chekhov and the festive atmosphere ... but we had to go to Moscow to rehearse.

Knipper

April 24
Sevastopol

Good day, dear writer! We're in Sevastopol station, half dead with exhaustion. We got to Sevastopol where I bought every kind of useless trash. The steamboat pitched and tossed. Some people lay down, I had breakfast in good company; after the meal I did a scene from

Act 4 of *Lonely People* with Meyerhold and sang a little song. It's boring to be leaving but I'm not sad because I shall be returning Yalta. Greetings, dear writer. Thank you for everything.

Your actress

Knipper

April 25
between Kharkov and
Moscow

We've got as far as Kharkov. The heat is stifling, like an inferno – where is your Yalta? We don't know what to do because of the heat. We drink, eat, play cards in the men's compartment. There's only one woman with us, we've called her Hedda Gabler because of her hair-do. She has a woman's journal and a check travelling bag. She knows Gorki. [...] I don't want to go back to Moscow, I don't want to!!! Greetings to all, to Gorki. Write to me. I press your hand in mind. Yalta – a dream!

Knipper

May 1
Moscow

It is May 1, dear writer. It is cold, raining and I am depressed. I'm ashamed to have written nothing to you before this. In some ways I'm still not used to my own room again, I wander about, not sure what to make of myself, or others. I would like to go south, to the warmth, to have sunshine in my heart – Epicurean ways, don't you think? I'm letting myself be spoiled a little, a lot, but that isn't good for me. Yalta has faded like a dream. It gives me such pleasure to remember how happy the first few days I spent with you were, when I was not an actress. Pity you are unwell. I have poor memories of Sevastopol. So do you, I think. In Yalta, however, it was one long, noisy party: visits from generals, good food, the opening at the theatre, applause, noise, congratulations and, to crown it all, supper on the roof at Tatarinova's house – like a fairy tale!

How are you, Mr Writer? What is happening in your heart, your head, what are you dreaming up in that wonderful study of yours? Were you happy with our stay on the whole?

Write me a beautiful, sincere letter and don't take refuge in jokes, as you so often do. Write what you feel. All right, I am being boring, I am clinging. Write what you want, whatever your pen dictates. Who are your most frequent visitors? Oh, woman! Yet another question!

I hope we shall see each other in June, if you are willing to have me. We will live quietly, but I have just remembered, you are off to Paris. I am not going to the theatre. I haven't been called. My people are very glad I am back, of course, they've been feeling very sour. Yesterday evening Uncle Sasha and Volodya drove Masha crazy with their silly mood.

The roses are in wonderful bloom, some consolation for my black mood. I am impatient for a letter from you, I would love to know what you are doing.

Addio, academicus, dawdle in your garden, tend your flowers if there are no women about.

I take your hand in warmest greeting.

Olga Knipper

Knipper, *Memoir*

Chekhov soon came to Moscow, it felt empty in Yalta after the life and laughter we had brought with us, but he did not feel well in Moscow and soon left for the south.

Knipper

May 18
Moscow

You were terribly down yesterday when you left, dear writer. Why? The thought of it gives me no peace and I just had to write a few lines to you.

I know we spent many, many happy days together! Is that your impression, too? Answer me. [...]

Tomorrow you'll be home – greetings to everyone. Live, don't be down, wait for me – I am coming to make your life a misery.

I kiss dear Masha [...] Do I kiss you?

Olga Knipper

Chekhov

May 20
Yalta

Dear, ravishing actress, good day! How is life with you? How are you feeling? For the moment, I'm in Yalta, I've been very unwell. My head was aching while I was in Moscow, I was hot, but I hid that from you like a guilty secret but now it doesn't matter. [...]

Be healthy, be lucky. I knew Masha had written to you so I hastened to pen these few lines.

Your A. Chekhov

Knipper

May 29
Moscow

Tomorrow is my last day in Moscow! A mass of things to do. I haven't started packing yet, my head is in a whirl. It's cool, grey here, I'm glad to be heading for the south to get a little warmth. I'm trying to see whether I can travel with mama. It's empty here right now; mother is at the dacha and my brother dashes off in the morning so I am alone. [...] Tell me: is Borzkhom your poste restante? And will you come to Batum? You haven't changed your mind, I hope. How can we correspond?

I press your hand in mine

Olga Knipper

Knipper, *Memoir*

At the end of May I went with my mother to the Caucasus and what was my amazement and pleasure when I met Chekhov and Gorki on the train from Tiflis to Batum. We travelled together for six hours, as far as Mikahilovo where mother and I changed trains.

Knipper

June 3
Vladiskavka 7.30 a.m.

Wonderful, luxuriant south. The southern sun always warm and the scent-laden air ... You won't believe me but the rain is bucketing down, the thought of the journey to Voenno-Gruz is dreadful. Everything is sodden. We'll almost certainly get stuck. We're travelling in a large carriage and we have two Armenian ladies with us. We shall suffer together. Mother is in despair, it's her first time in the Caucasus and all she can see is vexation. Now we're gathering speed.

What are you doing? Write to Borzhom as soon as you can. I send you greetings, and to your mother [...] Mother bows.

Your actress

In early July Knipper went to Yalta to spend the holidays with Chekhov's family, leaving for Moscow on August 5. During her stay, she and Chekhov became lovers.

Lover

Knipper

Good day, my darling! Did you have a good night?

I've just got up, washed, drunk some very bad coffee and sat down to write to you. To my great chagrin, two travelling companions have appeared on the scene: an elderly lady who is going as far as Kharkov and a Polish woman with a flat face. She is still sleeping in the upper berth but I don't like the look of her. I don't know where she is going.

The carriage is swaying badly. Yesterday, after I left you, I stared into the darkness for a long time, my heart was heavy. I had a cry, of course. It's just that life was so full during my short stay with you! I can't write clearly, because my thoughts are so disjointed. It was awful to be alone, leaving everything behind yesterday, suddenly, I was overcome. I thought about you all the time – he's on a bus, he's visiting Kist's inn, he has finished his business and has gone for a stroll round the town.

Yesterday's trip was glorious, wasn't it? I've such rich memories of it – you, too? My dear, my darling!

I'm writing, looking out of the window – endless space stretching away – I like this view after the heady beauty of the south. Next year we will try and live in the north, won't we? And if that doesn't work? Well! We can dream anyway.

It will be strange, getting back – I won't feel at home. What did you do in Sevastopol? Write to me. Damn, the carriage is swaying so much I can't write.

We'll be in Kharkov at 3 and I'll post this letter, I'll wire home and have dinner. [...]

Keep well, live, don't be sad, write for everyone, for me in particular.

I kiss your intelligent head, feel my burning kisses. *Addio*, my academician. Love me and write to me.

Your actress

Knipper

August 7
Moscow

Here I am in Moscow, my dearest darling!

It's late, I'm terribly tired, my brains are addled, but I want to write just a few lines to you.

Did you get home today, as well? Did you wander round Sevastopol?

In Kursk, a young girl got into the train, she has just finished school, a wonderful girl, full of the joy of life, in 5 minutes she'd told me all about herself and her family, it was like a breath of spring. I was very happy she turned up. The disagreeable Polish woman got off at Kursk, I would have been afraid to sleep in the compartment with her – she was very strange.

The girl is a devotee of our theatre, especially Chekhov's plays. She has seen *Seagull* 4 times and didn't suspect she was talking to Arkadina. I didn't enlighten her.

The train was late, so I didn't get home until 11, only to find a message from the theatre that there was a rehearsal at 12. I just had time to wash, drink a little tea and dash off. The rehearsal had already started. Everyone greeted me warmly and asked after you and when you were coming. What could I answer? [...]

Nemirovich asked when you were sending the play, everyone kept asking me about it, thinking I was bringing real news. But can I really get any sense out of Anton Chekhov? Judge for yourself. [...]

For God's sake, write the play, don't keep everyone in suspense, it's almost complete in your mind.

So, peaceful nights, dreams, rest, love me, be kind to Masha and your mother. I kiss you, my dear writer [...]

Your Olga

Chekhov

August 9
Yalta

Greetings my darling Olya, my joy! I received your letter today, the first since you left. I read it, reread it and am writing to you, my actress. After taking you to the station I went to Kist's inn and spent the night there. The day after, because I was bored and at a loose

end, I went to Balaklava. I spent my time avoiding fashionable ladies
who recognized me and wanted to organize a reception in my
honour. I spent the night and in the morning took the [steamship]
Tavel for Yalta. The sea was devilishly rough. Now I'm in Yalta,
I'm bored, bad tempered and fretful. Stanislavski came to see me.
We talked about the play and I promised to finish it by September at
the latest. You see what a good boy I am.

I keep thinking the door will open and you'll come in. But you
don't, you're rehearsing in [Moscow], far from Yalta and from me.

Goodbye, may the angels watch over you. Goodbye, good little
girl.

Your Antonio

Knipper

August 9
Moscow

It's so dull without you. I so want to see you, so want to caress you,
look at you. I feel as though I've been thrown overboard.

What are you doing, what are you thinking?

Everything's awful, dreary, I'm tired out and can't rest.

We rehearsed today, there's a great deal of work to do, and I do
want to work, otherwise my acting will be as messy as it has been
the last two seasons. [...] I talked to my uncle's doctor and didn't
quarrel with him. When I told him about the bald patch and the
brownish spots on my temple and hand he said my nerves were
really playing up. He took me himself to see a throat specialist – you
see what a dear he is. [...]

No letter from you, won't I get one before the 11th? Perhaps
you've stopped thinking about me? Do write. I kiss you with all my
heart, my dear Anton (and what will you call me?).

Are you working?

Your Olga

Knipper

I sat down, sorted out my desk, took out your photo, looked at it and thought for a long time. And I felt terribly good inside as I realized you love me. My heart melted and I wanted to write to you again. Am I teasing you? – No, it's good that I'm writing, particularly as yesterday I sent such a sour letter. I was in a very bad mood yesterday. [...]

I come to the most important question near the end: when are you coming? You must come. It would be too cruel to be apart the whole winter. The weather is warm, dry. I imagine going to meet you, I can see your face, your smile, I can hear your first words.

You know, I just can't show myself in Moscow. A lot of people are convinced we're already married. Savitskaya stated it as a fact in Kastropol. Elka heard it in a bath house in Alupka. [...]

Don't you find that funny? Do I see you smile?

Have a peaceful night, it's late ... Big kisses, my darling, I expect a letter from you tomorrow – will I get one? I shall be terribly hurt if I don't.

Your Olga

Chekhov

Dear glorious, wonderful actress, I'm alive, in good health, thinking of you, dreaming of you, pining away without you. I've been in Gruzuv for three days; now I'm back in Yalta, my prison. A fierce wind is blowing, the boat isn't sailing, there's a heavy swell, people are drowning, there's not a drop of rain, everything has withered and faded, in a word everything's been awful here since you left. Without you, I'll hang myself.

Be healthy, and lucky, my little German. Don't be down, sleep sound and write soon.

Big, big kisses, 400 of them.

Your *Antonio*

Chekhov

August 14
Yalta

Dearest, I don't know when I'm coming to Moscow – I don't know because, can you imagine, I'm writing a play. I'm not writing a play but some kind of mish-mash. There are many characters – I may, possibly, get it all wrong and stop writing. [...]

Knipper

August 14
Moscow

I've finally had a letter from you, my darling Anton! I didn't know what to think, I was sick with waiting, I was in torment. Yesterday I dashed off a desperate letter to Masha. This morning, I ran down to the post-box and found your letter. I was terribly happy, I could scarcely believe it. Are you laughing? Then do. I love it when you laugh and then, suddenly, go glum again.

So, you're working? In Gruzuv or not?

Write and tell me how the play is going, how you are working – really hard, is it coming easily? Don't get angry, don't get bored, don't pine. We'll see each other and forget everything. I wish you had healthy, fresh air. But where shall we see each other? You don't mention it anywhere. [...]

Knipper

August 16
Moscow

It seems an age since I wrote to you, my dear Anton. But I'm not exactly spoiled by letters from you, either. I've been in Moscow for over a week and not one letter from you. Now I feel melancholy: I heard Uncle Sasha's confession: his dissatisfaction, his sense his life's been stupid, his debauchery, his drinking bouts, his morbid soul-searching to see if he can find one speck of purity, humanity, remorse, his desire to make reparation, and all of it delivered in a dull monotone by the light of a single candle. On the table there were a sausage and a dish of green redcurrants which I ate as I listened. He is a pitiful sight, he is talking of shooting himself, but of course he won't. He kept asking if I had faith in him, if I believed he had improved after a life in a military camp. I'm sorry I wasn't kinder to him, but I really am disgusted by some of the things he has done this summer. I just listened in silence, and made no answer. He felt it. He dropped a hint that he'd like to tell you everything, that perhaps you would understand him better than I! I really do feel sorry for him.

Does it bore you, my telling you all this?

I would love to sit in your study, in the alcove, and for everything to be very, very quiet. I would like to rest at your side, then pester you, say silly things and play the fool. Do you remember when you took me up the stair and the way it creaked and gave us away? I absolutely loved it. My God, I'm writing like a schoolgirl.

I have just taken a long break, crossed my arms and looked at your photo and I've been thinking about you, me, the future. What are you thinking about?

We talked so little and everything is so vague, don't you think? My man of the future!

Have you forgotten what I'm like? Do you love me? Do you believe me? Are you lonely without me? Do you eat well at dinner? Do you quarrel with your mother? Are you kind to Masha? Try and answer all my questions from now on. Write more about yourself, tell me everything. Now let me take your head in my arms and wish you goodnight.

Your Olga

Chekhov

August 17
Yalta

Good day to my dear, good little actress. I'm writing a play but guests are an infernal nuisance. Yesterday they were here from 9 in the morning till night and today for lunch. My head is in a mess, my mood is superficial, I get angry and have to start from scratch every day.

The headmistress of the girls' school arrived with two of her relations, young ladies. They arrived, settled themselves in the study and now they're drinking tea.

Nemirovich's wife is staying at the Rossiya, waiting for him.

Wind. There's a swell. I abandoned the study and am writing in a corner of my bedroom. If our visitors don't shatter my mood and I don't get angry, I'll finish the play between September 1st and the 5th, i.e. I'll write it and make a fair copy. Then I'll come to Moscow, in all probability.

I haven't had a line from you for ages. That's very poor, my dear. Be healthy, don't be in the doldrums.

Your *Ant*

Chekhov

August 18
Yalta

My darling, I shall answer all the questions in your letter. I'm working in Yalta, not Gurzuf, and am being abominably frustrated at every turn. The play is in my head, it's already shaped and running smoothly, all it wants is to get written down but as soon as I pick up a piece of paper some ugly great mug or other peers round the door. I don't know what the rest will be like but the opening seemed to come quite easily.

Shall we see each other? Yes, we shall. When? Early September, probably. I'm bored and angry. Money just disappears, I'm ruined, going broke. A bitter wind today, storms, the trees have withered.

One of the cranes has flown away.

My dear little actress, I could run across a field in pure idiot delight, by the wood, the stream, the sheep. It's a funny thing to say, but I haven't seen real grass for two years. Darling, it's so boring!

Mother leaves tomorrow.

Be healthy. I haven't seen Stanislavski and his wife or Mme Nemirovich.

Your *Antonio*

Knipper

August 19
Moscow

Good day, dear Anton. It's late and I've just got back from the Hermitage garden where I tried listening to an operetta but found it utterly crude, trite and vulgar. [...] I didn't want to be at home alone today. I've spent a lot of time at home these last few days, particularly as I wasn't well yesterday and spent the whole day, by myself, lying down. Today I had a rehearsal. [...] I went to the theatre at 7 for my salary, saw a bit of *Enemy of the People* and went to the operetta with Vishnievski – an agreeable companion? What do you think? There we met Sanin, saw 1½ acts and watched the gymnasts, but once I'd had enough of the delights and was feeling chilled to the bone, I headed home and sat down to write to a dear and distant friend.

You sent me a sad letter today, didn't you? I went to rehearsal this morning and, as I went downstairs, I wondered if there would be a letter from you in the box and my heart leaped when I saw the envelope. You write to me so seldom! However, knowing you, it can't be otherwise. I hope the expression 'don't change me' is a joke. Aren't you ashamed?

I'm terribly happy you've settled down to work. The play *must* be first class, you hear? I feel it will be riveting. How I long for the two of us to read it together! Nothing must get in the way. My God, how my heart will leap when I go to meet you, my dove. I will clean you up, you will be well groomed, we'll clean your shoes, get rid of all the fluff and dust and examine our hearts. Don't call me German, you hear?

Masha will be here tomorrow – I'm so happy, so happy! You have chained me to you both, horrid people! I need to love you and don't want to!

I don't feel like tidying my room, or doing anything, I don't like it any more. I went to the doctor: they're going to massage my throat, give me electric treatment and lubricate it. I don't want to go anywhere or see anyone. But I want you, you, you, you, you, you, you ... I kiss you, many, many big kisses, my darling.

Your, your Olga

Chekhov

August 20
Yalta

What is all this, my darling?!! You write that you've only had one letter from me but I write every, or almost every day. What does it mean? My letters never get lost.

Yesterday I went into the garden to rest when suddenly – horror of horrors! – a lady in grey approached me. [...] She talked rubbish but gave me to understand she could only stay from one till three. Only! [...]

The play seemed to get off to a good start, but now I'm disenchanted with the beginning, it seems vulgar to me and I don't know what to do. A play needs to be written non-stop without a break, but this morning was the first time I've been alone without interference. But what does it matter, anyway? [...]

Knipper

August 23
Moscow

I had letters from you yesterday and today, my dear, my darling Anton, and am terribly happy. Happy that the play is coming right, but I really don't understand why you don't fend off these troublesome visitors at a time like this. It's completely understandable for you to be cross and bad-tempered when all these minor irritations prevent you from working. [...]

You Slav layabout. I think if you really intend working, you will guard against all these visitors.

It's two days since I wrote to you – a veritable age, isn't it? [...]

So, are you coming, my dear? At the beginning of September? Do you want to see me? Or are you doing fine without me? You'll be a cold man in the future!

I have to stop now and run to rehearsal, my dear. [...]

I kiss you, my dear, and wait.

Your Olga

Your letters aren't very affectionate.

Chekhov

August 23
Yalta

Good day, my darling. In your letter [August 19], you are angry because I write to you so little. But I write to you often, you know!

Stanislavski was here yesterday. He stayed until 9 and then we went (or rather I took him) to see the headmistress of the girls' school. There is a very nice Hungarian woman at the school who speaks very funny Russian. She played the harp and made us laugh. We stayed until 12. [...]

Still no rain. They're building a shed in the courtyard. The crane is bored. I love you.

Will you come to the station to meet me? And where am I to stay? In which hotel – is there a comfortable one near you that's not too expensive? Think about it and write to me my darling.

The house is quiet, peaceful, I get on well with mother, we don't quarrel.

You go to the operetta with Vishnievski? Well now ...

Write to me soon, don't be mean. I'll reward you for it, I will love you wildly like an Arab. Be healthy and happy, Olya. Don't forget, write and think often of your

Antoine

Knipper

August 24
Moscow

I've just got back from the baths, there's no one at home, everything's quiet and I want to talk to you, Anton mine. Are you mine? You've never called me by my real name, only in your first letter. Don't you like it? [...]

My darling, my dove, get rid of people, do something so that you can write in peace without all these irritations. In your place I would go through agony if I had to write in such conditions. Of course, there's no comparison between what I do and what you do, but I would guard against useless visitors. Personally, I lock myself away from everyone and everything. That's why I'm writing. You know all this perfectly well. I want a letter from you in which you tell me you are finally writing and are able to devote yourself entirely to work. Will you? I'll be so happy [...]

Your actress

Knipper

August 26
Moscow

It's awful, rainy, Anton. I've just got back from rehearsal with soaking feet because I had no galoshes and holes in my shoes. Vishnievski calls me the 'dowerless bride'[1] and laughs long and loud when he sees me with holes in my shoes and in an old frock. [...]

No letter from you yesterday or today – I'm sad. [...]

Your Olga

Knipper

August 28
Moscow

It's one in the morning already, my dear Anton and I've just got back from a rehearsal of *Snowmaiden*.[2] [...]

You asked me about hotels? But I thought you would be staying with Masha. Her tenant won't be back for a while and you'll be better, more comfortable than in a hotel – aren't I right? [...]

How's your health, your mood? You should tell me so much more! We need to talk to each other very soon. Right?

I don't go anywhere except to the theatre and to see Masha. [...]

So, a peaceful night, my dear writer, I expect a letter tomorrow. I give you a big kiss, love me wildly like an Arab. What shall I love you like?

Your Olga

We had tea with Vishnievski. Nemirovich was there, too. Vishnievski lives in grand style. Everything in his home is dazzlingly clean and impeccably tidy and I'm thinking of marrying him. What do you advise?

---

1. The title of a play by Ostrovski.
2. Play by Ostrovski, premièred September 24, 1900.

Chekhov

August 30
Yalta

My dear Olga, I'm alive and healthy and hope you are, too. I've not been writing to you because of the weather and because I'm writing the play. It's turning out rather tedious but reasonably intelligent all the same. I'm writing slowly – that is absolutely to be expected. If the play doesn't come off as it should, then I'll shelve it till next year. But, at all events, one way or another, I'll finish it now.

Oh, if only you knew the frustrations. I can't refuse to see people, it's something I can't do.

Is it cold in Moscow? Dear me, that's bad.

So, be healthy. You are hurt because I don't call you by your right name in some of my letters. Word of honour, it isn't intentional.

I kiss you seventy times.

I've been rather unwell, but it's all right now, I'm in good spirits again.

Your *Antoine*

Knipper

September 1
Moscow

I haven't had a letter from you since August 23. Anton, my dear, that's unkind. I'm waiting, waiting. I only ask you to forgive me if you are working really hard. You don't write to Masha, either, you horrid creature! Are you in good health? But I won't press you. I'll stop making a fuss. But why this long silence? Don't you want to write?

It's cold here and quite horrid. Sometimes I'm at home, poor thing, sometimes at Masha's, seeking refuge: though I quite like living this way. My mood is a mixture of this and that, very uneasy.
[...]

Your Olga

Knipper

September 4
Moscow

At last a letter from you, dear Anton! I'm so glad you're in good health and working, I want you to be happy, not down, so you will come quickly. Oh, I feel troubled in my mind ...

I have a terrible headache today, the last two days have worn me out. [...]

You know Gorki and Sulerzhitski[3] are here. We talked about you – a lot. Gorki has been coming to rehearsals, he has been moved to tears. He lunched with us the day before yesterday, delighted everyone, told a lot of stories, talked about himself a lot, told us how, this summer, he had read your story, *In the Ravine*, to some peasants and the impression it made. He kept moving about and shed a few tears as he remembered. And the peasants looked at your photograph with such curiosity and affection, and listened so attentively to his reading. [...]

Your Olga

Chekhov

September 5
Yalta

My dearest, my angel, I've not been writing to you, but don't be angry, don't give way to human weakness. I've been working on the play the whole time, doing more thinking than writing. [...] I'm writing the play but not rushing it and it's very possible I'll come to Moscow without having finished it: there are so many characters, crowds of them, and I'm afraid it will turn out confused or colourless, and so I think it would be better to put it off till next season. [...]

I have guests. [...]

No rain in Yalta. The trees are withering, the stream dried up long since; the wind blows every day. It's cold.

3. Leopold Sulerzhitski, a friend and disciple of Lev Tolstoi, who later became Stanislavski's friend and assistant.

Write more often, your letters gladden my heart and lift my mood, which is parched and black every day, like the Crimean soil. Don't be angry with me, my darling.

My guests are leaving, I must go and see them off.

Your *Antoine*

Chekhov

September 6
Yalta

Darling Olya, my angel, it's so very, very dull without you. I'll come when you have finished rehearsals and performances begin. When it will be cold in Moscow, i.e. after September 20.

I'm at home and have the impression* I'm writing.

Be healthy, old thing.

Your *Antoine*

* I say I have the impression because some days I just sit at my desk, walk about, think, then sit in an armchair and get engrossed in the paper, or think about this or that, dear old thing!

Write!

Chekhov

September 8
Yalta

[...]

I leave for Moscow on September 20 and will be there on October 1. I'll stay in the hotel all day and write the play. Write it, or make a fair copy? I don't know, dear old thing. One of the heroines is a bit shaky. I can't do anything with her and I find that very annoying.

[...]

I'm afraid you'll be disappointed in me. My hair is falling out, it's awful, so bad I shall be bald as an old coot in a week. It's the barber's fault, apparently. So, what do I have to do to become a monk?

Is Gorki writing a play or not? Why do they say in *Novosty Dnya* that people won't like the title *Three Sisters*? What nonsense! They may not like it but I wouldn't dream of changing it.

I'm terribly bored. Do you understand? Terribly. All I eat is soup. It's cold in the evenings and I stay home. There are no pretty ladies. Money is running out, my beard is going grey. [...]

Your *Antoine*

Knipper

September 10
Moscow

It's so many days since I wrote to you, Anton darling!!! Are you downcast? I've been walking, I've been out of town two days, taking in the pure autumn air, admiring the wonderful autumn hues. Now I'm at home alone for the first time in two weeks or more. There's been such confusion recently I didn't try to sit down at my desk.

The trip to Vorobevy Mountains was better than we could have anticipated: I only had one regret, that Masha couldn't be with us, she was busy at school. There was Uncle Sasha; my brother Volodya and his fiancée; Lev, my cousin, back from the Transvaal; and I, your humble servant. We gathered in the morning, on the spur of the moment. The weather was warm, balmy, it was easy to breathe, easy to walk, everything around was smiling, pensive, gentle. [...] A few days ago, I was going down Tverskoi Boulevard, greedily inhaling the scent of the autumn leaves, it excited me and made me want the open country. We took the horse tram as far as the Novodevichi Monastery, then walked a mile or two through the kitchen gardens which smelled of dill and cabbages, then crossed the river and reached Vorobevko. There wasn't a soul about, fortunately, an unusual silence, not a sound in the air, not a leaf stirring, and I wanted to be alone, quite alone, and sit with you in this autumnal heaven and feel nature all round. You would understand what I mean. I can feel that mood now, I could be living it now. In the woods, the maples and beeches are golden, the aspens are turning red; the oaks are still green. The earth is damp, you can smell the mushrooms, there were my favourite late flowers and gossamer in the air, in a word, such beauty I wouldn't have torn myself away. The sun was loving, in a kind of reverie, and the clouds in the sky had such soft shapes. We spent a long time admiring our golden-domed mother, Moscow, lost in a haze; the sun seemed to throw patches of light on it. I have loved this view since I was a child. We drank tea on the terrace, played the fool a little, laughed a little, ran a little and roamed the woods and ravines. Uncle Sasha and I were in lyrical mood and gathered bunches of every conceivable kind of autumn leaves, grasses and flowers. I brought Masha a huge bunch – she loved it. On the way back, we took the ferry to the Doromilovski bridge. There were geese on the river banks and we saw two wild ducks land. We got back home very happy, refreshed and had a noisy meal. [...]

I've just received your letter, my dear! I want to see you awfully, but how can you come in the cold? That worries me terribly you know, my darling. What it will be like? You'll stay with Masha, of course, and find bed and board, don't worry. We will love you and nurse you – no, not me. Is it true my letters make you happy? My dearest one. Big kisses.

Your Olga

Knipper

September 12
Moscow

Why do you want to come after the 20th and not now? It's warm, the sun is shining. And it would be better for you to write here than in your Crimean exile. Aren't I right? Don't think of going to a hotel – Masha's home is so comfortable. I'll give you an excellent remedy for falling hair. Take half a bottle of alcohol, add 9 grams of naphthalene and rub it into your scalp – it will be a great help. Do you hear me? It wouldn't do at all for you to come to Moscow bald, people will think I've torn your hair out. [...]

Chekhov

September 14
Yalta

[...]

I've been at home for the last 6 or 7 days and haven't been out at all. I've been very ill – temperature, cough, catarrh. Today things seem a little better, I'm on the mend but still weak and useless, and sick at the thought that I've done nothing, written nothing for a whole week. The play stares balefully at me from my desk and I am baleful about it, too.

You don't advise me to come to Moscow? Mother is coming in early October. I shall have to send her as, obviously, I can't come to you. That means during the winter you'll forget who I am, I'll fall for someone else, just like you and everything will be as before.

I'll write again to you tomorrow and, by then, I'll be well, my darling. Dr Altschuler came. Be healthy and happy.

Your *Ant*

Chekhov

September 15
Yalta

[...]

As regards my play, it'll get finished sooner or later, in September or October, or November, maybe – but whether I decide to have it done this season or not is an open question, my dear baboon. I may decide against it, because first, the play may not be finished and it can lie on my desk, and second, because I must be at rehearsals, I must! Four crucial female roles, four young, intelligent women, I can't entrust them to Stanislavski, however great my respect for his intelligence and understanding. I must keep half an eye on rehearsals.
[...]

Write me another interesting letter. Go back to the Vorobevy Mountains and write. You're a clever woman, write the essentials so there won't be two stamps on the envelope. But at the moment you're not in the writing vein: first, because you've many things to do, second because you're already drawing apart from me. Isn't that so? You're damnably cold, but then that befits an actress. Don't be angry, my dear, that's the way I am, you know.

No rain, no water, the plants are dying. It's been warm again. Today, I'll probably go into town. You don't write anything about your health. How are you feeling? Well? Are you putting on weight or losing it? Write about both.

I kiss you till you swoon and go mad. Don't forget your

Ant—

Knipper

September 19
Moscow

My dear, you write such strange things. I don't want you to come to Moscow? *I* don't want? When I'm in torment and angry because it's warm and you're not here? I decided you'd gone cold on me, that you felt no inclination to come to Moscow. My God, I would love you to be here with me, to go to rehearsals, I would rest on your shoulder. I'm thinking you might die! Can't you understand that? I deliberated whether you would genuinely feel well, quiet and physically better – aren't I right, dearest? Bring your mother and stay as long as she does, you'll be fine here, believe me. I will love you, cherish you, sing to you; my throat is getting better, thanks to the massage, my voice is getting stronger. I'm healthy but I'm not putting on weight, I'm losing it. I'm losing my hair, too – you see, in sympathy. I misled you – you need 1.5 grams of naphthalene, not 9, in ½ bottle of alcohol. Be sure and do it. Rub your scalp 3 or 4 times a week.

Do you know, I got your letter of Sept. 15 yesterday evening and the letter of the 14th on the 19th – isn't that strange? You've finally written me a human letter – but you only sent a short note as though it were a burden to you to write. [...]

So, you've decided to forget me and fall in love with someone else? Do so! And I'll catch someone's fancy. What nonsense this all is. [...]

Chekhov

September 20
Yalta, Telegram

Mother arrives Moscow tomorrow. Play not finished. Will come later. I bow, I kiss your hand.

Antonius

Chekhov

September 22
Yalta

Good day to my darling Olga, my dove. How are you? It's a long time since I wrote to you. My conscience pricks me a little although I'm not as guilty as it would seem. I don't want to write – what would I write about? My life in the Crimea? [...] Mother leaves for Moscow tomorrow and I may come soon although it's not at all clear why I should. Why should I? To see you and then leave again? How interesting. Arrive, see a crowd of theatre people and leave again.

I'm going to Paris, then, probably, to Nice, and from Nice to Africa, if they haven't got the plague. I have to get through, or drag myself through, this winter somehow. [...]

Are you angry with me, sweetheart? What can I do? It's dark for writing, my candles don't burn properly. My darling, I kiss you, forgive me, be healthy, be happy! [...]

Your *Ant*

Knipper

September 24
Moscow

Why don't you come, my dear Anton. I don't understand. I've not been writing because I've been waiting for you and want to see you again. What's stopping you? What's worrying you? I don't know what to think, I'm very worried.

Or maybe you don't feel the need to see me? I'm hurt that you haven't been open with me. I feel like crying every day. Everyone says you are going abroad. Can't you understand how painful it is to hear that and to have to answer hundreds of questions?

I know nothing. You write so vaguely – 'I will come later'. What does that mean? It's warm all the time here, the weather is fine, you would be perfectly all right, we could love each other, be near each other. Then it would be easier to endure several months of separation. I shan't get through the winter if I don't see you. You have a loving, tender heart, why harden it?

Maybe I'm writing nonsense, I don't know but the thought that we must see each other keeps nagging at me. You must come. The thought that you are all alone thinking, endlessly thinking, is awful.

My dear, my beloved Anton, come to me. Don't you want to acknowledge me, or is the thought of linking your fate to mine irksome to you? Write to me in all sincerity, everything must be frank and open between us. Tell me what is in your heart, ask me any questions you like and I will answer. Do you love me? That feeling should make you feel good, and I need to feel warmth, not confusion. We need to talk of many things, simply and openly. Do you agree?

I expect you almost daily. The season opens this evening. I'm not playing. I shall be out front with Masha. Gorki's here. Sulerzhitski comes to see us. I'm not well, my heart is heavy and troubled. I eat little, sleep little.

Think about all this and send an answer to

Your Olga

I'm sorry, my letter is very disjointed.

Chekhov

September 27
Yalta

My dear Olga, my wonderful little actress, why this plaintive, bitter tone? Am I really as much in the wrong as all that? Then forgive me, my darling, but don't be angry with me, I'm not really as bad as you seem to suspect. I've not been able to come to Moscow because I've been ill, for no other reason, I assure you, I give you my word. Word of honour! Do you believe me?

I shall stay in Yalta until October 10, working, then leave for Moscow, or go abroad, depending on my health. At all events, I will write to you.

I haven't received a line from my brother Ivan, or my sister. They are obviously angry about something, I'm not sure what.

I went to see Dr. Sredin[4] yesterday, he had a lot of guests, most of them strangers to me. [...] He is suffering from rheumatism.

Write and tell me all about *Snow Maiden*, what the opening of the season was like, what state of mind everyone is in, what the audiences are like etc., etc. You're not like me, you have a lot to write about, a lot to pass on, while I've nothing to offer – oh yes, one thing: I caught two mice today.

4. One of Chekhov's doctors.

Still no rain in Yalta. A drought to end all droughts. Poor trees, especially on this side of the mountain, not a drop of water and now they have turned yellow, like people who never know a drop of happiness in their lives. That is inevitable, I suppose.

You write: 'You have a loving, tender heart, why harden it?' When did I harden it? When, come to think of it, have I displayed any hardness? I've always loved you in my heart and showed affection towards you. I never hid it from you and you accuse me for no reason at all.

Judging by your letter, you are waiting for us to sort things out, you want a long discussion with serious faces and serious consequences, but I don't know what to say to you, nothing that I've not said ten thousand times and will in all probability go on saying: that I love you, that is all. It's not my fault, or yours, that we aren't together but the devil's, who put a bug in me and the love of art in you.

Farewell, my dearest darling, may the angels watch over you. Don't be angry with me, my dove; don't be sad, be good.

What's new in the theatre? Please write.

Your Antoine

Chekhov

September 28
Yalta, Telegram

Had a very nice letter yesterday. Will probably come in October.

Antonino

Knipper

September 30
Moscow

Is there some misunderstanding between us, my darling? I'm here waiting, endlessly waiting and all you give me is: 'I'll probably come.' I don't want probably, I want *positively*.

I sent you two wild letters – you're not angry with me? Forgive me, my dove, but I was sick at heart; I'm not exactly sweetness and light now. Do you remember me or not? If you love me, you'll understand ...

This winter will be exhausting for us both. It will quickly pass and then, in spring, there'll be warmth and so much, much more ...

You have so little trust in me! I find it almost funny. What do you think about me? Don't imagine I take your hints seriously. I laugh quietly when I read them. Oh, writer dear, you are a hermit. Come quickly; you said you didn't feel like writing, but wanted to talk. So do I. It's almost a week since I wrote to you, waiting for something. When your telegram arrived my heart skipped a beat, I thought you were wiring me to announce your arrival. But when I read it, I was so hurt I nearly cried. Come, I'll do everything to make you comfortable here, to thaw you out, make you better and feel well in the comfort of my love. Will I feel well in the comfort of yours? Darling, darling, I so want to live a full life.

I just don't want to talk about events, the daily round. That now seems unimportant to me. I eat, I get upset. Today I was terribly happy to perform *Uncle Vanya*.

I'm bombarded with questions about you and when you are coming. Masha sends people to me when they ask, and what can I say? [...]

Love me and believe in me.

Your Olga

Knipper

September 30
Moscow, Telegram

Come quickly, I'm all impatience.

Knipper

October 1
Moscow

Yesterday we played *Uncle Vanya*, dearest, with such pleasure, such delight! It's the first play this season the public has greeted with such warmth and friendliness. [...] I thought of you, my dear. I wanted you to be there, for you to see how actors and audiences love you, their delight in its success. [...]

I hear you are hard at it, writing. I felt it because you don't say anything about the play in your letters. Write, my dear, write a good play so that the two of us can live many happy moments together. [...]

Chekhov

> October 4
> Yalta

Dearest, if I come, it won't be before the 12th. I'll wire you, without fail. There's been a slight hitch with the play, I haven't written anything for ten days or more because I've been ill and also because I was rather weary of it, so that I wasn't sure whether to write to you about it or not. I had 'flu, a sore throat, a hacking cough; I scarcely went outside, my head began to ache, now I'm on the mend and can go out. Whatever happens, the play will be written but won't be done this season.

Think about a hotel or furnished room. Please do! A room where it won't be tiresome to go down the corridor and it doesn't smell. In Moscow I'll probably make a clean copy of the play. From Moscow, I'll go to Paris. [...]

So, be healthy, my golden, beloved girl. [...]

> Your *Anto*

Knipper

> October 7
> Moscow, Telegram

Wire the day of your arrival, waiting, sending no letter.

Chekhov

> October 8
> Yalta, Telegram

Definitely the 21st

Knipper

October 11
Moscow

You're waiting for a letter, dearest Anton, amazed or cross I haven't written to you. In your letter you talk of arriving on the 12th and then on that day I get a telegram – definitely the 21st. I decided that was a mistake and the numbers had been reversed. [...] Yesterday, by chance, I heard from Nemirovich that you were indeed coming on the 21st so I hasten to write to you, my dear. It hurt me to think of you all alone, I can't bear it. And why lose the gift of these beautiful autumn months? I usually have few regrets about the past, but the thought of the recent past and the present causes me pain and distress. And you? I don't know how I'll get through this winter, I don't know where to look for comfort, only in work, maybe. My darling, don't be angry if I complain a little, I know things aren't easy for you either. But our sufferings will be rewarded, won't they? The spring will bring us much light, warmth, joy, renewal. You must be laughing wryly reading these lines, but in your heart you agree with me, don't you?

How is your health? [...] Don't be afraid, I don't want a conversation with serious faces and serious consequences, as you feared. [...]

Chekhov

October 14
Yalta

Darling, I'll be coming to Moscow on October 23 at 5.30 p.m. The express train has stopped running. If you have an evening performance, don't come to meet me.

We have amazing weather in Yalta, the like of which you haven't seen. Everything is in full bloom, the trees are green, the sun shines and warms the air, but it isn't hot.

It rained for three days, including yesterday, violent rain but today the sun is out again. Don't ask about the play, it doesn't matter if it'sn't done this year.

From Moscow I'll go abroad. [...]

I'll be at the theatre on the 23rd, definitely.

Your *Anto*

Knipper

October 16
Moscow, Telegram

Wire me, I'm worried

Chekhov

October 17
Yalta, Telegram

Coming Monday, definitely.

Knipper

October 18
Moscow, Telegram

Come quickly, I want to see you.

Chekhov

October 22
Lozovaya, Telegram

I'm swimming.

Chekhov

Knipper

November ?
Moscow

Unfortunately, I have a rehearsal call for the crowd scene in Act I [of *When We Dead Awake*]. Farewell, darling, I'll come after rehearsal.

Your Olga

Chekhov went to Moscow with the intention of staying a few days but, in the event, stayed seven weeks. He spent as much of his days as he could with Olga and spent the nights at the Hotel Dresden. This arrangement enabled them to continue their liaison without undue embarrassment to Chekhov's sister and mother, although both were aware of the situation, which caused them increasing distress.

Knipper, *Memoir*

When our favourite writer read his long awaited play, *Three Sisters*, to the actors and directors there was a stunned silence. Chekhov gave an embarrassed smile, coughed nervously and wandered among us ... Snatches of remarks were heard: 'This is an outline, not a play', 'It's unactable, no real characters, just a few hints'...

Chekhov revised the first two acts in Moscow, then left for France and Italy with the intention of rewriting the rest. The slowness of the post and his constant shifting from place to place made his correspondence with Olga, and indeed with everyone else, highly erratic, resulting in certain tensions. He despatched the revisions of Three Sisters *as he completed them.*

Knipper

December 11
Moscow

I can't get used to the idea of our being apart. Why have you gone away when we should be together? Yesterday, as the train drew out, taking you with it, I felt with a pang, for the first time, that our separation was real. I walked behind the train as though I didn't believe it was really happening, and suddenly burst into tears and wept as I've not wept for many a long year. I was glad that Sulerzhitski was with me, I knew he understood and I wasn't ashamed of my tears. He was so tactful, so caring, we walked in silence. We waited a long time at the end of the platform for all the people who had come to see you off to leave. I couldn't have borne to see them I loathed them so much. It felt good to cry, hot plentiful tears. I've been unaccustomed to crying these past few years. I wept and felt better for it. I went to see Masha, I sat in a corner and cried gently the whole time. Masha sat beside me and said nothing. Marya Timofeievna was talking quietly to Sulerzhitski in the other room. Then they all came to our house, Sulerzhitski started quizzing the two Maryas about physics and geometry, to make us laugh. I heard it all in a dream, my face buried in a pillow. He was telling them lots of things about his life, doing tricks for them, but I was completely disengaged, my mind was with you, I could hear the rhythm of the rails, I had the particular smell of the carriage in my nose, I tried to guess what you were thinking about, what was going on in your mind, and, can you believe, I did ...

Afterwards we had a quiet dinner. Sulerzhitski and Drozdova made us laugh, they went into all sorts of weird postures and spoke in a very peculiar way. They left and we went to bed. I slept badly, heavily and woke late. I went to the theatre around 12 and found there was not any rehearsal because they were rehearsing *An Enemy of the People*. Raevskaya is ill and Kocheverova is taking over so they don't have to cancel the performance. After I left the theatre I went to see how Raevskaya was. I felt fine, and in sympathetic mood. It was good to see the snow falling. I like that impression of calm and softness. Raevskaya can hardly speak, she is in bed with very bad bronchitis and a temperature of 39. Then I went home, chatted for a while with Elia and Volodya, had lunch, read D'Annunzio and started this letter to you, my dear, my good Anton.

You'll get this letter on Saturday. It takes five days, doesn't it? How did you get there? What were your travelling companions like? They didn't worry you with their cigars? Did you talk to them? It's not yet 5 and you will be in Warsaw at 9. Take care not to catch cold changing trains and, for God's sake, wrap yourself up and don't be angry with me for talking to you like this and go on calling me 'sweetheart', 'doggie' and 'glorious girl' as you always have, please.

You know, Anton, I'm afraid to dream, I mean to interpret my dreams, but it seems to me that something good and strong will grow out of our feelings and when my belief is strong I feel so at ease, my heart glows, and I want to live and work, the pettiness of the daily round can't touch me, and I stop asking questions about the meaning of life. You feel this belief, this hope I have, that we'll be able to spend three months apart, won't we dearest? I don't know why, but I think you will be able to work again and you will be able to rest in Nice, you will go for walks and that will make you want to get back to your desk all the more.

Shall I know what you are writing? Just a few words?

I keep remembering the way we said farewell in Sevastopol and yesterday. Yesterday when we parted our feelings were stronger, clearer, weren't they?

I shall live and work, I won't be sad, I shall think of the spring and our reunion. You, too, my dearest darling? I kiss your dear head, your lovely eyes, your soft hair, your lips, your cheeks, your clever forehead, I clasp you in my arms. Love me, love me and write more often to

Your doggie

Chekhov

December 11
4 in the afternoon Brest

I've reached Brest. Everything is fine. Still no sun. I wish you health and all that's best!

A. Chekhov

Chekhov

December 12
Vienna

My dear, I turned into a complete idiot! I got here and all the shops were shut because it's German Christmas![5] So, here I am, sitting uselessly in my room, not knowing what to do, calling myself every kind of fool. [...] Some restaurants are open and they are packed with dandies who would make me look like a scarecrow. So, what was I to do?

Tomorrow I leave for Nice and in the meantime I cast a lustful eye towards the two beds in my room: I shall sleep and dream! I'm only sad that you're not here, my little scallywag, my sweetheart. How are you getting on, there in Moscow? Are you in rehearsal? Have they got far? Dearest, write and tell me every day, all the details! Otherwise God knows what kind of mood I'll be in.

There was no snow from Brest to Vienna. The earth today was acrid as in March. It isn't like winter at all. My travelling companions were boring.

5. Because of the difference between the Russian and the western calendar, December 12 for Chekhov was December 25 in Austria.

I'm going downstairs for lunch or dinner, I don't know what to call it, then to bed. Big kisses, I press your hand in mine, my wonderful girl. As soon as I get to Nice I'll go straight to the Post Office – perhaps your letter will have arrived.

Write, little one.

Your *Ant*

Knipper

December 12
Moscow

Now you're in Vienna, my darling. [...] I got back from the theatre before 12, had a meal, undressed, washed, put on a dressing-gown and sat down to write to you. That's what I'll do every evening, if I'm not too tired. Tomorrow or the day after I'll get a line from you. [...] It's so empty without you, so very empty. I can still see your face there, in front of me, so alive, I can hear your voice so clearly. [...]

Knipper

December 12
Moscow

Good day, Anton. Are you still on the move? Tomorrow you'll be in Nice, you'll see the sun, the sea, the greenery – lucky man! I've just got back from the theatre, after *Seagull*, and found your postcard from Brest – I was overjoyed. [...] Today, my dear, we had a glorious rehearsal of *Three Sisters* – we are beginning to get the general feel of Solyony, Chebutykin, Natasha, Irina and me. [...]

I've found the walk and I talk in low, chest tones, which, you know, you find in these aristocratic women who have a kind of elegant abruptness. But don't worry, I'm not overdoing it. [...] Yesterday we played *Seagull* in aid of the war veterans.[6] There was a lot of laughter. We had a four-year-old boy in the audience who made comments all the time. Looking at the set for Act I, he said for the whole house to hear, 'Mummy, let's go into the garden and run about!' Of course, the audience laughed.

6. The Russo-Japanese war.

'There's the samovar' – 'She's drinking water' (me in Act Three) etc. – those of us on stage could scarcely contain ourselves. [...]

Chekhov

> December 14
> Nice

Wonderful little actress mine, my angel, my little Jewess, good day. As soon as I got to Nice I had a meal and then the first thing I did was write to you ... My head is spinning from travel fatigue, I've not been able to write today, I will tomorrow but for today just let me kiss you 10,000 times, little girl. It's raining a little but it's warm, wonderfully warm. The roses are in bloom and flowers of all kinds, you wouldn't believe your eyes. There are young people in light clothes, not a hat in sight. [...]

Vienna was boring, the shops were shut and you ordered me to stay at the Hotel Bristol, apparently the best hotel in town; they're terribly snooty and won't let you read newspapers in the dining-room and they're all so dressed up I would have felt ashamed to be among them, like some clumsy Boer. I left Vienna on the express, first class. [...] I had a compartment to myself.

So, be healthy, sweetheart. God and the heavenly angels keep you. Don't change me, even in your thoughts. Write and tell me how rehearsals are going. [...] I implore you.

> Your *Ant—*

Knipper

> December 15
> Moscow

I couldn't write to you yesterday, my dear. I went to bed late and my head was absolutely splitting. [...] Today I seem better.

My dear, you left just in time, today it's –14, so cold! I dislike this intense cold, it depresses me. Now you're in Nice, you're warm, lucky man. Write and tell me how you feel, if you're settled, if your room is a good one, light and warm. Because in the south, rooms are usually chilly in winter. [...]

I think of you often i.e. you are with me all the time, wherever I go. Oh for the spring, the spring!

Chekhov

December 15
Nice

My dear, strange as it may seem, I feel as though I had landed on the moon. It's warm, the sun shines everywhere, it's hot in an overcoat and people wander about as in summer. The window in my room is wide open and so, it seems, is my heart.

I'm rewriting my play and am amazed at the fact that I can even write this farce, and at the reason I'm writing it. Oh, my sweetheart, why aren't you here? You would look, rest, listen to the singers and musicians who wander through the courtyard now and then and, above all, warm yourself in the sun. Now I'm going to go down by the sea and read the papers. Then I shall come back to the house and get down to writing – and tomorrow I'll send Act III to Nemirovich and Act IV the day after – or perhaps both at the same time. I've made a few changes to Act III, added a little but not much.

Sweetheart, send me a photograph. Be a darling, do. There are a lot of flies. [...]

I hug you, kiss you a thousand times. I'm impatient for a letter from you, a long letter. I bow right down to my knees.

Your *Ant*

Knipper

December 16
Moscow

I've just got back from rehearsal, frozen and bad-tempered, I become so sluggish in weather like this, –27 today, can you imagine?! You would go mad. I cried in the street, my eyes hurt, my cheeks hurt, my lips hurt, everything hurt. I'm losing any kind of energy.

At home I found your letter from Vienna which I expected today. [...] Why get so upset? You could jostle your way through the festive crowds and look, and you can buy things that are just as good and cheaper in Nice. Did you really have to stay in your room? Didn't you take a walk on the *Ringstrasse*? Didn't you go to the theatre? You're just a slav sourpuss. I wouldn't allow you to go abroad! But really, in the west you do feel that you are quite ungainly. In Vienna I felt so inelegant, such a sledge-hammer! The people there are so chic, svelte, they all move quickly and beautifully, they have such bearing. Russians abroad look like rag-bags. [...]

Tolstoi came to see the 'Chekhov Evening' recently and, I hear, split his sides with laughter, he liked it so much.

Chekhov

[December 17]
Nice

Sunday. I can't remember the date.

This is the third night I've spent in Nice and not a line from you. [...] My dear Olya, don't be lazy, my angel, write to this old man very soon. It's wonderful here in Nice, the weather is amazing. After Yalta the local countryside and weather seem like heaven. I bought a summer coat and am cutting quite a dash. I sent Act III to Moscow yesterday and will send IV tomorrow. I've only made a few changes to Act III but I've made drastic alterations in Act IV. I've given you a lot more lines (say, thank you). And so, write and tell me how rehearsals are going, tell me everything. Because you don't write to me I don't feel like writing either. Enough is enough! This is my last letter. [...]

Give Vishnievski my address if he wants it.

They feed you enormously here. After lunch you have to take a nap and do nothing, which isn't good. I must change my way of living, eat less.

The residents at the *pension* are Russian and dreadfully boring, dreadfully. And mostly ladies.

A big kiss and a hug for my dear old thing. Don't forget me. Remember me once a week. I hug you again, and again.

Your *Antonio*

Knipper

December 18
Moscow

Forgive me for writing in pencil, my dear. Today I've taken to my bed because I'm afraid I'm developing bronchitis. The theatre doctor came to see me, sounded me, listened and said there was a lot of catarrh in the throat, no bronchitis and my temperature was up a little. I don't know whether I shall be able to play *Lonely People* tomorrow and *Dead* the day after. The doctor will come again and give the theatre an answer. They're rather worried. Nemirovich came back from Petersburg and dropped in to find out how I was. I've a temperature of 37.5 and a painful cough. I could play of course, but what about after? I've been feeling off-colour for some time, I've had three attacks but pulled through by taking quinine. I felt awful yesterday and got back from rehearsal feeling an absolute misery, I didn't even write to you, I didn't know how I was going to play *Uncle Vanya* in the evening. My voice went but I played Act 2 quite well and differently. Yesterday I put a turpentine compress on my chest, drank tea with rum in it, took quinine and today I'm staying in bed. Oh, it's so tedious – so very uninteresting. [...]

Why no letter from you? There wasn't one yesterday, or today. You could write a few lines. I deliberately didn't write to you this morning because I was expecting a letter from you but it's nearly evening and still none has come. It's bad to cheat, you know, my dear.

I haven't had a line so far from Nice. How are you getting on, how is your health, your mood? Do you go for walks, how do you divide up your time, will you start writing soon? Why don't you scribble a few lines to your mother? I rather foolishly let out that I'd had a letter from you and immediately felt I should have kept quiet. She was hurt. You always write to her first, why are you now so inconsiderate? She thinks you've changed towards her because of me. Be kinder to her, please. She loves you and you've always got on well together, so why the change? Will you write to her, my dear? It's awkward writing lying down, so I'll finish. Do you remember the Dresden? Do you dream of spring? I kiss you, darling one, write, write and love your doggie-girl.

Knipper

December 19
Moscow, 8 p.m.

So, Antonino, my darling, at last I've had a letter from you from Nice! That means the roses there are blooming, it's warm, fine and your letters are cheerful, although you must be devilishly tired from the journey and lazy Russians who make themselves a nuisance even on foreign trains. But I love them!

I'm still in bed today. The doctor's been twice, keeps prescribing things. [...]

I have a painful cough, thick phlegm. At nights I make a strong mustard plaster. The doctor says I've aggravated splenitis but I just laugh at him. [...] Nemirovich came and combed my hair: today they're doing *Fyodor* instead of *Lonely People* and tomorrow *Dead* instead of *Terrible* with a loss of 7–800 roubles, all because of me. So, I shan't be playing until the 26th. I'm terribly sorry about the *Sisters* rehearsals and in two days I'll wrap up well and go to the theatre. I'm lying down, reading, resting, I'm calm, I'm not at all embarrassed. [...]

Knipper

December 20
Moscow

I'm still writing in pencil, my dear, sweet Anton, I'm still lying down, my cold won't relent. I didn't sleep a wink last night, I read. A senseless, wild cold started – I don't know why, my head is like lead. My cough seems better, my throat isn't so ticklish. I don't leave my room, I keep covered up and drink *apomorphin*. I don't know what's going on at the theatre. *Terrible* was scheduled for yesterday instead of *Dead* but yesterday, during the evening, the theatre secretary came and told me that Meyerhold has a bad throat and can't play – what do you think of that! They'll probably cancel the show.

It seems the cold isn't quite so intense.

I want to see you, Anton, chat with you, sit at your side, look into your eyes. How do you spend your time? I want to read beautiful, beautiful profound poetry. I take Heine and leaf through his *Buch der Lieder*, which I love. [...]

Chekhov

December 21
Nice

I've just received your letter, little actress mine. [...]

The play is finished and has been despatched. I've added a lot for you in Act IV. You see, I spare no efforts on your behalf, I do my best. Write and tell me about rehearsals, whether there are any misunderstandings. Is Nemirovich coming to Nice? If so, when?

I take my meals in a vast company, almost all women and so gross! I haven't been to Monte Carlo yet.

My little ballerina, life is so dull without you. [...]

I now have two rooms, one large one and one slightly smaller and my bed makes you smile every time you get into it: it's amazingly soft and wide. I speak a little French but I'm forgetting what little I ever knew. I often see you in my dreams, when I close my eyes I can see you clearly. You are the woman I need.

Be healthy, sweetheart, may God who made us all keep you. Be clever, work, and come here in the spring. I've something for your ear. A big kiss, a hug and another kiss.

Your *Antonio*

Write and tell me about all the rehearsals.

Season's greetings. It's New Year here, January 3 already. Spring will soon be with us.

Knipper

December 23
[January 5] Moscow

You staggered me yesterday, dear writer! You hadn't received a single one of my letters by the 17th when you should have had at least two; in all I sent eight letters. Strange! I expect a postcard from you in reply to my letter. It would have been better had I written to you poste restante, I shouldn't have listened to you, although it's insane the way letters get lost abroad!

This is the first day I've wandered round my room a bit. I felt all right. Only very weak. I didn't feel well yesterday, so I didn't write to you. I have to play on the 26th. I hate being flat on my back, I mope. [...]

I try to picture you in a summer coat, strolling down the street, sitting by the shore of the sparkling sea and in the *pension* with all those boring ladies. Only eat more and rest after lunch for as long as you want, it won't do you any harm. Don't starve as is your wont. I want to see you hale and hearty, you understand, sweetheart? Have

you really got to know many people? Write and tell me all. I can't
say anything about rehearsals, I've not been to the theatre for 6 days.
The doctor says that yesterday they rehearsed Act 2 until 1 in the
morning, with great cheerfulness and energy. [...]

Have your picture taken and send it to me with something intimate
written on it, I'll keep it hidden. [...]

Knipper

> December 24
> [January 5] Moscow

My dearest, darling Anton, I really am getting terribly alarmed that
you don't answer my letters. Can it be you haven't received them? I
find that incomprehensible.

Today is Christmas Eve, so there's the traditional hustle and bustle
at home. I remember when I used to be part of it and loved making
sure that everything was perfect and there was a surprise for everyone. Now I don't really care, in fact I find it all burdensome. I want
you to be with me, or me to be with you and for everything to be
other than it is. [...]

Chekhov

> December 26
> Nice

Dear little actress mine, this letter will reach you in the New Year.
New year, new fortune. I kiss you, if you will, a thousand times and
wish you everything you wish yourself and that you remain as good
and glorious as you always have been.

How, by the way, is your health? Your last two letters were
written in pencil and alarmed me, but I wasn't convinced by your
splenitis. I'm rather afraid you have mild typhoid fever and that
means you won't be allowed inside the theatre and my plays won't
be done and I shall have to play roulette. But are you well? Yes? So,
fine, my wonderful darling. I wish you the best.

It's suddenly turned cold here, actual frost. Can you imagine? As
never before. In Marseilles snow covers the mountain tops and the
flowers have faded overnight and here am I going around in a
summer coat! The papers are complaining about the unusual cold.
[...]

Knipper

December 27
[January 8]
Moscow, Telegram

Inquiète envoyé dix lettres répondez

Olga

Chekhov

December 27
Monte Carlo, Telegram

Salue ma belle

Knipper

December 27
[January 8]
Moscow

I don't understand you, Anton! I'm worried that you aren't getting my letters and can't think what it means. I sent a telegram so you could send just one word in reply to say whether you had received my letters. Think about it: in your last letter you write that you had received nothing and wouldn't write anything either and since then I've had not one letter – does that mean you haven't received them or how do you explain it?

I've sent *ten letters*, as I said in my telegram. You're presently in Monte Carlo as is evident from your telegram? Are you playing roulette? Or not? [...]

Yesterday I played *Uncle Vanya* for the first time again, today I'm doing *Lonely People* and tomorrow I'll go to the *Sisters* rehearsal. [...] Gromov's Solyony isn't working, as they say. Sanin may play it. Vishnievski [Kulyagin] is best of all and the others praise him. Meyerkhold [Tusenbach] is nothing special and Artiom [Chebutykin] hasn't quite found the tone. I'm relaying other people's comments as I haven't seen for myself. [...]

Chekhov

December 27
Nice, Evening

Little actress mine, why so worried? I had your telegram today and was at a loss for an answer for quite a while. Shall I tell you I'm as strong as an ox? How is your own health? Are you still at home or have you been to the theatre? My dearest darling, it's better not to be sick, of course, and better still not to be sick at heart. When you are far from me, I've all sorts of ideas running round my head, terrible ones sometimes. Don't be ill, dearest, without me, be clever.

Today I went to Monte Carlo and won 295 francs. I had a telegram from Nemirovich in Mentone.[7] We'll see each other tomorrow. I've bought a new hat. What else? Have you had the new version of your role?

You write that you have sent me two letters, evidently they've been delivered in Moscow in my name. If you sent them, I didn't get them. Judging from the papers, it's cold in Yalta, stormy weather, frost; mother is bored to death.

Your last letter [December 21] is very touching and poetically written. [...]

Chekhov

December 28
Nice

Imagine, doggie mine, the horror! A short while ago I was told a gentleman was asking for me. I went downstairs and there I saw an old man who introduced himself as Cherkov. He was holding some letters, which apparently were addressed to me but had been delivered to him because his name is similar to mine. One of your letters (there were three in all, your first three) was open (!).

Your reproof as regards Vienna, when you call me 'a slav sourpuss' comes very late; 15 years ago I was indeed somewhat lost and didn't go anywhere I should, but this time I went to the only place possible, the theatre, but all the tickets were sold. [...] I bought a splendid wallet at Klein's. He opened his shop on the second day of the holiday. I also bought straps for my luggage. You see, my sweetheart, how thrifty I am.

---

7. Nemirovich had been obliged to leave Moscow to look after his sister in France.

You give me a ticking-off for not writing to my mother. Dearest, I've written to my mother and to Masha many times but never had an answer and probably won't. I just gave up. Not a line from either of them so far and, you're right, I've always been a sourpuss, I'll always be in the wrong although I'm not sure why. [...]

It was cold but now it's warm and I'm wearing a summer coat. I won 500 francs at roulette. May I play roulette, sweetheart? [...]

I was in such a rush over the last act, I thought you needed it, all of you. Now it seems that you won't start rehearsing it until Nemirovich gets back. If only I could have hung on to this act 2 or 3 days more it would have been meatier, you know. [...]

Many ladies eat with me, there are Muscovites but I don't utter a word. I sit there moodily, say nothing and stubbornly eat or I think of you. The Muscovites sometimes talk about the theatre evidently wanting to draw me into the conversation, but I say nothing and go on eating. I'm pleased when they praise you. And, can you imagine, they praise you a lot. It would seem you're a good actress. So, little girl, be healthy, be happy. [...]

Your *Antoine*

Chekhov

December 30
Nice

Dear actress, today is just like summer and I'm starting it by sitting down and writing to you. Your last letter was a little gloomy, but no matter, it will pass. The main thing is not to be ill, my joy. [...]

I had a letter from Vishnievski yesterday in which he tells me he was splendid in the run-through of the first two acts. Have you left the house and gone to rehearsals? You know the changes I made to Acts III and IV, but do you know Act I? Have they rewritten the parts for you? Or are you still working from the old copy-books? [...]

No letter from my mother, or Masha and, naturally, there won't be. I wrote to a doctor in Yalta and asked him to tell me what state my house is in. They don't exactly spoil me at home, my dear, don't think I'm an ungrateful brute. Are you leaving the house and going to rehearsals?

1901

Knipper

January 1
Moscow

[...]

Today I went past the Dresden for the first time and I remembered ... [...]

I went to rehearsal yesterday and today. Today we marked out Act 3 without Stanislavski. Tomorrow we'll do it with him present. Yesterday Sanin joined the cast. I don't know what he'll be like. I was ill and didn't see a single rehearsal. [...]

You write that Masha spends the whole of Act 4 in black, or can it be in a grey or white blouse? [...]

Your little actress

Chekhov

January 2
Nice

My sweetheart, dear, glorious girl, your letter of December 11 has just arrived. A wonderful, splendid letter, thank heaven it didn't get lost. [...] No letter from mother or Masha, although they've had my right address since December 20.

I live here quietly, know many more people than in Yalta, there's nowhere to hide. But I just don't know what to do. I had a long letter from Stanislavski. He wrote it before December 23 but I only got it yesterday. He writes about the play, he praises the cast and you especially. [...]

The weather here is wonderful. I wear summer clothes. It's almost good enough to be perfect. I've been to Monte Carlo twice, sent you a telegram and a letter. Dearest darling, you're angry because I don't write to you and you're afraid you don't write to me. But without your letters I pine away. Write more often and longer letters. Your letters are very good, I love them, I read them several times. I didn't know you were so clever. [...]

Knipper

January 2–14
Moscow

Good day to you, my dearest Anton! It seems an age since I wrote to you but I've only missed one day. Thank you for your telegram. I'm glad you're feeling well again. Has it been warm in Nice? Have you seen Nemirovich? Write and tell me everything, there's a good boy. Have you started writing anything or are you just idling about? Both are equally good. I'm healthy again, although I'm coughing and my throat is infected. I'm free today and tomorrow. [...]

Yesterday was Luzhski's name day and the whole company went to his home. We played *Lonely People*, then went in a body. The house is a good solid, old bourgeois building. Mama is stout, in a mantilla, very good natured, there was an army of young waiters, the usual meal with things in aspic and a *sauté* of grouse and young men to dance with, they pulled you onto the floor with strings. If I were a young lady of good family, as it was in my youth, I would have been desperately bored and yawned but now I feel quite differently. You sit, watch and chat, in a word you feel fine, and quite happy not to be part of the throng. Luzhski's house is enormous, there are endless rooms. [...]

The hosts are dears, very cordial and Luzhski's wife Pereta is sheer benevolence – she likes everything in life, everything is good, everything is a blessing. Two groups of mummers came. The first of about 15 to 20 people, Neapolitan fishermen and signoras with tambourines. A plump baritone fisherman sang Italian songs and a choir came in making a racket with tambourines and castanets, trying to do some mime, and gave a feeble rendition of a wild tarantella. [...] The second group was interesting. It was the chairman of the Society of Art and Literature's idea. He had a red wig and a long nose and demonstrated his arsenal of puppets. [...] We never stopped laughing. [...] The Snow Maiden created a furore – 'a useless doll on sale at the Art Theatre' as the puppet-master called her. Terrified at being lost in Moscow, she began to recite parts of all 5 acts of the play with clever remarks aimed straight at Stanislavski. It was very amusing and witty. [...] I got hold of Stanislavski and we danced a quick mazurka, *solo,* so did Luzhski, though he's no dancer. We danced rather well, I may say. When the outsiders had gone, we gathered in the dark, comfortable library and sang gypsy songs, accompanied on the guitar by [Stanislavski's brother] Boris, his wife sang, she has a sweet voice. Then we sat and talked and parted at 7. I got up at 11½. Naturally they put off today's rehearsal and here I am now, writing to you, my dear, distant Anton. [...]

Let the winter pass soon!

Tomorrow we rehearse Act 3 without the books. The staging is interesting. I'll write the day after. I still haven't read Act 4, I hear I've a scene with Chebutykin, I'm glad about that. I do so want to play Masha well! Soon there'll be a run-through of 3 acts and I'll write more then, everything's only roughed in for the moment.

That's what I wrote to you today. Don't you dare feel low and pine. We'll live, we shall! Live and love! Isn't that so, my dearest? Love me [...] and think of me more, and more often. *Addio* until the next letter. [...]

Chekhov

January 2
Nice

Are you sad now, my heart of hearts, or happy? Don't be sad, sweet one: live, work, and write more often to your Venerable Antonio the Sage. It's a long time since I had a letter from you, apart from the one dated December 12, which I received today, and in which you tell me you cried when I left. What a wonderful letter, truly! Of course, you did not write it yourself but got someone else to do it for you, didn't you? An admirable letter.

Nemirovich hasn't been to see me. I sent him a telegram the day before yesterday asking him to come and see me *alone.* We need to meet to talk about the letter I've had from Stanislavski. I'm spending the whole day indoors, as I did yesterday, I'm not going out. The reason is I've had an invitation from some big wig. I don't have tails and I'm not in the mood. Malakov, from Moscow, came to see me today. What else? Nothing.

Describe at least one rehearsal of *Three Sisters* to me. Is there anything that needs adding or cutting? Are you acting well, my darling? And look here, don't put on a gloomy face, not in one single act.

Angry, yes; gloomy, no. People who are used to being sad inside just whistle and are often lost in thought. You often become pensive on stage when people are talking. Understand?

Of course you do, because you're bright. [...]

Your *Toto*

Knipper

January 4
Moscow

I'm just writing you a few lines, my dear. I've only just got back from rehearsal and sat down to a meal – Khotyaintseva and Zvantsova came and are still here and in ¼ of an hour I have to go back to the theatre to perform *Dead*. I've dreadful catarrh, I simply can't speak. The 'flu won't relent. I didn't sleep last night. – I've just got your letter. Your letters are calm, no low spirits. Enjoy yourself, my dear, while you're there. You can come back. You're a notorious fidget. You know, I'm right to be worried about my letters falling into other people's hands! [...] Tomorrow we run all 3 acts. I'm pleased with my Masha but I haven't had the new version of Act 4, so I don't know. [...]

Chekhov

January 6
Nice

Dear, clever girl of mine, it's a long time since I had a letter from you; you've obviously given up on me. I'm happy to say I've had all the letters you sent. [...]

I've finally had a letter from Masha. Now I shall write to mother every three days so she doesn't get bored. [...]

How is *Three Sisters* going? Not one of those miserable hounds writes to me about it. You don't write about it either and I could give you a hiding for that. [...]

Knipper

January 7
Moscow, Morning

I've just got up, my dear, although it's one in the morning. Because in your last letter you write that I don't understand how much you love me. I read that yesterday evening and decided that you wrote that idly but then thought you might mean it seriously – yes or no? You think I don't feel how much you love me? Quite the contrary, my dear, I know that no one ever loved me as much as you, or ever will. What was the matter, were you bored?

I haven't written to you for two days. Yesterday I paid a lot of calls with mama and then had a headache that turned into a migraine and then went to perform *Lonely People*. Yesterday I went to see Fedotova, chattered endlessly. [...] She showed us old posters, pictures, gifts. As we talked, I was horrified at the difference between what the theatre was like then and what it's like now. [...] On the 14th there will be a daytime run of 3 acts of *Sisters*. I still don't like Sanin, I don't know what will happen on the day. I don't like Meyerhold either – no gaiety, no strength, no life, – dull. Only you keep quiet, don't say anything, let others tell you what's going wrong – I'm still wheezing, my catarrh won't give up, another bout started before the other had finished. As soon as I'm well again, I'll have my photo taken and send it to you – happy? [...]

I often think of you, my dear. When shall we be together, how and where? [...]

I'm glad you're so well and warm over there. I felt like running to you, if only for a few hours, chat with you, kiss you, criticize you because of your hair – *o pardon, academicus*!

I kiss you, hug you, and
love you
Your – who?

Chekhov

January 7
Nice

Dear little tippler, I've just had your letter and the description of the evening at Luzhski's. You ask what happened to the letters, or rather, the three letters that all arrived in the same envelope. Don't worry, dearest, I got them. Thank you. [...]

You tell me nothing about how the play is going, what I can count on etc., etc. It's highly possible I shall go to Algiers on January 15. But still write to the old address, i.e. in Nice and they will forward them to Algiers. I want to see the Sahara. [...]

Knipper

January 7
Moscow

For some reason I'm in 'terribly good spirits', dear Anton, and I just wanted to tell you. I don't know why, I have such a strong desire to live a happy life, to feel and understand everything – all the beauty, the wholeness, the immensity of life. I want to smile at everyone, help everyone so that all is light and warmth around me.

You're not laughing at me? You do understand? Ah, Anton, how I long to be with you right now! Tell me, do we really understand even a fraction of life? [...]

Knipper

January 9
Moscow, 1 a.m.

A restful night, my dear Toto. I've just got back from the Bolshoi theatre and am going to bed to read *Kramer*.[8] [...] Today we set Act 4. You've given me a lot, dearest, but it's difficult to play. But I love the role. Concerning Act 3, Stanislavski said I'm like Carmen, I need to be more dreamy, more restrained. I like the Act 4 décor. Tomorrow we'll wait and see what Nemirovich says. I think we open on the 24th. [...]

8. *Michael Kramer* by Hauptmann, opened October 27, 1901.

I don't know where my letters get to. I write almost every day, I haven't missed more than 2 days. Ask at the post office. [...]

Your doggie

Chekhov

January 11
Nice

Heartless, savage woman, a century has passed without a letter from you. What does it mean? Now my letters are being sent to me properly and if I don't get them the only one responsible, my faithless one, is you.

If the sea isn't too rough in the next few days, I shall go to Africa. [...] I won't stay long, two weeks.

It's wonderful summer weather here all the time, warm, marvellous, flowers, ladies, bicycles but it's all an oleograph and not a picture, for me at least.

Write, doggie! Red-haired doggie! It's so mean of you not to write to me! If only you would tell me what's happening to *Three Sisters*. You still haven't written anything about the play, absolutely nothing except about rehearsals, mostly whether there was a rehearsal that day or not. I'll surely give you a thrashing, dammit. [...]

Your *Toto*

Knipper

January 11
Moscow, 1 a.m.

My own dearest, you complain that you're not getting any letters but I'm writing all the time, every day, or every other day! Why are you grumbling at me? – I'm terribly tired today. My brother and his wife and little girl will be here until the 25th and go to Petersburg in 3 weeks. Yesterday I stayed up late reading Act 4. I got up early to the sweet prattling of 5-year old Adochka. [...] We ran the third act twice. Nemirovich saw the runs and, apparently, has changed a lot. Stanislavski created tremendous commotion on stage with everyone running about and getting excited, Nemirovich, on the other hand, suggested creating a lot of noise off-stage and a feeling of emptiness on stage, with a measured pace, which will be much stronger. Everyone has the right tone and we have reason to hope the play will go well. Yesterday, Stanislavski talked to me for more than two hours at a stretch, a thorough examination of me as an artist, lecturing me again on my inability to work, saying I had played far too many roles in the last three years and that I'm never ready at the 1st performance, only on the 15th etc ... I find him difficult to talk to; [...] I didn't see Nemirovich, only I was staggered by one or two things he'd said. He told Sanin that people were getting on your nerves, you weren't at ease with them and were going to Africa?!!! That's news to me! My dove, don't be angry if for the present I write often but badly. Things are hotting up over *Sisters*. Then there are rehearsals, fittings and evening performances! [...] I've to spend time on the role. Act 4, you know!

Don't talk nonsense, that I've fallen in love, I've forgotten you – there wouldn't be time, even if I wanted to. My silly old 'Venerable Sage Anton'!

[...] Have you thought when we'll meet? And where? [...]

Olga

Knipper

January 13
Moscow, 2 a.m.

Night again, late again and again I am writing to you, my dearest darling. Thank you for not forgetting me, for writing often. Life is easier when you write. First things first: Stanislavski has asked me to ask you about the end of Act 4. Can we dispense with carrying Tusenbach's body across the stage, as that would mean a crowd scene that could break in on the trio of the three sisters and, above all, would make the set wobble since, as you know, our stage isn't deep. For the moment we're rehearsing without it. For heaven's sake, answer immediately. Don't delay. Of course, the sisters can't sit there indifferent if a body is brought into the house. What do you think?

Tomorrow there is only run-through of three acts at 12 – that means getting up early. The tram-tram[9] is causing a problem. Nemirovich thinks we should sing out these signals like bugle calls, with mimed actions, of course. If we just speak them, they'll come out as

9. A secret signal between Masha and Vershinin.

crude or incomprehensible. Write about that, too. [...] I've just come from the theatre where we've given the 99th performance of *Fyodor*, it's 2 in the morning. I'll read through *Sisters*, as I've hardly rehearsed the 1st and 2nd acts – I've been ill. Nemirovich is discussing the next season with the actors. Sanin told me I would get an increase of 400 roubles. I'm not greedy, but really, given the work I do, it's not very much, don't you think, because I've to spend more than others on wardrobe? Anyway, I shall persuade the management they should bear the cost of my wardrobe. For the rest, I have to resign myself to the fact there are no [new] parts for me next season. Well, we'll see. [...]

Your Olga

Uncle Sasha read *Sisters* and says it's the best thing you've written.

Chekhov

January 14
Nice

Dear actress, I'm worried. First you write that you've been ill and second, I read in the *Russkie Ved.* that *Uncle Vanya* has been taken off. Why, oh why, dear girl, are you ill, if you really are ill? Why don't you look after yourself, why do you bounce about and not sleep till 7 in the morning? You need taking in hand. I get your letters as I should and read them two or three times. Why don't you write anything about *Three Sisters*? How is the play going? All you write about is Sanin and Meyerhold and I suspect that my play is a flop already. And when I saw Nemirovich here, it was very boring and I had the impression the play is an unmitigated flop and that I won't be writing for the Art Theatre again.

I was a little unwell but it's all right now, everything's fine. [...] I'll write to you on the boat and from Algeria almost every day, dearest and then you'll remember me from time to time.

The consular secretary has been to see me so I couldn't write to you. I got your letter while he was here. I get all your letters, but you don't write every other day, sometimes less, my dear. Well, God be with you. [...]

Your *Toto, ex-physician
and part-time dramatist*

Knipper

January 15
Moscow

In your last letters, dearest, you're very cross with me for not writing. But I must tell you again that I never miss more than two days, I'd say, in fact not more than one. I don't know what becomes of my letters – they probably go to some gentleman or other. I write the address out in full.

I haven't been able to write anything about the play up till now because we've been at the nappy stage, so what could I write? Yesterday we had a dress run of Act 2. Everyone was pleased on the whole, although everything's not quite right yet. There's nothing to say about the play, people watch it with enormous interest, oh great master. The interpretation, they say, is concert-like. Not everyone is happy with Meyerhold. Andreeva and Savitskaya are good. Luzhski and Vishnievski, too. Stanislavski hasn't joined the cast yet.[10] I had a long discussion with Nemirovich yesterday about my Masha. Stanislavski says I'm over-dramatizing it. The role hasn't come to the boil yet, you see. The point of disagreement with Nemirovich is Masha's confession in Act 3. I want to do the third act in a state of nerves, in fits and starts, that means the confession is strong, dramatic, i.e. the darkness of the situation gains the upper hand over the joy of love. Nemirovich wants this joy of love, so that, despite everything, is full of this love and doesn't confess as to a crime. The second act is full of this love. For Nemirovich, Act 4 is the climax; for me, it's Act 3. What's your response? Nemirovich suggests we do it this way: Masha asks for a continuation of Vershinin's motif, i.e. humming quietly, of course with an eloquent face. The staging here is very important and I'm not sure Stanislavski has got it right, we'll probably have to change it. He asks once more: Masha asks him (not humming) without looking at him, face out front, embarrassed, as it were, by this declaration. In a word we must make sure the audience understands. We'll try it many different ways.

[...]

---

10. Stanislavski took over the role of Vershinin ten days before the opening night.

Chekhov

January 17
Nice

Sweetheart, don't worry, your letters are getting here all right and
I'm willing to bet not one has gone astray. Thank you, dear doggie.
And if recently, as you write, I get short letters from you and don't
get them very often, so be it. You have work to do, a great deal of
work, although I don't think the play will be done this season, only
in Petersburg. [...]

I'm in top form. We're intending to go to Algeria but not soon, I
think, because the sea is rough. Today, for example, there's a storm.
A lot of people come to see me, stop me working a lot and get on
my nerves. I can't write, mainly because I feel such fury. After
Algiers I want to go straight back to Yalta. [...]

Your Venerable Sage,
Antony

Knipper

January 18
Moscow, 1 a.m.

Last letter January 15
Anton, darling, dearest, why the sad letter, the despondency? Why
the rust in the heart? [...] Throw off the gloom, my dove, my
darling. Do you love me? We'll soon be together. Yesterday I sent
you a greetings telegram [on your birthday] (ask at the telegraph
office) but in the evening I got a reply: *Tchekoff inconnu. Adresse
insuffisante – what do you think of that! I'd forgotten to put Pension
russe*! How I cursed myself! Did you really think the actress had
forgotten the 17th. Did you forget yourself?

You ask about the play? What nonsense to think of failure! God
help you! The play is terribly interesting to see. We haven't been
through it all yet. Everything is going well for all of us, only
Meyerhold lacks *joie de vivre* and Sanin still hasn't found the tone.
Today we did really good solid work on Act 2. I'm not writing much
because I'm still not clear about everything. You, after all, don't like
talking about things you're working on, and I don't want to chatter.
Don't be cross, my darling, and don't worry.

This evening, Nemirovich and I did good work on Masha, I understood everything, consolidated it, and I do love this role so terribly. It plays itself, really, doesn't it?

I won't play the confession in a loud voice but with strong inner drive and feeling and a glimmer of happiness if I can so express it. There is almost no movement, the eyes ... oh, I'm chattering on like an actress and you can't understand me. In the second act, Nemirovich insists that Vershinin and Masha shouldn't be lonely but that there should be the impression they have discovered one another and feel the joy of love. Stanisl. has decided that Irina and Rodé should dance to the waltz Tusenbach is playing while Masha becomes engrossed in a Russian waltz at the words 'The Baron is drunk'. Fedotik catches hold of her but she pushes him away and whirls around alone. In the 3rd act I'm not comfortable with the fact that Stanisl. has Masha take care of Irina, who is sobbing hysterically and, on Andrei's entrance, has the sisters take her behind the screen because she doesn't want to see him. But that, I think, will be altered and the sisters will stagger downstage on the beat.

The décor is charming. A wonderful pathway; lined with fir-trees, a house with a large terrace and a porch where officers pass and Masha and Vershinin part. Does it matter if I make a tiny cut in my last speech? If I find it difficult to deliver? Does it matter? I really like the shaping of Masha in the last act. The whole role is a marvel. If I ruin it, I'll give myself up as a bad job. [...]

Sweetheart, I'm not in a sour mood. I feel fine if I don't wear myself out and if I sleep well, i.e. six or seven hours. I can live without food but not without sleep. Do you sometimes see me in your dreams? [...] Write to me from Africa every day, *without fail*, either a postcard or a few lines because I shall get terribly worried if we don't write. [...]

Your Olga

Knipper

January 19
Moscow, Telegram

Télégraphie santé inquiète – Olga

Knipper

I'm just writing you a few lines, my dear. And I shall write every day so you won't growl at me. You wrote to Masha that you have not been well. Write and tell me in detail what's the matter with you. I'm not a doll and that kind of attitude towards me will only make me angry. I sent you a telegram today in the heat of the moment. [...] I'm exhausted. I get no rest. I spend all my free moments away from the theatre with my family, as mama works all day. I'm surrounded by people all the time and so I'm nervy. I've just quarrelled with my brother Kostya about our theatre, straight after *Lonely People*. Usually I keep quiet. All I want right now is to go to bed and not move. I don't read at all, not even newspapers – quite shameful! Why is there so little time? We polished the 2nd act, tomorrow we tidy up the 3rd. On the 26th there's the 100th performance of *Fyodor*. Dearest darling, how life rushes by. Let winter be over soon.

I so want to rest with you! I don't know how I'd keep going if I didn't have that to look forward to. A peaceful night, my darling and restful sleep.

Chekhov

Santé merveilleuse   Antoine

Chekhov

Darling little actress mine, exploitress of my heart, why send me a telegram? It would be better to wire about something yourself than for such silly reasons. How is *Three Sisters*? Judging by your letters you're all spreading utter and complete nonsense. Noise in Act III? Why noise? There's only noise in the distance, offstage, muffled, confused but on the stage itself everyone is drowsy, half-asleep. If you ruin Act III, the whole play goes for nothing and, in the twilight of my years, I shall be hissed off the stage. In his letters Stanislavski praises you highly, Vishnievski, too. Though I can't see you, I praise you, too. Vershinin delivers tram-tram-tram as a question and you as an answer and to you this is such an original joke that you speak this 'tram-tram' with a smile. She says 'tram-tram' and laughs, not loudly, just a very little. We don't need a character as in *Uncle Vanya* here, but someone younger and livelier. Remember, you are easily amused and easily angered. Well, my hopes are in you, sweetheart, you're a good actress.

I have already said that carrying Tusenbach's body across wouldn't work on your stage but Stanislavski insisted that the body was essential. I wrote so it wouldn't be done, I don't know if he got my letter.

If the play flops, then I'll go to Monte Carlo and gamble and drink myself silly.

I feel the urge to get out of Nice. But where am I to go? I can't go to Africa at the moment because the sea is rough and I don't want to go to Yalta. I shall have to be in Yalta in February and in Moscow in April. And then we'll leave Moscow for somewhere.

I have absolutely no news at all. Be healthy, sweetheart, my despondent actress, don't forget me, love me just a little, even a pennyworth. I kiss you, hug you. I wish you joy.

Keep well.

Your Venerable Sage
Antony

Knipper

January 22
Moscow

My dearest, darling Anton! People are being a nuisance again and annoying you, so why not go to another hotel? As I write, people are chattering all round me and asking me questions. I spent the night with Masha in her new apartment, which is very comfortable, almost in the country, quiet and very pleasant. We gave a good performance of *Seagull* yesterday. [...] The opening of *Sisters* is fixed for January 30. Stanislavski has now joined the cast. Nemirovich says Kachalov should play Tusenbach. What do you think? Why have you still not said anything about Tusenbach's body? [...]

I must dash to rehearsal. I kiss you, hug you. Think of the spring and the beauty of life. You love both, don't you, poet mine!

Your doggie

Knipper

January 23
Moscow, Midnight

Another day and no letter from you, my dearest! Life is so dreary without them; when I get back from the theatre I dash from one table, one corner to another – is there anything from Nice? I go around in a strange, confused and sometimes quite furious state. I can't be alone for a minute and that does me no good at all. I get worse with time. On the 27th my brother and his wife leave for Petersburg and I shall rest before *Sisters*. On the 27th there will be a dress run of Act IV with Stanislavski. Masha, good soul that she is, will write to you. I'm afraid to say anything beforehand.

Enough about the theatre. Did you get my telegram of the 17th or not? I'm so happy you're in good health again. Why don't you write and tell me how you are? That grieves me. Then I've the feeling you are cooling off me. Send me your photograph *without fail*. [...] I've no idea where we'll spend the summer together, where we can rest, love each other, without other people being a nuisance. I want you to be happy with me, I want us to have our *own* life, the two of us, without intruders. I know the kind of life you like, poet mine, you admire everything that is beautiful and graceful. [...]

Chekhov

January 24
Nice

Sweetheart, wonderful woman, I'm not going to Algiers because the sea is rough and my companions refuse to leave. So, I wash my hands of the whole thing and am going home to Yalta. Fortunately, I'm told, the weather's fine and mother is alone.

I'll send my photograph. [...]

I hear from you that in Act III you lead Irina by the hand. Why? Is that in keeping with your mood? You shouldn't move from the sofa. Doesn't Irina come to you? Honestly! Colonel [Petrov][11] has written me a long letter complaining about Fedotik, Rodé and Solyony; he complained about Vershinin and his immorality; he's going astray with someone else's wife! [...] He praises the three sisters and Natasha, I'm happy to say. He also praises Tusenbach.

Father *Antony*

Knipper

January 26
Moscow

Bonjour, mon très cher Antonio! Comment ça va? La santé et l'humeur vont bien, sans doute?

I receive all your letters and give my academician a big kiss in return. I really don't know how I feel. It's as though someone were pulling a string and I were just obeying, without thinking. I'm only really alone when I sleep, which means I'm not me, I'm living by inertia, unconsciously. That is awful!

Tomorrow there's a dress rehearsal of *Sisters*. I'm very emotional in the 4th act, I cry my heart out; I'm told – sincerely. In the 3rd act, I talk to my sisters or, as I put it, I confess, holding back, in fits and starts, with pauses, it's hard not to do it loudly. I only shout 'Oh, you're so silly Olya! I'm in love, that's my fate ... etc' ... then, quietly once more, tense. She sits quite motionless, hands clasped on knees until the off-stage 'tram-tram'. Then she lifts her head, her face lights up, she jumps up nervously and takes leave of her sisters. I've decided that by 'tram-tram' (in your version *she* calls, *he* answers), she is saying that she loves him i.e. the admission he has been seeking for so long. I sit down at the desk, by the footlights, agitatedly scrawl something in pencil. When he sings, she looks, smiles, turns away i.e. bends her head and asks 'tram-tram'. After his response, she says, even more anxiously, 'tra-la-la', and finally, decisively, 'tram-tram'. If this is all done with a smile, it can't be vulgar, seeing it's a mere *rendez-vous*. Because up to that night their relationship has been pure, yes? I think everything is going well now. I'm told the fourth act, starting with the parting of Masha and

11. The military adviser to the production of *Three Sisters*.

Vershinin, creates a considerable impression. I'll write about the dress rehearsal the day after tomorrow. Today was the 100th *Fyodor*. [...]

Chekhov

January 26
Nice

Today, my dearest, I shall in all probability go to Algiers. Still write to Nice and they will forward my letters or write one or two letters to: *Alger, poste restante*. From Algiers, I'll move on to Yalta and then go somewhere with my doggie. [...]

How did *Three Sisters* go? Wire me *Alger, post. rest.* – don't spare me. It's been cold here the last few days, as cold as Yalta and I'm glad to be leaving. If, my darling, the sea is rough this evening, then I shall obey my travelling companions and go to Italy. Not Algiers, to Naples, but I'll write to you about that not later than this evening. I shall go to Marseilles overnight ... brrrr!

But I'm in good spirits, I love to travel. For the last few days I've dreamed of going to Spitzbergen for the summer, or Solovka. [...]

Chekhov

January 28
Nice, Sunday

I'm writing this letter from Nice, sweetheart. From here I'll go to Florence, then Rome, then Naples, where I'll get your letters forwarded from Nice. My address for letters and telegrams is: *Naples, post. rest.*

Has my play been done, or not? I know nothing. [...]

By Lent I shall be at home in Yalta. I'll probably leave Italy by sea, going via Corfu.

Your *Antonio*

Chekhov

January 28
Nice, Sunday

Dearest, Masha's confession in Act 3 isn't one, it's just a frank conversation. Play it highly-strung but not desperate, and don't raise your voice, smile from time to time and above all play it so that one can feel the exhaustion of the night. And so one can feel that you are more clever than your sisters, or at least, that you think you are. As regards 'tram-tram-tram', do it your way. You are my interpreter.

I'm writing, of course, but not with much relish. *Three Sisters* seems to have worn me out or I'm simply tired of writing and getting old. I don't know. I may not write for five years, travel for five years and then come back and work.

So, *Three Sisters* won't be done in Moscow this season? You'll première it in Petersburg?

Only, remember, there's no hope of any success in Petersburg at all. [...] In Petersburg there'll be polemics but not a whiff of success. I'm sorry. [...]

Academic *Toto*

Knipper

January 29
Moscow

Many, many thanks, darling, for the photograph. Only you look so lack-lustre, as always in amateur photographs. [...]

Chekhov

January 29
Florence, Monday

Dearest, I'm writing from Florence and will probably stay here for two days. I can only say it's wonderful here. People who haven't been to Italy have never lived. My room's so cold I'd put on a fur coat if there were one.

Has *Three Sisters* been done? Are you in low spirits? Darling, it's all irrelevant nonsense. [...]

Your *Antoine*

1901

Three Sisters *opened on January 31, 1901. Knipper wired Chekhov immediately after the performance.*

Knipper

> January 31
> Moscow, Telegram

Grand succès embrasse mon bien aimé   Olga

Unfortunately, the telegram was sent to Algiers from where it was forwarded to Yalta. Chekhov did not receive it until he got home, and thus remained in ignorance of the success of the play for some time.

Chekhov

> February 2
> Rome

Dearest girl, I'm in Rome. Your letter arrived today after a whole week. I think my play is responsible and has flopped. Not a whisper about it – obviously it misfired.

Oh, what a wonderful land this Italy is! Marvellous country! There's not a corner, not an inch that isn't food for the mind.

So, I'm in Rome. From here I go on to Naples, where I'll spend five days (that means I'll get your letter there, if you sent one), then to Brindisi and from Brindisi by sea to Yalta, via Corfu, I think. You see, my darling, what a traveller I am. Going from place to place, looking at everything, is much nicer than sitting at home writing, even for the theatre. We, i.e. you and I, will go together to Sweden and Norway. Yes? A memory for our old age.

I'm now in perfect health, perfect, my darling. Don't be anxious and be healthy, too. [...]

I'm eating a terrible lot. I had a letter from Nemirovich; he praises you.

> Your *Antony*, the
> venerable sage

Chekhov

Rome
le 4 Fevral

Dearest sweetheart, I'm still in Rome. From here I shall go to Naples and from Naples to Corfu, but only if I hear that there's no plague in Constantinople; if there is, I'll go to Russia via Vienna. [...] Yesterday I had a telegram from Naples, from Nemirovich notifying me *Three Sisters* had been done. He says the female roles were the best. Now I'm waiting for a letter from you. [...]

Tomorrow I leave for Naples where I'll spend five, maybe four days. Your letters have been forwarded to me here from Nice, not one went astray. And so by February I shall be back in Yalta; once there, I shall write a great deal till we meet and go somewhere together. Yes?

A big kiss. Be healthy, don't be down.

Your *Ant*

Knipper

February 5
Moscow

I need to talk to you so very, very much, my dear Anton! There's so much to tell! [...]

Moscow talks of nothing else but *Three Sisters*. A success for Chekhov and a success for our theatre. À *propos* of your doggie, they write in the *Novoe Vremya* that Miss Knipper and Mr Gromov stood out in a superb ensemble – isn't that wonderful? [...]

I had a letter from my brother in Petersburg about rooms. A good one can cost as much as 80 r. a month. If two share, it's easier on one's pocket. And everyone talks about the legendary cost of living, terrible. [...]

I've played every night all this week, except on the 8th when they did *Dead* with Munt.[12] Are you bored without my letters. I like that. But my letters have been so awful, my dear, that I'm ashamed.

---

12. Ekaterina Mikhailovna Munt, member of the Art Theatre, Meyerhold's sister-in-law by his first marriage.

You're not angry with me and haven't stopped loving me? Anton, you haven't changed? You still have your nose, teeth, hair, eyes, beard?

I'm so sad you can't see me playing Masha. I would play for you with such joy!

So, a peaceful night, my dear? How are you in yourself? Is it true Florence is beauty itself? *La bella Firenze*, they call it, and rightly. Did you see the Palazzo Pitti and the cathedral with the beautiful façade? I live on the banks of the Arno, in the *pension Bellini*. [...] Why aren't I there with you? We would lounge about and enjoy ourselves gloriously! [...]

Your little actress

Chekhov

Rome
le 20 Feb [February 7]

My darling, I shall be leaving for Russia, for the north, in two hours. It's very cold here, it's snowing and I have no desire at all to go to Naples. So, write to me now in Yalta.

Not one letter from you about *Three Sisters* although I was told in a telegram that the *Novoe Vremya* said you stood out as the best of the lot. Write all the details to me in Yalta, I beg you, dearest. [...]

Your *Antonio*

Knipper

February 8
Moscow

I simply wanted to tell you that I thought a lot about you today and that gave me serenity of heart. My darling, how far away you are from me! I can't wait for the end of winter, the end of the season when I shall be with you at last every day, every hour! If only you knew how I look forward to that! Where shall we meet?

If the play is done without me, I could be free in May. I'm so tired, so worn out, I feel like someone else. I expect you're laughing at me. People say: she wears herself out, goes frantic like a squirrel in a cage and imagines she's doing something practical. Laugh at me, Anton, but I couldn't live without all that. It doesn't tire me at all, sometimes I'm calm and can live the kind of life I want. I can't live the life I want at home i.e. find the right *train*, so as not to be driven mad by people who don't interest me, and so that time doesn't go to waste. I so want to see you, Anton. I look at your picture and I can hear you laugh, I can see all of you, the look in your wonderful eyes, I can hear you calling me 'glorious girl'. I love that.

You're loving Italy – life is so full there, nature, poetry and history!! [...]

Your Olga

Sisters is all the rage. Yesterday there was an ovation after the fourth act. We're going to Petersburg on the 14th. Two bookings sold out. We open with *Uncle Vanya*.

Knipper

February 10
Moscow

Yesterday and today, I expected a letter from you and finally got one. What a difference there is between your life and the mess mine is in. You have only fresh, wholesome impressions, so much space, freedom! I drag myself through the season, tired out, indifferent to everything, and there is just a glimmer of light in the distance – the summer break with you, somewhere we'll be comfortable together. I so want to talk to you, my dear! I shall be in a desperate state before our meeting. That's what I dreamed! ... What do you dream? ...

Today we played *Seagull*. After the 4th act there was an ovation, and tomorrow, after *Three Sisters*, farewell to the audience. I can imagine what will happen. Everyone's talking about *Sisters*, talking, talking about Chekhov ...

Chekhov

February 11
Volochisk, Telegram

Wire Odessa [Hotel] London going to Yalta. Greetings.

Chekhov

Knipper

February 12
Moscow

I've received a telegram and your letter, my darling. So you will
soon be in Yalta. But why didn't you go to Naples? Let's say that
the winters are unpleasant in Italy because the houses are 'draughty'.
And they don't have stoves – I shivered desperately myself – you
only come alive again in the sun, in the street. Soon you'll be in
Yalta and I can already feel you near me. At the moment I'm sitting
in the dining room, writing to you, there is total silence. Darling
little Adochka is asleep in the next room. I've grown very attached
to her these last six weeks and parting will be difficult. The samovar
is simmering on the table, there are children's toys everywhere,
there's no one at home, everything is quiet and I'm beginning to pull
my thoughts together. I leave for Petersburg the day after tomorrow.
I've to pack and there is a lot to do, I have to remember every silly
last thing, every shred of clothing.

Yesterday the season ended with *Three Sisters*. We've played it
seven times! Full houses of course, even the house seats were sold.
There was a tremendous lot of noise last night. Bouquets were presented to Lilina and Andreeva; after the fourth act the whole company took a bow. The audience went mad. We all took flowers and
threw them out front. Applause was ringing in our ears. But I'm
always depressed at moments like that. And yesterday I wanted to
cry, I felt so alone.

I couldn't begin to describe to you that feeling of sadness and
unease. Added to which I'm very tired and gave the last performance
everything I had. At the end the audience crowded round me, pressed
my hands, girls kissed me, they raised me shoulder high and dragged
me right through the theatre to the exit. I thought I'd go mad because
of the heat, and because I disliked it all so much. They pushed
Masha away from me. I spent the night with her. Today I went shopping. Tomorrow I'll be rushing about the whole day. I shall have to
have a good rest in Petersburg and play *Uncle Vanya* with renewed
strength on the 19th.

I've sent many letters to Naples and Nemirovich wired you, why
have you had nothing so far? What I ask myself is whether you've
actually been to Naples. That means everything is waiting for you. It
could be this letter will reach you before the correspondence from
Italy and so you should know that *Sisters* had a huge success; both

the play and the interpretation produced a sensation. [...] I play
Masha with such delight. You see, she has been of great use to me.
I've found out what kind of actress I am, I've understood myself.
Thank you, Chekhov! Bravo!!! [...]

Your Olga

*The Art Theatre left for its first tour to St. Petersburg on February 14,
1901. Everyone was aware of the risks involved. The contempt in which
the aristocrats of St. Petersburg held the 'tradesmen' of Moscow was
notorious. The notion, therefore, that anything artistically superior
could come out of Moscow was dismissed out of hand. Chekhov, who
profoundly mistrusted critical circles in St. Petersburg, anticipated
nothing but grief for his beloved Olga.*

Knipper

February 15
St Petersburg

Here I'm in Petersburg, my darling! I'm writing to you in pencil
because I still don't have any ink and my brother and his wife are
having lunch downstairs and their room is locked. I'm very tired, I
got here this morning by the express, chatted with the family, ran
around town, went to the theatre and have only just got up – I had a
little nap. I'm staying at 16 Boulevard Morska, room 37, that's
where you should write. These furnished rooms are very good, I
hear. Well, we'll see. I shall have a room for 60 r. in a few days but
for the moment I live more expensively. I shall be by myself, which
pleases me, at least I shall get some rest. The journey here was good.
Andreeva, Stanislavski and Nemirovich had a private carriage on the
same train. In the morning I sat in their sitting room and read aloud
two articles from the *Novoe Vremya* in which we are soundly criticized. Petersburg has gone crazy, they've gone mad about our arrival,
they're expecting something special and of course they'll be disappointed. Tickets are being sold with incredible speed. What is
going to happen?!!! I'm terribly worried. I have the feeling I shall be
playing *Uncle Vanya* for the first time, I'm thinking about the role,
as though it were a new one. We open on the 19th, on the 20th we
do *Lonely People*, on the 21st *Uncle Vanya* again and *Lonely People*
on the 22nd. Will you think of me? I'll wire you after the first per-

formance. [...] I'm impatient for a letter from you. How was your journey, how are you? [...] A big kiss for you, will you give me one back? I hug my writer.

Your doggie

Knipper

February 20
St Petersburg, Telegram

Huge success for Chekhov and the theatre healthy happy receive no letters.

Chekhov

February 20
Yalta

My dearest, wonderful darling, a big hug and a kiss. I've been travelling for two weeks, had no letters, and thought you'd gone cold on me and suddenly they all turned up from Moscow, from Petersburg and from abroad. I left Italy so soon because there was snow, and it was cold and because, suddenly, life palled without your letters, and because I was in the dark about everything. I only found out about *Three Sisters* here in Yalta; in Italy, all I got was ifs and buts. It was like failure because everyone who read the papers kept their mouths shut and because Masha was full of praise in her letters. Well, never mind. [...]

Knipper

February 21
Petersburg, Night

I so want to see you, dear Anton! I so want to talk to you about all the events of the past few days. I'm completely alone now. Kostya and his wife left for Moscow today.

We've just played *Uncle Vanya* for the second time. The audience was receptive but the papers roasted us shamelessly. And such a roasting! They absolutely tore me to pieces. The reviews were illiterate, stupid and venomous. But we hold our heads high, we go on playing. At the first performance we were all infernally nervous, like schoolchildren. *Lonely People* got an all-round roasting, both the play and the performance.

Night has set in, my day is ending. Sanin showed me all the papers – the abuse was awful – none of us is a decent actor, only Stanis. and Sanin were praised. Meyerhold and I were completely savaged, as were Andreeva and Moskvin. In short, it was terrible, my darling!

I've been terribly upset tonight, I confess it openly. You can't imagine how disgusting, how insulting the attitude towards our theatre is. I'm sick at heart. They attack our whole enterprise; they tore Elena to pieces, so now of course they'll savage *Three Sisters*. But I'll survive! It may be all to my good—[...]

It's now the evening of the 22. I couldn't finish my letter, I was in such an absurd mood. I haven't become a stranger to you, Anton? You haven't forgotten me? You haven't fallen out of love with me? I received your telegram at a very happy moment, after the glittering first night of *Uncle Vanya*. It was your success, too. The audience insisted you be sent a telegram and when the curtain went up Nemirovich wrote one and read it to them. Cries of 'write something more enthusiastic' were heard! Were you happy to get a message from the public? Or don't you care? Audiences like us, despite the roasting in the papers. [...]

So, sleep sound. [...] And do write, I haven't had a letter for an age – what does it mean? [...]

Your doggie

Chekhov

February 22
Yalta

Sweetheart, how is life in Petersburg? I think you will all soon be sick of that town and come to loathe its coldness and tittle-tattle and, poor darling, you will start to feel weary of it all. Yesterday I had a telegram from Nemirovich, telling me *Lonely People* was a failure. That means the trouble has started. Whatever happens, I don't think you'll ever be going to Petersburg again. [...]

Why don't you write? So far I've had one letter and one telegram. You're happy, thank God, my darling. You mustn't mope.

Evidently you're taking bookings until the fourth week in Lent. Then what? Are you all coming back to Moscow? Write to me, darling. [...]

Your Father *Antony*

Chekhov

February 23
Yalta

Darling little actress, my wonderful doggie, why are you angry with me, why don't you write to me? Why don't you wire me? Do you grudge the money for the telegram? Wire me for 25 r., I give you my word of honour, indeed I pledge myself to love you for 25 years.

I've been ill for three days, maybe it's nothing, I'm a little better. I was ill and alone. I only get *Novoe Vremya* among the Petersburg newspapers and so know absolutely nothing about your triumphs. Send me [other] papers i.e. the pages where they talk about your theatre. But that's tedious – the hell with them.

You didn't write how long you are going to be in Petersburg, who you see there, what you are doing. [...]

Nothing new here. So, I wait for a letter from you, my glorious little actress [...]

Your *Father*

Knipper

February 24
Petersburg

Do you realize your last letter was dated February 7, or have you forgotten? And today's the 24th and not one letter! You see how angrily I began, it's just as well I broke off. After a few hours I finally had a letter from my Father. It means you're healthy.

I was terribly heartened by your letter, dear Antonio! Yesterday was a difficult day. I hope Lent and this tour will soon be over. I'm just about to go and play Elena in a matinée. My performance was savaged in *Rossiya*. Why were they so incensed? I'm a touring actress, an outsider. According to them I should be a 'lustful predator' (what a disgusting expression!) and so they decided I wasn't an actress and there was no character. In my opinion, she's boring, episodic, she only appears lustful to Astrov, who sees an idle aristocrat. [...]

Knipper

February 25
Petersburg, Telegram

Wire me no letter strange

Chekhov

February 26
Yalta, Telegram

Sent three letters happily await telegram more genuine as to mood

Chekhov

February 26
Yalta

Dearest, today is February 26 and no letter from you at all! Why so? Is there nothing to write about or has the Petersburg press exasperated you so much you've given up on me? It's all so trivial, my darling. I only read *Novoe Vremya* and don't get worked up about the Peters. papers because I've known long since how it would be. I didn't, and don't expect anything but muck from the *Novoe Vremya*. [...]

I've been unwell, coughing etc., but now I'm better and even went out for a walk on the quayside. [...]

Your Father *Antony*

Knipper

March 1
Petersburg

Good morning, darling! Spring is in the air! I'm writing to you with the window half-open, the sun is shining, it's already quite warm. I can hear the sound of wheels, the rumbling of carts. The air has its effect – it's like being out walking, because the house makes me feel so sleepy. I love that feeling. The real spring will soon be here! The 25th was our anniversary – did you feel it? Oh, you! We gave the 50th performance of *Uncle Vanya* and our 100th of a Chekhov play. Nemirovich sent wonderful flowers to our dressing room [...] and after the show we drank champagne and the first toast was, of course, to you. Our mood is good despite the abuse in the papers.

There are no reservations about our success with the audience. They're saying straight theatre has never created such a commotion in Petersburg before. *Uncle Vanya* and *Enemy of the People* are the shining stars. Yesterday we played *Three Sisters.* It was very well received and we played, so they say, better than in Moscow. That's all I read. On March 4 the Union of Russian Writers is giving us a lunch at the Kontana[13] – there was an announcement in the papers – isn't that wonderful? And on Saturday they invited us there for a soirée.

Yesterday I really 'played' in *Sisters* and in the fourth act I was really carried away. I repeat, this is my favourite role – do you feel that? I'm tired of the theatre. I want to go somewhere, I want open space, I want to fill my lungs, freely, easily after a stifling winter and all the nervous wear and tear. I'll finish my letter and go for a stroll. I like the look of Petersburg. I like to walk by the river, I like the crowds, the wide pavements, there's a kind of European patina over everything. But you don't like it, do you? [...]

Chekhov

> March 1
> Yalta

My dear, don't read newspapers or you'll wear yourself out. Let it be a lesson to you: listen to your venerable sage. I told you, I assured you no good would come of Petersburg – you should have listened. Still, your theatre will never go to Petersburg again and thank God for that.

Personally, I'm giving up the theatre. I'll never write for it again. You can write for the theatre in Germany, in Sweden, even in Spain, but not in Russia, where playwrights aren't respected, get nothing but kicks and are forgiven neither for their success or their failure.

---

13. One of the finest restaurants in Petersburg.

You've been the object of abuse for the first time in your life, that's why you're feeling so bruised, but it will pass in time, you'll get used to it.

The weather is wonderful here, warm, sunny, the apricots and almond trees are in blossom. I expect you in Holy Week, my poor, berated little actress, I'm waiting, waiting for you.

Between February 20 and 28 I sent you five letters and three telegrams. I asked you to wire me, but no word in reply. [...]

I'm in good health, word of honour.

I hug you.

Your Father

Knipper

March 2
Petersburg

You've been unwell, dearest Anton? You felt lonely? Poor darling! I would look after you, comfort you, fondle you!

Yesterday I sent you two clippings from the *Rossiya*. But the gutter press is of no interest at all so I don't buy them or send them to you. Why bother with telegrams? What did you wire me about? Nothing special here. We live, we perform. We're all fine.

Today we perform *Uncle Vanya* and then a whole week's rest.

Knipper

March 3
Petersburg, 2 a.m.

I can't go to bed without writing you just a few lines ... I've just got back from the soirée at the 'writers' union'. It was very simple, friendly, masses of people, so many expressions of goodwill towards our theatre, sensitivity towards us actors! I felt splendid. Weinberg gave a short speech of welcome and said that for the first time they could feel the link between literature and the theatre etc ... applause. [...]

But I won't be coming to Yalta at Easter all the same; think about it and you'll understand why. It's impossible. You're such a kind soul and so you invite me! But don't you understand? [...]

Your doggie

Knipper

March 5
Petersburg

I write letter after letter from Petersburg and you say you don't get them. Don't be upset, darling for your berated little actress. Only the press abuses us but the public loves us and all these backbiters are shamed. I'm praised for *Sisters* and even yesterday at the writers' lunch someone spoke at length and referred to the parting of Masha and Vershinin and the whole room – 150 people – applauded me. I heard a lot about the 4th act, many people wept when they talked about it. Why are you so angry with the theatre? Surely not because of the backbiting? They are people of limited ability, can you really call them educated critics? Don't get into a bad mood! Spit on them. [...]

Don't dare sign yourself Father, I don't like it.

Chekhov

March 7
Yalta

I received an anonymous letter, according to which you fell head over heels in love while in Petersburg. I've suspected for a long time that you are a real miser, a pinch-penny. It would appear you don't love me because I'm a spendthrift and wanted you to bankrupt yourself by sending one or two telegrams. What of it? But I still go on loving you, it's a habit [...].

Skinflint, why didn't you write and tell me you were staying on in Petersburg and weren't coming back to Moscow? I waited here and didn't write because I thought you were coming home.

I'm alive and in good health, apparently, although I cough as furiously as ever. I work in the garden, where the trees are already in flower; the weather is wonderful, as marvellous as the letters that are starting to reach me from abroad. The last are those from Naples. How good, how clever you are, dearest heart! I read each letter three times, that is the *minimum.* I work in the garden, but work in the study is very slow, I don't feel like doing anything. I am reading proofs and am happy that it passes the time. I go to Yalta rarely, there are no attractions for me there, on the other hand the Yaltese spend a long time here and each time I lose heart and swear I will leave, or get married, so that my wife can throw them out – the guests I mean ...

Let me propose.

I have brought back some excellent perfumes. Come and collect them in Holy Week. Do come, my darling, my angel, but if you decide not to come, I shall be very put out and my life won't be worth living. I'm waiting for you now, counting the days and the hours. It doesn't matter if you love someone else and have betrayed me, just come, please. Do you hear me, doggie? Because I love you, you know I do, and now life is hard without you. And if the theatre says you have to rehearse over Easter, tell Nemirovich it'll be a dirty trick.

I went downstairs a moment ago and had tea and rolls. I had a letter from Petersburg from academician Kondrakov. He went to see *Three Sisters* and is thoroughly enthusiastic about it. You have written nothing about the supper parties you are invited to, do so now, please, if only for friendship's sake. I'm your friend, your real friend, doggie.

I had a long telegram from Kiev from Solovtsova telling me *Three Sisters* was performed in Kiev with devilish success. My next play will certainly be funny, very funny. At least, that's the way I see it.

Well now, old thing, take care, be happy not sad, don't worry. [...]

I kiss you eighty times and hug you. I'm waiting, remember. Remember!

> Your Venerable Sage,
> Antony

Knipper

> March 9
> Petersburg

Dearest darling, I want to speak a few words of affection so you won't be angry because your little actress has become so coldhearted in Petersburg, and written you such disagreeable, unfeeling letters. I've been run off my feet, rather. I'm ashamed of my letters, terribly ashamed! There was nothing of me in them, nothing of my real self, my warmth and I know you felt it and thankfully said nothing.

You're such a good man, Anton! As you can see, I'm aware of it
and if you had uttered a word of reproach, I would probably have
been very pig-headed. [...] But do you know how I feel?! I gather
I'm going to be free in April and May – does that please you? If
they're rehearsing *Kramer* and Ibsen's *Wild Duck*, then there's nothing for me to do. I might still play Kramer's daughter, but I don't
think so. I've 4 months free and I have to think of the best, the most
sensible, the cosiest way to spend them. Do you agree? Answer me
very soon, in detail, affectionately what you want, what you dream
of. Only, remember, dearest, that for the moment I can't go to Yalta.
What would be the good? To hide once again, to see your mother
unhappy again, that's very difficult for me, believe me. Either you
don't understand or don't want to. And I find it difficult to talk
about. But you do understand how hard, how agonizing it was last
summer. How long are we going to go on hiding? And why? Because of other people? They will soon shut up and leave us in peace
once they realize it's an absolute fact. And we will find things easier.
I can't bear all the ambiguity, why make life difficult? Do you understand what I mean, do you agree? [...]

Chekhov

March 11
Yalta

So you don't want to come to Yalta, dearest. Well, as you wish, I'm
not going to force you. Only I really don't want to leave here! I
don't want to bother with trains, hotels ... Still, those are trifles –
I'll come to Moscow – enough said!

You're happy, you're not in low spirits and in that you're clever,
glorious girl. You write that I don't like Petersburg. Who told you
that? I love Petersburg, I have a weakness for it. I have so many
memories of that city! It's the theatre in Petersburg I can't take. [...]
I reject it completely, I dislike it. [...]

Your sweet, glorious letters give me unusual pleasure. Only why
don't you want me to sign myself Father? I'm living like an absolute
monk. All right, I won't do it any more. [...]

Well, sweetheart, a restful night! Be healthy and happy and don't
forget me.

Your *Antoine*

Knipper

March 11
Petersburg, Night

I'm writing to you, dearest, before going to bed. Your letter [March 7] gladdened me, I smiled when I read it. Anonymous letters always tell the truth. I fall in love and am unfaithful to you at every turn – quite true. But I will still come to you and be yours alone. And we'll be fine. Only where are we to meet? I just want to be with you. You find it a nuisance going away? We won't run far away – yes or no?

How many of my letters did you receive abroad? It's all so stupid. I keep writing, so please don't complain. Will you be able to work when I'm with you? Will life be better when I'm there than when you're alone? Answer you horrid recluse! [...]

I have to be in Moscow in Holy Week as we have a problem over our apartment. Our house is being sold and we have to vacate it by May 1. Mother is quite lost, she's desperate, I've to help her because she is busy the livelong day. Do you understand, my dear? If the weather is good, you could come to Moscow? Couldn't you? And in the summer we could go to Sweden or Norway? I like the idea very much. Don't say no. [...]

Little actress

Knipper

March 15
Petersburg, Night

[...] I've just given an appalling performance of the 4th act of *Sisters*; sorry, dear writer! Don't swear at me. I couldn't wait for the show to end. I've felt so weak these last few days, I've been taking Valerian drops three times a day with bromide and have felt better. I think it helped but it doesn't matter. [...]

Where shall we meet? I'll go wherever you want, but not Yalta. Vishnievski is hurt you haven't replied to the photo he sent. I kiss you, Anton, hug you. Don't dare cough.

Chekhov

March 16
Yalta

Good day, little one! I'll certainly come to Moscow, but I don't know if I'll go to Sweden this year. I'm tired of travel and my health is like an old man's. I'd look like your grandfather, not husband. I idle away the days in the garden, the weather is wonderful, warm, everything's in flower, the birds sing, there are no visitors, not life, sheer heaven. I've given up literature altogether, and, when I marry you, I'll make you give up the theatre and we'll live together like planters. Would you like that? Well, go on acting for five years and then it will be obvious.

[...]

Write to me, my darling, your letters give me such pleasure. You're deceiving me, because, as you write, you're human and a woman. Well, deceive me then, but stay the fine, glorious person you are. I'm an old man and if perchance I should deceive you, then you'll forgive me, as you'll understand that there are grey hairs in my beard but a demon in my extremity. Isn't that so? [...]

I hug you, traitress, a hundred times, and give you a big kiss. Write to me, write to me, my joy, because when we're married I shall beat you.

Your Venerable Sage
Ant—

Chekhov

March 18
Yalta

So, little actress, in a few days you'll be back in Moscow; that means I won't write to Petersburg any more. What's the Moscow address? Do I write to the old one or wait for the new one?

The weather is extraordinary, amazing, the most wonderful spring in a long time. I'd enjoy it but the trouble is I'm alone, completely alone! I just sit in my study or the garden.

My glorious actress, don't do *Michael Kramer*, you'll have to spend the whole of May and June in Moscow working on a trifling, totally uninteresting part. Listen to me, my dearest, if we are alive and healthy, you can play a thousand more roles. Ah, what charming weather! The barometer has risen tremendously. [...]

Your Venerable Sage

Knipper

March 21
Petersburg, Morning

Yesterday you sent me a flirtatious letter, do you know that? Something's slipped. I'm joking, I'm joking.

What do you write about your health? I'm worried that you might not be well, Anton. I'm very anxious that you want to come to Moscow, who knows what the weather will be like? I want to see you. I would come to your home but we really can't go on living like good friends, you must see that. I'm tired of all this hole-in-the-corner business, it's oppressive. It's awful to see the hurt your mother suffers and the embarrassed look on Masha's face. I feel caught between two fires in your house. Tell me what you think about it all. You still say nothing. I've been exhausted recently. I've kept to my bed. I spent the whole day flat on my back, unable to lift a finger. Today they thought of replacing *Lonely People* with *Enemy of the People* but I had a good night's sleep and got up feeling quite well. Nemirovich has just been to see whether I can play or not. [...]

Darling, write to me straight away, as soon as you receive my letter – tell me where we can meet and send me a telegram in Moscow about your health, you must, you hear. Don't dare come to Moscow if you aren't feeling yourself. We can see each other somewhere in the south, if not in Yalta – I'll come. I'll leave on the 24th. [...]

Your little actress

Chekhov

March 26
Yalta, Telegram

Healthy will come after Easter greetings waiting for letter.

Antonio

Knipper

March 27
Moscow, Telegram

Coming Yalta tomorrow   Olga

Knipper spent two weeks with the Chekhov family in Yalta, then returned to Moscow with Masha. She had decided upon marriage.

Knipper, *Memoir*

I decided to join my life to Chekhov's, despite his poor health and my love of the theatre. I believed that life could be beautiful and so it was, despite the sorrow of our frequent separations.

Knipper

April 14
Sevastopol

Soon we'll be on the train. I have awful toothache. I went to the dentist's in Sevastopol. He made an incision in the gum, gave me oil. Masha massaged my face. I'm not saying a word, I don't open my mouth. I feel awful. If only I can reach Moscow. The boat was steady. I heard one beautiful lady lauding Chekhov, she was happy to have seen him on the pier, she says he's thirty-eight, we talked about the Art The. [...]

Knipper

April 15
Kharkov

Hallo, my darling Anton, we're in Kharkov. The journey has been good, the lower berth was free – I'd hoped for a miracle and got it. I didn't sleep all night for the pain and well and truly disturbed Masha as I cried terribly and was an awful coward. She was an angel and looked after me; by daybreak it was better, the damnable abcess on my gum may not get any worse. I've never known such pain in all my life. I cursed everyone and everything [...] I'll write a better letter from Moscow. [...]

Your Olga

Chekhov

April 16
Yalta

Dear Knipschitz [...] Life is thoroughly wearisome without you. Today I received your unsealed letter [April 14] in which you complain of toothache. My poor little darling. Write and tell me how your teeth are, how you are getting on and how you're feeling in general.

Oh my dearest darling, I thought I could sit down at my desk and work without you but as usual I'm doing nothing and feeling quite insignificant. [...]

Chekhov

April 17
Yalta

I received a large poster today, my *Uncle Vanya* has been done in Prague with unusual success. Darling, it rains every day in Yalta, it's damp. Because of the abundance of moisture, my tulips should be huge.

What are you doing in Moscow? Write, little one, don't be lazy. I'm in the doldrums without you and your letters. [...]

The roses aren't yet in bloom but soon will be. [...]

Knipper

April 17
Moscow

I'm finally in Moscow, my dear Anton! I can't throw off the idea
that we parted for no good reason at all, since I'm a free woman. It
was for appearance's sake, wasn't it? What do you think? When I
said I was leaving with Masha, you didn't breathe a word about your
not wanting me to go. You said nothing. I concluded that you did
not want me in the house after she had left. *Que dira le monde?* Is
that the real reason? I don't think so. I've racked my brains, imagining all kinds of things. Although I'm quite clear about your feelings,
or perhaps because I am, I found it difficult to talk about the things
that were most important to me. Do you remember how unsociable I
was on the last day? You thought I was angry with you. Now I'm
very uneasy and I would like to write many things, everything I feel
but so that you will understand and not turn things round the way
you always do. What are you thinking? Should we pass off the
things we don't want to say in silence or not? I know your hostility
to sorting things out 'seriously' but I don't want to sort things out, I
need to talk to you as to someone close. In some ways I find it painful to think about my last visit to Yalta, although we had a great deal
of fun. I've a kind of aftertaste, the impression of something not
said, shrouded in mystery. Perhaps you dislike my talking about it?
Tell me, frankly, I wouldn't want to annoy you, I lived in such expectation of the spring and of being somewhere with you, of our
living for each other if only for a few months, of our getting closer,
and there was I a 'visitor' in Yalta once again, leaving again. Don't
you find that strange? Sincerely, though? I've scarcely written all this
and regret it already, I think you feel it, and understand perfectly.
Answer this letter right away, if you feel like replying sincerely; tell
me what you think, take me to task if you must, but say something.

Now I kiss you, my darling. May I?

Everyone in Moscow is amazed to see me back, they can't understand it. I tell everyone that my mother sent for me to resolve a
problem over the apartment. I dropped in at the theatre today. I was
bombarded with questions about you – if you were happy with the
success of *Three Sisters*, when were you coming etc., endless questions. Vishnievski tells me you sent him a very sad letter, is that
true? There was a discussion about *Kramer* this evening, at 7, not

particularly interesting. Nemirovich is going to Yalta soon, you'll see him. What is the weather like in Yalta? How is the garden? Are the irises in bloom? Is the grass growing?

[...] My mother is very happy I'm back. Egorovna[14] is making our home Easter cake, they are generally spoiling me. Tomorrow I'm going to have a tooth out, my lower jaw is still painful. I've been in such pain I don't want to think about it. I know one thing: if I'm ill, the only person I will allow near me is Masha, she does me such good. Will you look after me? Everyone agrees I appear in better health, have more colour and haven't put on weight. But all you did was make remarks! ... Sleep well. I will write again tomorrow, a big kiss – do you want it?

Knipschitz

Come early, we will marry and live together. Shall we, my dear Antonioni? What will you do all day long? Write me even the smallest detail and don't take refuge in jokes.

I kiss you
Olga

Give my best to your mother.

The weather is fine and sunny, I go out in just my frock, although the air is fresh in the evening. The willows are in bud.

Knipper

April 18
Moscow

It's 2 in the morning again and I'm writing to you again, dearest Anton! I can't get you out of my head, I think of you every moment. I suddenly have the feeling that you're already tired of me, that you don't love me as you used to, that you just like having me around, and see me as someone near you and nothing more. I can't imagine life without you. I'm sorry, my dear, to raise this again. I won't do it again – you don't like this woman's talk. Don't be angry with me.

Today I finally went to the dentist and he told me there was no need to take the tooth out and that he would give me a filling that would last 20 years. Today I found an apartment very close to Leon-

---

14. Anna Egorovna Sutugina, cook to the Knipper family for most of her life.

tievski Lane.[15] Mother asked me, oh so discreetly, whether I would be living with you or would make other arrangements. We haven't decided anything and I just don't know what to tell mother. I can't live alone on my salary, i.e. I could if I weren't working in the theatre but somewhere in government or the law where you can control your expenditure. That's very difficult in the theatre. I think I'll arrange things as follows: I'll take two rooms on the side in the new apartment and pay mother 200r., as this one is 200r. dearer than our last, besides which I'll give mother as much as I can. If I don't live with her, then we'll have to find her decent tenants in the town, as the apartment costs 1400 and is very comfortable and economical. Mama is terribly upset, it's pitiful to see her. We have to find an apartment by the 15 May. If you come soon, I would like to discuss it with you. You'll give me an answer about it? Or just get angry with me for writing to you about nothing. But, for me, this isn't nothing – I have to find a quiet corner for the winter so I don't go through all the bother I've had so far.

Chekhov

April 19
Yalta

Dear actress, sweetheart, couldn't we go along the Volga together, to Astrakhan, say, what do you think? Think about it and I'll come quickly to Yaroslavl, or Nizhni or Rybinsk. We must spend the summer as pleasantly as possible i.e. as far away as we can from other people.

It's raining in Yalta. [...]

Chekhov

April 19
Yalta

Little doggie Olga! I'm coming in early May. As soon as you get a telegram, find out from the [Hotel] Dresden whether room 45 is free. What I mean is, find a cheap room. [...]

If you agree, we'll go down the Volga together and be little sturgeons. [...]

15. Now known as Stanislavski Lane, off Tverskoi (Gorki) Street.

If you give your word that no one in Moscow will know about our marriage until it has actually happened, then I'll marry you the day I arrive. Because I have a horror of weddings, the congratulations and the champagne, standing around, glass in hand with an endless grin on your face. [...]

Knipper

April 21
Moscow

I saw you in my dreams last night, dearest! Do you know where? – In a compartment on a train, we were travelling together and you were kissing me – and I woke up. You are coming soon, aren't you?

You're not yourself, I can feel it all the time, and yesterday your letter confirmed it. Dear Anton, be more simple, more open with me, more truthful, it will be better than keeping mum. Don't be angry if my letters make you depressed but I've not been happy either. So, you're doing nothing. Do you go into the town at all? Who visits you? Are you marrying Olga Mikhailovna soon? How big is the dowry?

Chekhov

April 22
Yalta

My dear sweet Knipschitz, I didn't ask you to stay on because I hate Yalta and because I thought that, in any case, we would soon be seeing each other wherever we liked. Dear heart, you are getting worked up over nothing. I have no secret thoughts, I say what I think.

I shall be in Moscow at the beginning of May. If possible, we will get married and take a trip on the Volga or we will take a trip on the Ga and then get married, whichever you prefer. We can take the boat at Yaroslavl or Rybiusk and go down as far as Astrakhan, from there to Baku and from Baku to Batum. Will that suit you? Or we could sail north up the Dvina to Arkhangelsk and from there to the Solovietski islands. We will go wherever you like. Then I will spend most of the winter with you, in Moscow, in the apartment. Provided I'm in good form and not ill. My cough drains me of energy, I think vaguely about the future and I write without enthusiasm. But you can think about the future, be my teacher, as you say, and then I will think about it, too. Otherwise we won't have a full life, only take it like a spoonful of soup every hour.

So, you have no new roles for the moment? How very pleasant. Today I was sent a review of *Three Sisters* in the *Revue Blanche*. I've been sent Tolstoi's reply to the synod on his excommunication. I've also been sent the magazine *Les Fleurs du Nord* with my story *Night at Sea* in it. Ivan writes to tell me he is ill. I received a telegram from the Olympia Theatre in Petersburg, asking permission to put on *Three Sisters*. It's raining today, there is the devil of a wind but it's warm outside, which is very pleasant. My dog Châtaigne, that you call Le Roux, has had his paw trodden on and I had to bandage it and the place reeks of iodine.

You forgot one rouble on my table. [...]

I haven't written any gloomy letters to Vishnievski.

What will I find when I go to the theatre? What is in rehearsal? Which plays? *Michael Kramer*? *The Wild Duck*? I've a strong desire to write a farce, or a four-act comedy for the Art Theatre. I'll write it if nothing gets in the way, but will not deliver until the end of 1903.

I'll wire you, tell no one and come to the station alone. You hear? Farewell, my heart, my dearest, darling girl. Don't be sad and stop imagining God knows what; I give you my word, there is nothing I want to hide from you, even for a minute. Be kind, not angry.

A big kiss for my doggie.

Your *Antoine*

Knipper

April 24
Moscow

I'm writing to you for the first time by daylight, my dear. Usually I do it at night – I undress, wash, put on a dressing gown and write in the dark, when the house has settled down and everyone's stopped rushing about and singing. It's cold here although it was a little warmer today. Yesterday was simply awful! My whole skin hurt from the cold and I felt dreadful. [...]

Yesterday I went to see a French company with my cousin. [...] It was very boring. We saw *Cyrano de Bergerac* – the acting was external and so made no impression whatsoever. Tomorrow I'm going to see *La Dame de Chez Maxime* with Masha.

I haven't been to the theatre. They're rehearsing *Wild Duck* and *Kramer* – I'm free. [...] I read about *Uncle Vanya* in Prague in the papers, and was very glad. My darling, are you coming soon? Life is so dull here without you. I think about you all the time, it's become a habit with me. [...] So, you're coming and we'll get married and run off somewhere. To Yalta, if you don't want to go anywhere else. [...] We'll see what winter brings. We'll live through this year somehow – if it turns out too uncomfortable, we'll have to do something to improve it.

Do you agree, my dear?

A big kiss for the present and I wait for you tenderly.

Your doggie

Are you really in love with Knipschitz?

Knipper

April 24
Moscow

I had just sent a letter to you and then found yours in the post-box as I was leaving the house. Your idea about the Volga is an excellent one – I'm terribly happy, delighted as a child. I've never seen the Volga. Darling Anton it's all going to be so wonderful! My heart is full of light. So, that's decided – to the Volga! I kiss you and wait for you.

Your Olga

Chekhov

April 24
Yalta

The same rotten weather in Yalta, sweetheart. Cold, rainy, windy. Nemirovich was here yesterday, gentle, but not in good spirits, he seems to have grown older recently. He wants very much to write. [...]

Have you decided where we'll go? Think about it, sweetheart. [...]

You write asking me to bring the documents we need for our marriage. But I don't have any documents, except a passport.

So farewell, my little Lutheran, be healthy, happy, don't pine. Be a real, rosy-cheeked German. You want me to call you Olya? Well, good health to my Olya. [...]

Your *Ant—*

Knipper

April 26
Moscow, 8 p.m.

My head has been aching ever since this morning but morale is good – I had a fine, a more than fine letter from you in which I'm rewarded by kisses. My head is better, as Masha and my cousin Lelia massage it thoroughly and I feel asleep. It's warm again today, sunny. [...] Sulerzhitski, Vishnievski and Masha are coming this evening. Horrid Vishnievski swears and vows by all that's holy that in a year or two I will be his wife! He's always making jokes like that and yesterday I almost got cross. It'll just happen, he says. Yesterday evening we saw *La Dame de chez Maxime*, a risqué farce; we laughed, although the cast was far from being first class. Lilina and [Stanislavski] were there [...] we sat together. What's this, darling, about your writing another play for our theatre? That will be wonderful! And a comedy, too!!! – Our itinerary – Yaroslavl, Astrakhan, Baku, Batum seems very good to me, dearest. I'm very attracted by the Volga. How wonderful, how beautiful it will be! If only you knew the pleasure the thought of our trip together gives me! I'm waiting for you, not just expecting you! How are you feeling now? Is your cough better? Don't go out when it's damp, otherwise you'll be running into town for something you don't need. [...]

Your doggie

Knipper

April 29
Moscow

I'm inclined to think that this letter won't reach you in Yalta because I know that if you come as you want, and intend, it will be on May 1 or 2.

The weather here is splendid, sunny but not hot, which is good. The trees are turning green, the bells are ringing as though it were a holiday. Yesterday I lay down to rest before going to the theatre and listened to their chimes. Sometimes they have a calming effect on me but yesterday they made me terribly tense i.e. they were pleasant to hear, but very painful, disturbing. And there were my thoughts. [...]

Your doggie

Chekhov

May 2
Yalta

[...] I leave Yalta on May 5 or 10 at the latest, depending on the weather. Then we'll go along the Volga. In a word, we'll do just as you wish. I'm in your power.

If Vishnievski marries you some time it won't be out of love but out of self-interest. But he's not such a bad chap, you might think, so marry him. Obviously he's counting on the fact that you'll soon be a widow, but tell him that I'm vindictive and am making a will in which I forbid you to remarry.

However that may be, darling, we'll soon see each other and talk everything over. It's evening and I feel better than I did earlier in the day, I'll probably get to Moscow in the morning, as from May 4 there's an express train. I'll send a telegram. [...]

Your *Ant—*

Knipper

May 6
Moscow, Telegram

Wire health arrival   Olga

129

Chekhov

> May 6
> Yalta, Telegram

Probably coming Friday [May 11] healthy

Chekhov

> May 9
> Yalta, Telegram

Have to come Friday definitely   Doggy

Chekhov

> May 24
> Moscow

Everything is ready at home. We must meet before 1 and talk. We leave on Friday for sure.

> A.Chekhov

True to his dislike of weddings, Chekhov arranged a private ceremony. Knipper's mother was furious when she was informed out of the blue that the wedding was to take place in secret and without the usual trappings. Chekhov devised an elaborate hoax to make sure no one knew of his plans. He arranged a dinner on May 25 to which all relatives and friends were invited. After a long and anxious wait for the bridal couple to appear, the news came that they had been quietly married and were already on their way to the station for the honeymoon. Their journey took them down the Volga, the Kama and the White river to their ultimate destination, a sanatorium at Aksyonovo where Chekhov could be looked after.

Knipper, *Memoir*

We were stuck at the 'Drunken Wood' by the Kama for twenty-four hours and had to sleep on the floor in a hut a few miles from the landing-stage, but got no sleep as we did not know at what time we could take the boat to Ufa. And throughout the night and at dawn we had to go out and see whether there was a boat coming. Chekhov liked the countryside around Aksyonovo: the long shadows on the steppe after six o'clock, the snorting of the herds of horses, he liked the flora, the river Dyoma where we went fishing every day. The sanatorium was situated in a beautiful oak forest but it was a primitive structure with the minimum of comfort. I even had to go to Ufa to get pillows. At first Chekhov liked the diet of fermented mare's milk but soon tired of it and we did not last the whole six weeks but returned to Yalta via Samara, along the Volga as far as Tsarinitsa and Novorossisk. We were in Yalta on August 20. Then I had to return to Moscow. Work had started at the theatre again.

Wife

Chekhov

August 21
Sevastopol

My dearest, darling wife, I've just got up, had some coffee and am listening with some alarm to the noise of the wind. [...]

I'm going to Yalta and expect to find a letter from you there. Don't be melancholy, sweetheart, don't be down, don't be angry, be happy and smile – it becomes you so.

I love you very much and always will. [...]

Your husband *Antoine*

Knipper

August 21
Lozovaya

I'm writing from Lozovaya, my darling. The journey is fine but I am so very sad. It's cold and wet. [...] How are you, how was your journey? Write and tell me everything. I hardly budged from my corner yesterday, when the train pulled out. I think of you all the time. In my mind I went with you through the station to the hotel.

A big kiss, be healthy, don't be down and above all write.

Your O

Knipper

August 21
Kharkov

My dear little Anton, my man of gold, right now you're probably having a meal in a restaurant! I can see your face so close to mine, feel it, and your sweet, loving eyes. Yesterday I stood at the window for ages and cried and cried – though you don't like that. I looked out at the moonlit night, and the silvery little path was so appealing I wanted to walk along it and feel myself in the open, not in a nasty carriage. When I am face to face with nature, every sensation, every feeling becomes more real, I understand them more. I expect you're once again damning me as a philosophical German! When I'd calmed down, I began thinking of our love. I imagined us spending the winter in Yalta, I found ways to occupy my time. That will probably be for next year. Don't you think? Well. Let's not make plans, this winter will show what the future holds.

The other woman in the carriage is very rich, evidently a landowner but what her nationality is, I can't say. Her husband talks like an aristocrat. She is splendid and doesn't say much – a considerable virtue in a travelling companion. The weather's now brighter and warmer. I slept well last night. I bought a paper and am reading. The thought of Moscow worries me. I'm already wondering how best to arrange things, how I can see you, my darling. Only my heart begins to ache when I think of the silent, deep well of melancholy within you. [...]

I love you, my sweetheart. Sit in your little alcove and think of me. Walk round the garden and tend your plants. Sit on the balcony and breathe in the air, if it isn't windy. [...]

We're in Kharkov already.

I kiss you, kiss you, love you.

Write.

Greetings to Masha and your mother.

Your Olga

Knipper

August 22
near Moscow

In half an hour I'll be in Moscow. No rain, but it's fresh. I slept splendidly. I think the family will be there to meet me. It's an awful long time since I had a letter from you, darling. I'll write to you this evening.

I kiss you, be healthy.

Your Olya

Once in Moscow, Olga had to turn her attention to the question of where they were to live now that they were married.

Knipper

I'm in Moscow, my dearest darling love, and I've been in an absolute whirl! It will soon be midnight and I'm still not in bed! I'm still shaking from the journey and I feel as though my eyes are dropping out. I've been talking about you, answering questions about you the whole evening, the whole day, the whole time. I'll start with all the events from the moment I sent you the card from Moscow station.

No one came to meet me and I was a little cross. I sat with my little trunk in the cab and drove round Moscow. It was fresh, almost chilly, but quite pleasant. The sun came through the clouds. [...] I was greeted very noisily at home. [...] Mother didn't come to meet me because she thought I was coming by another train. [...] At 12, I washed and dressed and went to the theatre. I was terribly, even stupidly worked up. There was no rehearsal so at first I only saw [one or two people] and then Nemirovich who, of course, asked me about everything. [...] He wanted to know, of course, how I stood with the theatre, was I tired of it? Everyone wants you to spend the winter here. [...] At 2, I went to lunch. [...] After lunch, mother and I went to see the new apartment. [It's] in the lane opposite the theatre, very roomy, high ceilings i.e. in 2 of the 4 rooms, the 5th room is dark, for the servant but, horror!, no lavatory. There's some kind of throne. That's the first snag. The second is that the room which was supposed to be all right for Masha is rather low and small and won't do at all, it's barely decent. We went through the other rooms, but nothing but snags. Finally we came across a very nice little place on Sniridonovka. There's a large European-style house fronting the street, but in the courtyard in the greenery there's a clean, delightful little lodge with 5 rooms, a wonderful kitchen, larders, a cellar and sheds, for 850 r. The rooms are low and not very big, but comfortable and there's a splendid room for Masha. Tomorrow I'll go and see the landlord and offer him 800 r. and if he doesn't come down I'll take it anyway. The house is warm and dry, they've been living there with their children for 3 years. Simply idyllic, dear Anton. A huge courtyard which will be covered in asphalt, it's clean, the landlord is someone eminent; he's an architect. If we don't take this little place, then mother will rent it next year, she's very taken with it. The air is excellent on Sniridonovka Street, many gardens, the street itself is clean. We're almost certain to take it.

You'll see how wonderfully comfortable it will be, my dear. I'm already pining without you. [...] How I would like to snuggle up against you, hear the way you call me 'sweetheart', see your tender, loving eyes. And how painful it is for me to think of you sitting there all forlorn ... Pleasant and painful. [...] Nemirovich said he wants me to play the wife in *The Wild Duck* as there's a gap. Only they hadn't mentioned it; I haven't given an answer for the moment. What do you think? [...]

Your Sweetheart

Mother still can't forgive herself for not having given you a proper wedding breakfast but says she was so browbeaten by my giving orders, there was no way she could hope you would come back to the house after the church; I didn't know that before the ceremony either.

Chekhov

August 23
Yalta

My wondrous wife, my dear friend. I returned to Yalta yesterday. Sevastopol was fine. There was a strong wind in the morning, I expected a swell but the sea wasn't heavy, everything turned out splendidly. Now I'm at home, at my desk, writing to you. How are you? What did you find in Moscow? How was your meeting with your colleagues? Write and tell me everything, glorious girl, I think of you all the time.

The armchair in your room is gloomy and lost in thought, I've told them to put it in mine. Your room downstairs is silent and lonely. Your mother's picture stands on the table. [...]

I didn't brush my clothes today – your absence is being felt already. My boots haven't been cleaned either. But don't be angry, I'll have it done, Masha will have it done and everything will be clean and fresh.

I love you very much, darling. Greet mother, Uncle Sasha, Uncle Karl, Vishnievski, Nemirovich, everyone from me. God keep you. I bless you. Write, write, write every day, otherwise you'll be beaten. I'm a strict, stern husband, you know that.

Your *Ant*—

It rained yesterday in Yalta. Everything is fresh in the garden.

Knipper

August 23
Moscow, 1 a.m.

How are you, my sweet? It's pleasant to think that at the end of the day I can sit and have a chat with you, dear Anton. I've just washed in the kitchen in a big bowl, washed away the dirt of the streets. Now the house is quiet again and I am writing to you again. All is warm and quiet in your house and, of course, you're already asleep. What did you have to eat? [...] Tomorrow I may have a letter from you, if you wrote it in Sevastopol as you promised.

Why aren't you here with me, Anton? It's absurd, strange being without you.

The less said about that the better, otherwise I'd just go on about it. I'll tell you about my day. I was awake before dawn, got up at 8 and at 10 went to see the house and decide whether to take it or not. They're asking 850 r., but I want it for 800 r., and although I've paid a deposit, I'll bargain with the landlord, he may be amenable. [...]

I haven't seen the landlord at all. From 1 o'clock the apartment will be ours, they're clearing it out. [...]

I forgot to tell you yesterday: Nemirovich and Sanin are talking about doing *Ivanov*. You won't say no, will you? You may need to make a few minor changes, but a production would be a very good thing. We can't do without Chekhov. But they probably won't let me play Sara and I shall die of jealousy.

Sanin asked me if it was a good thing to be married, didn't I find it limiting? Idiot! His 'heart is empty', 'I feel I should be married, but to whom?'. I gave him some advice. – I'm not needed at the theatre today. [...]

I look at your photograph and my heart is happy because I know every line by heart. Do you rub spirit in your hair? Tell Masha to prepare some fresh for you. A big kiss, my dearest. Write and tell me how you are?

Your Olya

Greetings from mother to everyone and to you especially.

Knipper

> August 24
> Moscow, Telegram

Have taken house warm comfortable write

Chekhov

> August 24
> Yalta

My dearest sweetheart, I had two cards from you and a sealed letter, thank you! You are good and kind and I love you, love you. My head's been aching since this morning, not aching, splitting, besides which I've not been alone from morn till night (night, too), what with one visitor after another. I can't work. [...]

I'll come to Moscow in September, whenever you write and tell me. It's deadly dull without you. I'm used to you, like a child, and without you I have no comfort or warmth. [...]

You write, 'my heart begins to ache when I think of the silent, deep well of melancholy within you.' What nonsense is this, my darling? I'm not melancholy and never have been and feel tolerably well and when you're with me I feel absolutely fine.

Write and tell me the kind of reception you got at the theatre, which plays are being done, what is happening and what you will be doing till September 15. Write properly, don't be lazy. I write to you at length but as my handwriting is small it seems short.

It's been cool, but now it seems to be warming up. It's quiet, glorious, the roses are in full bloom, I mean we're not just living but in clover.

I hug my wonderful wife, kiss her and bless her and humbly beg her not to forget me and to think of me as often as she can. When I come I will kiss you non-stop for an hour, then we'll go to the baths and the barber's, then lunch, then the evening, then bed. Yes? Sweetheart! What a dreadful picture of you in the [paper]. Oh, goodness me!

> I kiss you on both cheeks
> Your *Ant—*

Knipper

August 24
Moscow, 1 a.m.

[...] The house is being cleared from now until September 1. I went to see the landlord. He assures me it's warm and he lived there with his children and they wouldn't be leaving if 'the boss' hadn't asked to vacate it because of the work in the courtyard. I like this little house enormously and I know that Masha will, too. The kitchen is splendid, light, clean, tell her. There's a garden all round and the air is wonderful.

[...] Darling Anton, write more about yourself, who you are, what you are doing, down to the last button. How are you sleeping, eating, who do you talk to? [...] Do you rub your neck with eau-de-Cologne, massage spirit into your hair? [...]

Doggie

Chekhov

August 25
Yalta

Today, darling is three months to the day since we married. I was a lucky man, I thank you, my joy, I kiss you a thousand times. [...]

You've rented an apartment on Spiridonovka street? A house? What does that mean?

I'm terribly tired, I've had visitors all day. Yesterday my head ached but today it's all right. I just feel weary. [...]

Anton

When shall we see each other?

Knipper

August 25
Moscow, 1 a.m.

Good day, sweetheart, good day my darling, my tender loving husband! [...] I am waiting impatiently for a letter from you. Write and tell me everything. Tomorrow morning I'll send you some raffia and two ribbons for your *pince-nez.* [...]

1901

Knipper

August 26
Moscow, 12 midnight

[...] Today I sent the furniture to be reupholstered so that it will be clean and fresh in our little home. You will have a wonderful *chaise-longue*, inherited from our grandmother, the furniture will be cosy. I'm getting a piano. We're arranging everything so you'll be warm and comfortable here, I will love you, my sweet one, clean you up, care for you, pamper you, feed you, water you. [...]

I shall have a kitten, Martin, which Savitsaya gave me. If you don't like it it can stay in the kitchen, although it's sweet, gentle, plump, with doggy ways, it sneezes and rubs its eyes with its paws when they open or shut. It's two months old. [...]

Olya

Chekhov

August 27
Yalta

Little doggie, I'm well, but doing no more work than before because it's autumn and a lot of people are arriving. [...]

There are a lot of big spiders in my room. God knows where they come from. They move very fast. [...]

They're demolishing the stove in the sitting room. Today I'll rub my head as my hair is still falling out.

I'm going into town on business. [...] You see, my dearest, I'm writing to you in detail, and only keep quiet or write very briefly about one thing and one thing only as I love you and life is very dull without you, my joy, my little German. Your second letter was even shorter and I'm afraid you're going cold on me or you're getting used to being without me. [...]

Your Anton

Knipper

August 27
Moscow, 1 a.m.

[...] You complain you haven't had a single letter from me? I wrote to you from Lozovaya, from Kharkov, from Kursk, from Moscow station and a letter on the evening of the same day, i.e. the 22nd and I've been writing every day, I haven't missed one.

You must, surely, have received them all by now? [...] What are you reading? How do you pass your days? You write very superficially. If I know what you're reading I'll know what mood you're in. There's bitterness in my heart because I'm not with you. I live by waiting, waiting ... For the moment, I have no home, no nest, I've been camping out since May. I'm waiting till I can move into my house, and for it to be quiet and comfortable when you come. I saw you in my dreams. I'm reading Maupassant's *Notre Coeur*. We've had a Chekhov evening. [...]

I took three pictures of you from the packet of photographs and look at them every day. Anton, do you think of me, you haven't forgotten me [...] or have you grown used to life without me? [...]

Your doggie

Chekhov

August 28
Yalta

Darling doggie, I've just received your letter [August 24] and read it twice and kiss you a thousand times. I like the plan for the apartment, I'll show it to Masha [...] everything's fine, only why have you put 'Anton's study' next to the offices? Do you want to be beaten?

I'll answer your questions. I sleep splendidly, although it's very tiresome sleeping alone (habit!), I eat a lot and talk to visitors all day. [...] Yesterday I massaged my head. [...]

You see the kind of husband I am: I write to you every day, a perfect model. It's so dull without you. It seems to me I've become very domesticated and can't live without my wife. [...]

Your Anton

Knipper

August 28
Moscow, 12 midnight

You see what a good wife I am, dear Anton, I write to my strict lord and master every day. You're not sick of reading my letters?

You know, Masha wrote to me that you were in excellent form and I couldn't help feeling stirrings of jealousy, why are you doing so well without me? – Forgive me for writing that, I can feel you calling me a little fool. [...]

I don't understand what I feel at all?! Expectancy, that's all I can say. I'm beginning to get tetchy, that only happens to me in winter. But when I'm with with you I think I shall be doubly affectionate. How I long to see you. I adore it when you say you love me ...

Vishnievski can't wait to see you. He'll enjoy his talks with you, the way he'll make you laugh and talk rubbish, and you will tell him cock and bull stories about your married life. He's quite convinced that you would be better off making a life for yourself here in Moscow. Tomorrow Nemirovich reads his play [*In Dreams*]. Apparently he's in quite a state. [...] I'm told Stanislavski is wild about the play and has already written the plan for Act I. We'll hear if it's interesting or not. But it will be terrible for Nemirovich if the play doesn't go down well. [...] How will he feel? You, on the other hand are philosophical about such matters and don't see anything awful in it – do you? Nemirovich would like to read it to you, or send it to you but so far he hasn't had a complete copy in his hands. Come, read it, discuss it with him. [...]

I've started to do some singing every day. Write and tell me what you're thinking, what you dream about, my darling. What are you reading? Do you get all my letters? Do they clean and tidy your room? My writer mustn't be in a mess. Darling, it's so dreary without you, dreary and incomprehensible.

Hot kisses.

Olga

Knipper

Anton mine, *bonjour*! It will soon be 2 a.m., I got back a while ago from Nemirovich's reading of his play, and I'm terribly tired.

There's muddle in my head and gloom in my heart. [...]

I need to read the play carefully once more. Do you understand my meaning? People seemed to like the play, there was a great deal of applause. [...] I saw Stanislavski for the first time, he was very kind and asked after you a great deal, thanked me on your account as he's heard you were happy and contented, and said that I was clever. He acknowledged he finds it difficult to talk to you, that you seemed short with him and that he only got through to you on the one evening you spent together in Degtyany Lane. Our Kostya[1] was very nice. Vishnievski was here till 2 in the morning and talked a great deal, and loudly, of course, about you. Now it appears that he is the chief architect of our marriage, because he arranged for me to meet Masha, when she invited me, but I refused, because I never went anywhere. [...]

Your Olga

Chekhov

Last night I had something like cholera: vomiting, etc., quite unpleasant. Why, I don't know. I didn't eat anything, except meat. I fell asleep around dawn and now I'm all right, I've taken some *olei ricini*[2] and feel limp. [...]

You write to me about your kitten, Martin, but – brrrrr – I'm afraid of cats. But I do like dogs. [...] Still, sweetheart, bring a crocodile if you want; you can do anything you like as far as I'm concerned, I'll sleep with the cat if need be.

1. Stanislavski was known as Kostya in the company but was never called it to his face.
2. Castor oil.

Knipper

You ended your letter with the question, when do we see each other? I open mine with the same question. Today I felt wildly jealous, I had savage thoughts against everyone near you. I had an irrational desire to throw everything aside and take you away somewhere, so you would have no one but me, do you understand that? Is that bad of me, Anton? But I often have outbursts like that and I find it very hard to pull myself together, i.e. to resign myself to circumstances.

Three months already. I thank you; it was so good to be with you, my darling, my dear husband. [...]

[...]

I expect Masha is in good form and good humour. I will always be caught between the two of you. And I suspect she will never accept me as your wife and that will create a distance between us, I can feel it. I am sorry now I wrote that. But I feel, I am not sure why, sad, uneasy. [...]

The house still isn't ready. Mother was here today and was upset by the mess. They'll clear everything out on September 1 and I'll start moving. The furniture probably won't be ready before the 6th. You can't imagine what a dear little house it is; only 10 r. dearer than the apartment opposite the theatre, and you'll see how comfortable it is, though the rooms are small. I wrote to you about all this, you must have had my letters, my darling. I sent the plan too. Don't you like it?

Today I read Nemirovich's play. [...] It is quite devoid of feeling. There's a lot of good dialogue. The 2nd and 3rd acts are interesting. Act 4 really changes and is rather weak. If you'd seen the state he, Nemirovich, I mean, was in yesterday! It will be interesting to see if there will be a talk soon and who will speak out. Meyerhold and Roksanova sat frozen-faced. [...] Today was much warmer, the morning was pleasant, the sun was warm, there was the smell of autumn leaves. Come, Anton; we'll run away from the town together, in broad daylight. God, you'll be with me again! I will hear you, see you [...] look after you. Will it be soon?!!! You'll come as soon as I wire the apartment is ready, won't you? I'll do everything to make sure you're comfortable and don't catch cold, sweetheart. Bring warm clothing with you. [...]

Your doggie

Chekhov

August 31
Yalta

Dear wife, I receive letters from you every day, the post is now working well. [...] I'll come to Moscow when you've moved into the new apartment and write to me. In any case, I have to be there before hostilities begin otherwise they won't arrange *Three Sisters* rehearsals for me to see, i.e. I have to come before September 16. Isn't that so?

It's very dull without you, I might as well be shut up in a monastery. I can't imagine what the winter will be like!

The new cook prepares good meals and for the moment everything is fine. Mother seems happy with the cook, satisfied and I'm happy, too, of course. It's cool in Yalta, can you imagine? And I can't go out without a coat and I close the window when I go to bed. I sleep quite alone, like an old bachelor, an old fogey.

You complain in your letters that mine are short. My dear, my handwriting is small. On the other hand, my ideas right now aren't wide-spaced, I hardly utter one or two words before there's a full stop; but I've still been writing to you almost every day and telling you everything, or so it seems to me. Don't be angry with me, dearest, darling wife. [...]

Your *Ant—*

Knipper

August 31
Moscow, Night

Dearest, today I'll only write a few lines. I'm terribly tired, my nerves are in a bad way, I hate everything and everyone, I understand nothing about life. [...]

Don't write nasty things to me because my letter is short. I can't get used to your absence. [...]

I love you as ever and think of you always, you know that. [...]

Your Olga

Chekhov

September 1
Yalta

Dear Doggie, you write to me every day, I love you, bless you for that, keep up the good work. Be a clever girl and ask Nemirovich if there is any possibility of getting to know his play. [...] I'll read it very attentively with great interest and pleasure. I hope he won't refuse my request. [...]

They clean me up every day but not like you. [...]

Tell Vishnievski that I'm coming up from Yalta so I can rehearse *Three Sisters*. If there aren't any, then I won't see the play. [...]

Antonino

Knipper

September 2
Moscow

Today is so wonderful, so warm, my dearest darling! The family asked me to go out of town but I don't want to, I don't want to because you aren't here and I feel dead and bewildered. But the sun is warm and the air is mild. I've just got up.

Yesterday I was so exhausted I couldn't write to you, just kissed your photograph, and felt you so close, so close ...

Yesterday there was such a glorious sunset, such wonderful colours and your favourite bells rang! And all that excited me, I wanted space, to be away from the constraints than bind us. I'm a silly kind of person. Other people find delight in town life, they really enjoy it. Town life soon palls for me, I live it but reject it. I find it so burdensome, I feel this isn't real life at all, then there's the disturbing thought that it could all suddenly come to an end, that you could be seized by an unknown force. Don't think I mean suicide. I love Sulerzhitski for his nomadic way of life, his passion for living without staging, or props. [...]

I'm meeting Masha tomorrow and she will tell me all about you, dearest.

Tomorrow I make a start moving into the house.

Mother worries me because she says you won't like it as the rooms are small and I'm afraid of that, too. But because the air is good and there are no other tenants, if the house seems very warm, we can leave one window open so that we have some ventilation. What do you mean that your study is next to the 'offices'? It's only that the doors to your room and to the other place lead off the same lobby, that's all. We can either take tea, or play croquet in the courtyard in front of the house. Just like the country.

You must come soon. The weather is glorious. [...] Yesterday I saw a run of *The Wild Duck* with the sets. It dragged on till very late and I was so tired I didn't write to you at night as usual. Come, we'll see it together and share our impressions. You're reading Nemirovich's play. [...] He's going to Zvenigorod to tidy it up, rewrite it, i.e. strengthen the last act. I haven't seen *Kramer* yet, but I'm very interested by it. [...]

> Doggie

Knipper

> September 2
> Moscow, Night

Darling Anton, I wrote to you only this morning and now I'm going to bed and writing again. What a good wife I am! I spent the whole evening talking about you. [...]

I saw Masha and enjoyed her company terribly. I chatted to her. Then we went to see the new apartment. She liked it.

Lunch was very spirited, everyone was on their high horse, talked loudly but didn't quarrel. Our family is terribly noisy. [...] Masha said that in the train everyone was talking about you and me – older people and students; everyone praised your choice, said you had taken a good wife – you see? [...]

> Olga

Chekhov

September 3
Yalta

Good day to my darling little Olga! I didn't write to you yesterday first because I had many guests and second because I had no time. Once my visitors had gone I worked on a story [*The Bishop*].

Thank you, my darling, my mother was delighted with your letter: she read it and then gave it to me to read out loud to her. She speaks very well of you. You may be justified when you write about jealousy; but you are intelligent, good-hearted and what you say about your supposed jealousy is out of character. You say that Masha will never accept you, etc. That's absurd! You exaggerate, as usual, your ideas are nonsense and I'm afraid that you'll end up quarrelling with her. Listen, be patient, say nothing just for one year and everything will be clear to you. Whatever anyone says to you, however things look, just keep your own counsel. For newly-married people, happiness, initially, consists in non-resistance. Do listen to what I say, my dearest darling, and be intelligent about it.

I'll come as soon as you tell me to, but not before September 15. Whatever you wish, but, I can't be patient any longer. I'll stay in Moscow until December and you throw me out.

Now, my little German, send me Nemirovich's play, I'll take it away with me. I shall read it very thoroughly.

I shan't bring many clothes, I'll buy the rest in Moscow – warm underwear, a coat, but I will bring a blanket and galoshes. (I will come in an old coat. In a word I will travel light.)

I'm having an enormous wardrobe made for me and my wife. She is a shrew. We have to make life pleasant for her. Yesterday, I washed my hair in alcohol.

I kiss my dear old darling. God keep you. We will see each other in a little while. Write, write, my heart, write! I will never love any other woman but you, none.

Keep well and be happy.
Your husband Anton

Knipper

September 4
Moscow

I didn't write to you again at night, darling, because Masha arrived. I was in a state all day and my head was full of nonsense.

I waited at the station for Masha from 9 a.m. till 1. Because one lady who knew me asked me if I was waiting for someone and said that Masha was coming by the express which was extremely late. [...] We went to the house and Masha didn't take to it at all. You can't find a decent apartment for less than 1000 r. I thought we would live modestly and not spend too much. Now I'm terribly worried that you won't like it and I bitterly regret trying to find an apartment at all. I have no experience at all in such matters and now that makes me very unhappy. If you don't like it, we won't take it and we'll live in rooms. That would be the best thing to do.

Masha will move today, tomorrow I'll move and the day after we hope to be back to normal, more or less. Masha's waiting for me. *Addio*. A big kiss, my joy! Thank you for your letter, many thanks. A big kiss.

Your doggie

Chekhov

September 5
Yalta

Dear little doggie, no letter from you today and yesterday's was short and cross. Why? I've been out of sorts for three days; my spine hurts, my hands hurt, my mood has been so-so. But still I'm cheerful I look to the future with hope, I even have two guests for lunch today. [...]

Your husband A. Chekhov

Chekhov

September 6
Yalta

Darling heart, I feel better today though everything's still pretty awful. I'm coming to Moscow on the 15th or the 17th – that's definite. [...]

Your *Antonio*

Knipper

September 7
Moscow, Telegram

Weather like summer apartment ready come soon wire day kisses *Hungarian*

Chekhov

September 7
Yalta

I am arriving on the 17th, as I leave Yalta on the 15th, that's quite definite. You'll get a telegram from me: 'Monday'. That means I arrive on Monday morning.

Today I'm in much better health and I'd be quite fine were it not for the cough which will soon pass.

I got your despairing letter about the apartment and don't understand what you're getting so worked up about. The apartment is probably fine and if it's a little small, where's the harm in that? [...]

Your *Antonio*

Don't get upset, dearest. Whatever happens, don't get upset, everything they say is for the best. Absolutely everything.

When I arrive on Monday I'll go straight to the baths and then spend the whole day at home. On Tuesday we'll go wherever you want.

But I still don't know the name of the house you're moving to. I don't have the address.

Knipper

September 9
Moscow, Telegram

Wire health day of arrival not sending letter waiting for you
Hungarian

Chekhov

September 9
Yalta

I don't understand. Why two days and no letter from you? Why don't you give me your new address? You write you're moving to Sniridonovka but I don't know to which house.

I'm leaving on Saturday the 15th (I have my ticket) so I can arrive on Monday the 17th. [...]

I'm now fully restored to health.

Your *Antonio*

Chekhov

September 9
Yalta, Telegram

Healthy leaving Saturday   Chekhov

Chekhov

September 10
Yalta

It's ages since I had a letter from you. There are 5 days till I leave on Saturday; that means 5 days with no letters.

I still don't have your address, so I am sending my letters to Leontievski Lane. No news, I'm healthy – more or less. [...]

Your *Ant—*

Knipper

September 10
Moscow

Dearest, darling Anton, I didn't think I needed to write to you. I thought I'd had a definite answer to my first telegram: I'm coming. And, instead of that, I've been waiting for a week! Why, why? Why the delay? You don't give me a reason. Ill health? But today I had news you were better. I was worried because it's so long since you had a letter from me. I haven't written for 5 days. I thought my letters wouldn't reach you in Yalta. – I think of you endlessly, dearest. I'm miserable and bored, I don't want to see anyone, I find them all antipathetic, I don't know what to talk about.

Yesterday was my birthday and I howled in the morning and howled in the evening and I would have howled all day had there not been other people about. The whole family was here, eating snacks and drinking tea with cakes then we all went out to lunch. [...] Our house is very comfortable and I'm sure you'll like it. The rooms are small but very cosy. The study is charming and I spend my days dreaming how we will spend our time here together. I'm lost without you. This year will be difficult then things will be different. It's miserable and tedious at the theatre, I almost don't want to go there. [...]

Your doggie

Knipper

September 10
night, Moscow

Darling sweetheart, I want to write to you again so that you'll have letters from your spouse right up to the last day.

Where did you catch cold, my dear? I was right to be anxious recently. 'Old granny', do I hear you say? As you wish. Visitors plagued you? Wanting to give idle people a whole chunk of your life. Is that how it will be in Moscow? I'll only have you for a few minutes and then wearisome visitors? I don't like that at all. Just come soon! Why can't you come earlier? But, like a real German, you decided on the 15th and so, without asking why, you're staying until the 15th. Or don't you want to come? I'll accept two reasons only – health or work, nothing else.

You'll beat me when you come? I'm glad. Terribly glad. [...]

We'll go to Razumovski. It's wonderfully beautiful there at the moment. I was there with Masha on the 8th and my heart grew heavy, I was exhausted by my impressions of the place. It was extraordinarily quiet and majestic and sad, painfully sad ... The silence was only broken by the falling leaves and I felt afraid. Ah, Anton, if only I could describe all my impressions! I only know my heart began to pound and my eyes were wet. We sat at the water's edge. Masha wrote and I sat silent and thought. In spring there isn't the same charm, despite the abundance of life. Oh, come soon! I want to be here with you. You never talk of your feelings though I can guess what they are from every part of you. [...]

So, sleep peacefully. [...] I kiss you, kiss you and wait for you, wait for you.

Doggie

Chekhov

September 15
Sevastopol

Monday *Antonino*

Chekhov stayed in Moscow until October 26. He was present at rehearsals for Three Sisters *and attended a performance. He wrote to a friend that he found the production better than the actual writing. He then left on the return journey to Yalta, going first to Tula.*

Knipper

October 26
Moscow, Night

Dearest heart, where are you now? I can see you sitting in the blue carriage with the mirror, with your gentle, kind face and your vague smile, which I love so much and your loving, tender eyes. I've just done Act 4 and when I was standing at the pillar and listening to the music I couldn't hold back my tears and I saw you and don't know how I managed to speak the final words; and when the curtain came down, I burst into tears and was hauled back to my dressing-room, so I didn't take any curtain calls. I couldn't pull myself together.

They fussed and bothered over me, and, like idiots, sent for the doctor. I didn't see him, of course. Now I'm at home and can't see my Anton anywhere. Everything's spick and span, no literary disorder – so boring. Masha's not here, either. She's out drinking. I didn't tidy your bed, I couldn't. I'll pretend you're still here beside me. Silence all round, you can make a noise without waking anybody ... [...]

I started to clean and tidy the rooms. It's always better to keep going and busy with your hands. When you feel like this. [...]

I'll write tomorrow after *Kramer*. [...]

Your doggie

Knipper

October 27
Moscow, 2 a.m.

Good day my dearest, darling traveller!

There's so much I want to tell you, I don't know where to begin. [...]

I may talk nonsense. Where are you, Anton mine?

I still don't fully realize that you're not here ...

Kramer is on. Not much feeling of success in the house. I think the audience behaved disgustingly, coughing, blowing their noses, fidgeting. I think their attention was caught for first time by the scene between the father and son in Act 2. Not many curtain calls, but a lot after Act 3 and insistent calls for Stanislavski [...] I hear he lost heart after Act 2. I didn't go and see him. The audience like Lilina and Moskvin. For the moment it is still difficult to sort things out in my head. I'll write tomorrow. I'm tired and shattered after yesterday. [...]

Nemirovich has offered me the role of Julia [*In Dreams*] ... and put me in an awkward position. Lilina wants to put off rehearsals for a week but we start tomorrow. Naturally, I refused and then he said Schwartz would play the role. [...] He said he would provide me with an understudy so rehearsals wouldn't tire me out. Cunning, isn't it? What am I to do? It would be petty to make a fuss and be difficult. But I really don't want this vacuous role. I find it all quite

horrid and dispiriting. What do you say? Write, darling! I was so
happy at the thought of having some free time. Now I'm going to be
taken up with work that is neither attractive or congenial. [...]

Your doggie

Chekhov

October 28
Sevastopol, Sunday

Very heavy storm at sea; I hear the packets are sailing past Yalta.
I'm going to the post.
  It's chilly. [...]

Your *Ant—*

I expect a letter from you at home. Write about everything.

Knipper

October 28
Moscow, Night

You must be home by now, my golden love! You're probably telling
your mother about Moscow, about us? How are you? Well? Awful?
Still probably feeling comfortless. The rooms smell empty, there's
none of your dear, poetic disorder, no newspapers lying about everywhere. [...]

  I'm in an excitable mood today – I had lunch with the family, we
talked nonsense and I laughed so much all my muscles ached and I
completely forgot that I'm a married woman, not a little girl. [...]

  I didn't want to get up this morning, I was tired. [...] I went to
the theatre at 12 when they should have been rehearsing to talk
things through finally with Nemirovich. There was no rehearsal as
half didn't turn up and Nemirovich wasn't there either. [...]

  In the theatre they're talking of failure, *the boss,*[3] apparently has
lost heart. All the actors are imitating Stanislavski's cough as Kramer
and making jokes but kind ones. The papers praise Moskvin and
Lilina. We'll read the reviews tomorrow. [...]

Doggie

3. A familiar way of talking about Stanislavski at the Art Theatre.

1901

Chekhov

Dear, darling, glorious, clever wife, good day! I'm at home and feeling very strange. [...] The journey was fine as I didn't have to take horses in Sevastopol because the steamer was going to Yalta. The journey was quick, although it was cold. [...]
Write!!

Your *Antoine*

Knipper

Dearest, it's 8 a.m. and I haven't been to bed – I'm writing to you in my dressing-gown. Why haven't you written to me about your journey? Just one letter from Tula. I expect I'll get one from Sevastopol tomorrow. [...]

It's winter outside – a lot of snow, although it's blowing away. Everything is empty and dreary without you. [...]

Yesterday I went to rehearsal. Sanin is in charge of the play. Nemirovich isn't in the theatre. I take part unwillingly, very unwillingly. Sanin is in the middle of the 'crowd' scene, i.e. the chorus of students in the 1st act. [...] I don't know how *Kramer* went yesterday. [...] It seems to me Moskvin isn't getting the praise he deserves. What was your impression when you read the reviews? [...]

Your picture is on my desk next to a photograph of the house in Yalta. I look at them and think and send my thoughts to you, in your room there, I feel how 'my own one' wanders round his study, sits at his desk or reflects in his armchair. Write and tell me you're well, everything is as it should be, write frankly about how you're being fed. How sad I shall feel at Christmas, knowing you're all together. Don't forget me, Anton. Big kisses. I long to look into your eyes, into your face. Write about yourself.

Kisses,

Your doggie

Knipper

October 31
Moscow, Morning

I just didn't want to get up this morning. I wanted to lie there the whole day and dream!

I'm desperate for a letter from you! I want to know what your journey was like, how your health is. [...] What was the crossing like? What's the weather like; warm? How did you find everyone at home? Have you settled down to your routine in Yalta? Write and tell me everything. Are you heartsick, or are you glad that we're apart?

Everything's going so slowly. I was at the theatre in the morning and in the evening both yesterday and today. I took an English book to rehearsals and sat and read it, I read the papers as there's not much to do on stage, Sanin is still busy with the chorus. It will be an eternity before this play gets on. Yesterday a reply-paid telegram came to the theatre for you. I opened it as I thought if it was important I would wire you immediately. They're asking permission to do *Three Sisters* in Petersburg [...] for a benefit performance. I asked Nemirovich to reply. Did I do right? You wouldn't mind not making the decision yourself, would you? The play seems to belong to us as much as to you, doesn't it? – They'll send you the repertoire. [...]

Doggie

Chekhov

November 1
Yalta

I knew you'd be in Nemirovich's play. I'm not blaming you, just answering your letter. Judging from the press, *Kramer* didn't have the success I anticipated and that pains me. Our audiences don't need plays, they want shows. And as for Stanislavski losing heart, as you write, that's stupid and terrible; it means he's not aware of how well he's done.

Your *Anto—*

Olga was worried by Masha's lack of enthusiasm for the new house and tried to find alternative accommodation.

1901

Knipper

You've been gone almost a week and only two cards from you.
Yesterday I looked avidly out of the window to see if the postman
was coming; I got back from rehearsal and scanned every table
where there might be a letter from you – but nothing! Finally, I got
back from *Lonely People* and found a card from Sevastopol. My
dear, how cold you must have been on the journey to Yalta! It must
have been freezing in the mountains. And such a boring journey!
Were you alone? Did you take food with you? Didn't you eat all
day? [...]

I'm going with Masha to see an apartment. Yesterday Vishnievski
sent to say that at the house he's in there's a street entrance and 5
rooms with electric lighting and heating for 1000 or 1100. We could
rent out one room. We'll see.

Nemirovich asked me to tell you: as soon as you write a short
story send it to him quickly. He wants to arrange a matinée for our
needy students at which Chaliapin and Sobinov will sing and he will
read your story, all tickets 10 r. A good idea. Write if you agree.
[...]

Yesterday, during rehearsal, I sat in my sad dressing-room and
thought about you, my darling. I found it very difficult to get up in
the morning – I didn't want to live, get dressed.

Till tomorrow, sweetheart, be healthy, write to me; do you get all
my letters? I think I'm writing my sixth – right?

Big kisses for my poet, a thousand kisses.

Your doggie

*Chekhov encouraged Gorki to write plays for the Art Theatre. As a
result, Gorki started work simultaneously on two plays,* Small People
and The Lower Depths.

Chekhov

November 2
Yalta

Good day, my darling doggie! In your letter you ask what the weather's like [...] It's fine, warm but hazy [...] the garden's looking good, the chrysanthemums are in bloom, the roses, too, in a word life's a dream. Yesterday and today I've been reading proofs, which I hate, and have just finished, completely finished, so they won't send me any more.

I'm healthy, though yesterday and the day before, in fact since my return, I haven't been quite myself and yesterday had to take some *ol. ricini*. But I'm glad you're well and happy, it makes my heart lighter. I would terribly like you to have a little half-German, that would amuse you and fill your life. You should! What do you say? Gorki will soon be on his way to Moscow. He wrote me that he was leaving Nizhni[-Novgorod] on November 10. He has promised to alter your role [in *Small People*] i.e. expand it, on the whole he's promising a lot and I'm glad because I believe the play will be the better, not worse, for it. [...]

Olya, my wife, congratulate me: I've had my hair cut!! Yesterday cleaned my shoes – the first time since I arrived. My clothes still haven't been cleaned. But I change my shirt every day and massage my head. [...]

I'm sending you a poster from Prague for *Uncle Vanya*. [...] I live like a monk and only dream of you. Although it's shameful to make a declaration of love at 40, I still can't help telling you again, doggie mine, that I love you deeply and tenderly. I kiss you, hug you close.

Be healthy, lucky, happy.

Your *Antoine*

Knipper

November 2
Moscow, Morning

Good morning, my dearest, darling one! I dreamed about you all
night, how they saw you off from Moscow: a horde of people, depu-
tations, speeches, verses, hubbub. You stood on the steps in a blue
suit and screwed up your eyes ... – I waited all yesterday for a letter
from you – in vain. I'm beginning to get worried.

Yesterday morning I went with Vishnievski to see the apartment
he's suggesting.

Very high rooms with central heating, electric light – 5 rooms –
with a large dining room and a Masha's room, the others are long
and narrow. The windows are huge. 4 steps on the lower floor. We'll
rent out one room. The apartment is 1300 r., but they'll agree to
1100 or 1200 with heating. I don't know what will happen. It's all
boring. We're still looking for an apartment.

Rehearsals are sad, dreary affairs and put me in a foul mood.
Sanin shouts and yells and hammers. We're discussing costumes
today. I'll tell Stanislavski to take me out of Julia – Lilina's rested
and can start rehearsals. We're playing *Three Sisters* today. *Kramer*
is all right. Young people and students like it. [...]

Will I get a letter from you soon? Life is empty without them.

Your doggie

Knipper

November 3
Moscow, Morning

Bonjour, mon mari?! A big kiss for your letter, your dear, loving
letter, my sweetheart! I'm glad you had a good journey and that you
are well, not gloomy, not sour, remember I am yours. Life here is
dreary for me, I fear I'll shut myself away and shrivel up. I don't
feel like going anywhere. Recently I've wanted to give up everything
and study, get right away from my own head. I hate stagnation. The
theatre is boring, there's no work, I mean, not for me.

What I'm saying may be very nasty and petty-minded. Perhaps. I
feel I have many inadequacies as an actress, I want to rework my old
roles. I have very little self-confidence. I'm in a phase when I don't

think I'm an actress at all. My acting is awful, crude and so I only give the impression of being a real actress.

You don't like it when I philosophize, do you? I'm sorry for the 'piffle'.[4] [...]

Everyone in the theatre asks after you and sends their greetings. [...]

Is it warm in Yalta right now? Darling, take a walk each day, even if it's only round the garden, move a little, it's good for you. Eat plenty. Are you drinking milk? Big kisses for my darling.

Your Olya

Chekhov

November 4
Yalta

[...] The weather is fine, quiet, calm, sunny but Moscow winters are still better. It's all so sad without you. I have to write a lot of letters. [...]

Gorki's expected. Yesterday [a friend] tried to find him an apartment but she couldn't. He'll probably stay not far from Gaspra where Tolstoi is living. I still haven't seen Dr Sredin. I haven't been into town. [...]

Your husband!!!

Knipper

November 5
Moscow, Morning

I didn't write to you yesterday, darling because I got up late after the [literary] circle and went straight to rehearsal. We played *Uncle Vanya*. [...]

I was still in bed when I got your letter today. Thank you darling. Believe me, I love you. You are the only one for me.

Till this evening.

Your doggie

4. She is quoting Solyony from Act 1 of *Three Sisters*, 'When a man philosophizes, you get philosophistry or sophistry, but when a woman, or two women, start, you get pure piffle.'

1901

Knipper

November 6
(started on the 4th)
Moscow

Good morning, dearest!

I didn't have a letter from you yesterday! I hope there'll be one today?! If you don't want to write properly, just scribble a couple of lines and send them. I feel so good when there's a letter from you.

Darling, yesterday I was out in 'society'. We had lunch at the Luzhskis and then went to the club. When I came out of rehearsal Dr Obolonski arrived. [...] He'll help us sort out the apartment. They'll let us have it for 1100 r. with heating with a contract until August. We'll make up our minds in the next few days. [...]

On Sunday I went to rehearsals and we started the 2nd act. Sanin was yelling, raging, talking irrelevant nonsense. [...] Nemirovich has gone away with his wife! He left on Saturday. [...] After rehearsal I had a quick lunch with mother and then went to *Uncle Vanya*. I played the first two acts very badly but Act Three was fine. [...] After the show Masha came and we drank away our evening until 4 a.m. [...]

It's 12 o'clock and I shall hurry to post this letter so that you have news of me every day, my darling, my golden one.

Your doggie
for all eternity

Late 1901 and early 1902 was a period of change at the Art Theatre. First, there was talk of building a new theatre. This would be substantially financed by Savva Morozov, a friend of Stanislavski and the main shareholder. Morozov also resurrected the idea, first mooted by Nemirovich that the actors should become shareholders in a newly formed company. This led to internal conflict and to the exclusion of important members of the company, including Meyerhold. Chekhov, who had originally intended putting some money into the new venture, withdrew in protest. This period also marks the beginning of a serious rift between Stanislavski and Nemirovich, of which Knipper was acutely aware.[5]

5. See *Moscow Art Theatre Letters*.

Chekhov

Well, darling, yesterday I went to see Tolstoi. I found him in bed. He's hurt himself and is now resting. His health is better although the weather is hardly warm in these late October days and winter is oh so near! He was glad of my visit. And so this time I was especially glad to see him. He expresses himself in a pleasant, kindly way although he's elderly, or rather, old, he listens with pleasure and speaks readily. He likes the Crimea. [...]

Are they going to build a new theatre? When? Write, dear wife, it's so dreary and I feel as though I've been married for 20 years and separated from you from the very first year. I'll come in January. I'll wrap up warm and stay indoors. [...]

Your *Antonio*

Knipper

November 6
Moscow, Evening

Darling Anton, I was looking at your picture and sat down to write and felt ashamed. I would so like to be with you, I curse myself for not giving up the theatre. I just don't know what's happening to me and that puts me in a rage. I hate to think of you there all alone, sad, dreary and here I am busying myself with things of no consequence instead of listening to my feelings. What stops me?! I so want a little half-German!

Why do I keep reading what you wrote: 'a half-German, to amuse you and fill your life'? Why is what you meant so clear to me? I know what you think of me. But perhaps not.

I'm confused, at war with myself. I want to emerge from all this as a human being.

I think I'm writing very disjointedly and you won't understand what I mean. But try. Don't just read the words.

How will I get through this winter!? Anton, write to me often, tell me you love me, I makes me feel so good. I can only live when I am loved. I have come to that conclusion.

I'm so weak! Anton, Anton!

How much life gives, and how we let it pass us by. It was awful when I came to the conclusion that I am worthless as a person. Awful.

Chekhov

November 7
Yalta

You're beginning to sound like a glutton, all you talk about in your letters is food, how much I eat. Darling, I eat a lot! Please don't worry. I don't drink milk because there isn't any in Yalta, but I lunch and dine like a pig, enough for 10 people.

You want to give up the theatre? That was my impression when I read your letter! Do you really? Think very carefully, sweetheart, and then make a decision. Next winter I'll come to Moscow – that's what I have in mind.

I left Sevastopol by carriage, no joke at all and the worst thing was that the coachman depleted my coffers with every passing moment. We had to spend ages on repairs, and pay 3 roubles an hour. [...]

Today I caught two mice. So no one can say I don't do anything. [...]

I still haven't had one long letter from you, not one in which you discuss anything. But I really love it when you talk about things.

I'm afraid I weary you, or you're growing apart from me, little by little. I can't express my fears more explicitly.

The weather's calm, but getting chilly, fresh, winter will soon be upon us. You had lunch with Luzhski? I've never been to his house. [...] On the whole you do *Michael Kramer* extremely well. Stanislavski is very good and if our critics had more open and fresh minds, the play would have had a glittering success.

Don't forget you have a husband. Just remember that!

The garden is fine, there's plenty of everything but it does look sorry for itself. I despise nature here, it's cold.

But what if you were to decide to spend two or three days in Yalta! The whole journey would take a week...I could meet you in Sevastopol...I could live in Sevastopol with you...Eh? God bless you!

I love you – you've known that a long time. I kiss you 1013212 times. Remember me.

Your husband *Antonio*

Knipper

November 8
Moscow, Morning

Dearest sweetheart, please don't be cross if I only write briefly for the next few days, or miss a day – tomorrow we move out, today we're packing things up and then we'll start sorting things out. It's quite a business. The rooms are very high in your apartment on the first floor, very airy, so there's the hope I may see your tender, living, lovely eyes here, if the winter's not too severe. Am I right? [...] Does my darling clean his teeth? Properly? [...]

I was good in *Sisters* yesterday. [...]

As Julia [*In Dreams*], I mutter through my teeth and mince. I talked to Lilina. She's not strong and says there's no way she can play [in the evening] and rehearse in the morning. [...]

Be healthy, be happy my love. I kiss you many times, your head, your breast, your eyes and gaze into them for a long time.

Your doggie

Give us an answer whether you agree to send a new story to Nemirovich: he asked me about it.

Knipper

November 8
Moscow, Evening

Dear Anton, everything's packed, the removal van comes tomorrow and we'll be [in our new home]. We shall live in a civilized apartment. I'm sorry that because of me you had to have to live in that little house. If you feel well, then come – it's very airy and you needn't go out.

A troubled day. This morning, at the theatre, we heard that as Gorki was on his way here he was picked up by the police and put on a train straight to the Crimea. [...] How silly of me to write all this, you'll be seeing Gorki, his wife and his mother very soon. He

can come straight to you. That makes me terribly happy. I'm sure
you have a good influence on him, he loves and respects you. Put
him up. You've nothing against that, have you? At the moment he's
like a hunted animal. This whole business has thoroughly upset me.
He'll tell you all about it himself. [...]

Your doggie

Chekhov

November 9
Yalta

Good day, darling heart. The weather is wonderful today: it is warm,
clear, no humidity, quiet as summer. The roses bloom, and the carnations and a few other yellow flowers. I spent a long time in the
garden today, thinking how wonderful the weather is here but it
would be much nicer to be driving in a sled right now. Forgive my
cynicism.

So Roksanova is in *Seagull* again? The play was taken out of the
repertoire until they got a new actress and suddenly here she is
again! How appalling! I gather from the repertoire list that *Ivanov* is
in rehearsal. In my opinion that is a wasted, a futile effort. The play
will be a flop because you'll do it in an uninteresting way for slow-
witted audiences. I shall persuade all our best authors to write something for the Art Theatre. Gorki has written something already. [...]
I ought to get a fee, say a rouble per person. I'm not satisfied just
with writing you letters. After all we have been through, they are not
enough, we should be together all the time. We are wrong not to.
But what is the good of talking about it? God be with you, I bless
you, dear little German, I am glad you have been enjoying yourself.
A big, big kiss.

Your *Antonio*

[...] Arseni has just gone out to fetch the things Satin sent me:
mushrooms, smelts, a coat and other things. Everything got here safely.

I am writing, but I cannot say with any great enthusiasm.

Tell Masha that Muir and Merrylees [store] have sent our
purchases via Novorosissk, so we won't get them before April.

Knipper

November 11
morning, Moscow

Darling one, I want to tell you I love you tenderly and life is dreary without you. [...]

I'm writing to you for the first time from the new apartment. It's splendid here, Antonino. So much space, so much air! You'll be fine here! All we have to do now is hang the curtains and lay the carpets and everything's ready! There's electricity in Masha's room, the dining-room and your study, come what may, three lamps at 45 r. per annum. We shall live like lords! You're not cross, sweetheart? You must come, you'll be no worse here, you needn't go out for a week and still move about – there's plenty of room here, you can walk around the apartment. The windows are big – the place is fresh in a minute. I'll send the plan then perhaps you'll understand. The rooms are 15 feet high, Masha's room is quite separate, the kitchen won't be a worry to her, the walls are solid. Your study is a beauty. Next to it is my own splendid little corner. In a word, everything's fine and you should be happy. We're near everything. I didn't write to you yesterday, darling, as I was sorting everything out and in the evening I was tired as the devil. I was excused rehearsals and was free in the evening. [...]

I'm glad you went to see Tolstoi and that you got on well with him. Are you still going to visit him? What did you both talk about that was particularly interesting? Did you wrap up warm when you went to see him? Take good care of yourself so that I shall find you hale and hearty.

We left the old apartment with pleasure. Of course we won't sue – they've been very kind to us. [...] Today has been a difficult day – rehearsal, a performance (*Seagull*) and the move. [...]

Nothing is known about the [new] theatre but decisions will have to be taken during November. I'll write and tell you everything. *Kramer* is on and is going down well. [...]

Your doggie

Chekhov

November 11
Yalta

Hallo doggie! I had your plaintive letter today in which you call yourself a total nonentity and all I can say is this. The winter will soon pass and I will come to Moscow in the early spring so we can be together for the whole of the spring and the summer. Then I'll spend the whole of next winter in Moscow. The boredom of Yalta right now is such there can be no thought of giving up the stage.

It's raining, hammering on the roof. It's been raining a long time, monotonously hammering and that makes you feel sleepy.

Countess Tolstoi took a picture of Tolstoi and me together; I'll ask her for it and send it to you, but God forbid you should let anyone make a copy. [...]

I love you, doggie, very much.

If Gorki is in Moscow give him my regards. Tell him I expect him.

I don't cough much but my health was better in Moscow. Not my health exactly but my stomach. I'm eating enough. Trust your husband.

Your *Antonio*

Knipper

November 12
Moscow, Morning

Dear Anton, you frighten me with strange words like: 'I'm afraid I weary you, or you're growing apart from me, little by little. I can't express my fears more explicitly.' My dearest darling, where do you get such ideas? It all comes of our being apart. But I find it easier if you tell me all your fears rather than conceal them from me. Only please don't worry. You are the only one for me. I live on dreams of seeing you again, of living with you...

There are alarming rumours that Tolstoi is dead. If it's true, why don't they make it public? I just don't understand. During yesterday's performance nobody talked of anything except his illness and death. Write and tell me everything.

I don't know how I will get through the winter. I so want to see you, have you, to know your each and every thought, know everything that is stored in your mind, and love you, love you ...

There's nothing more I want to say to you. I live in the sole expectation of having a real kind of life, and perhaps it will be soon. Why is that? I want to discuss ideas with you, my poet. Anton darling, write something. I long to read your new story, and for the feeling it will give me. Write, dearest, it will make the time we're apart seem shorter. We shall see each other in winter. But spring is coming and we shall be together! [...]

> Your doggie

Chekhov

> November 12
> Yalta

To your new home, my joy! Only why haven't you or Masha given me the new address? [...]

In Dreams is a good title, pleasant, gentle. I'd be only too pleased to send Nemirovich a story but everything I'm writing at the moment is rather long and unsuitable for public reading and everything I'm currently writing is censored, i.e. not allowed to be read in public. It would be better to ask for me to be excused. [...]

> Your *Antonino*

I've just heard on the telephone that Gorki is on his way. I expect him here. Wire me your address if you haven't already sent it by letter.

Knipper

> November 13
> Moscow, Morning

I'm expecting a letter from you today, darling. I didn't have one yesterday. I'm 'terribly' fond of your letters. – What are you up to, what are you thinking? Anything new?

We had a snowstorm today, I'm in a bad mood, very tired from acting. [...]

We won't have a half-German again, Anton!

I'm sorry. Why should you think this half-German would fill my life? Don't you fill it? Think about it.

Write and tell me if Gorki is with you and how he is. Do you talk a lot? How is his health? Where is he going to live? Is it true Tolstoi has had a stroke? Yesterday rumours were flying about his death.

We're rehearsing Act 3. A difficult act. Noise and din the whole time and a host of small transition scenes against this background. I don't know if it's any good. We haven't reached the end of the act yet. In Act 3 I'm free because I'm not in it. I have very little time to myself at present, only the mornings. I'm at rehearsal from 1 to 4 and acting in the evenings. This week I'm only free Tuesday and Friday. And I have a lot to do – I have to repair my clothes, my fur coat because Mme Chekhov's falling to pieces – shameful isn't it?

What are you reading at present? How glad I am you've finished correcting proofs – what a bore for you! [...]

> Ever your doggie

Knipper

> November 13
> Moscow, Evening

Nemirovich has just been here to bring me sweets for the new home, he sat and talked. [...] They're not going to build a new theatre but alter our present one. Morozov gave me 500 r. today for Julia, i.e. for her clothes, but in actual fact they'll be more expensive because she is always dressed in the latest Paris fashion. I can imagine how much this play is costing him! [...]

> Your doggie

Chekhov

> November 14
> Yalta, Telegram

Health and happiness in the new home.   Anton

Chekhov

November 14
Yalta

I received your new address today and wired you – now I'm writing.
If the apartment is all right, if the heating (air?) doesn't give me a
headache and make me cough, then I'll come in January or
February and live with you till summer. [...]

Your *Ant*

Are you near the theatre now? That's good, sweetheart. It's been cold,
up to three degrees of frost.

Knipper

November 15
Moscow, Morning

Thanks for your little telegram, my dearest, darling sweetheart. I
didn't write to you all day yesterday and it seemed strange. I feel the
letters I write you are awful, but appropriate, because I am the way
my letters sound.

How wonderful, how quiet it is in our garden right now! You say
the roses, carnations and chrysanthemums are in bloom? How I
would love to sit quietly with you so that I could know some clarity
of mind. Do you really think it's a sin we don't live together?

You write that I'm enjoying myself? What an idea! You call our
mania for evenings out enjoyment? It's just nonsense.

Don't worry about *Seagull*. Lilina will soon start working on Nina
with Nemirovich.

Don't worry about *Ivanov*. I think it's being done to keep the
actors quiet. [...]

Sisters played to an almost full house yesterday – no free seats –
happy? *Uncle Vanya* brings in 1000 r. whereas *Kramer* doesn't take
1000 and *Wild Duck* hardly 400 r. [...]

Tell me more about your health. What suits are you wearing? Are
you all right? Are you drinking Ems spa water? Have you done as I
told you? Get your lady admirers to find some cream for you in
Yalta and drink it – do you hear? And eat properly. I'm beginning to
lose weight. I bought myself a wallet, for the first time in my life.

[...] I'm having your picture framed, Gorki's, too, yours for 7 r. 50 and Gorki's for 3 r. – you see how dear you are to me! Tomorrow I'll go to the baths.

Be happy, healthy, love me dearly. I kiss your dear head a thousand times.

Your doggie

Chekhov

November 15
Yalta

I got your address yesterday and sent you a telegram, my joy. Congratulations on your new apartment. You describe it and then you suddenly ask: 'you're not cross, sweetheart?' Where did you get that idea? Why should I get angry? Don't worry, my dear, I am content and happy. [...]

Knipper

November 16
Moscow, Morning

My dearest Anton, I hasten to write a few words to you, I don't want to miss a letter so that you get something from me every day. [...] *Lonely People* took 600 r. yesterday. We can call our theatre Chekhov's theatre. Are you happy?

No letter from you yesterday and none today. What does it mean? You say you don't like your letters to me but don't stop, write even if you don't feel like it otherwise I'll get worried.

The weather's warm here, I'm wearing autumn blouses. I go on foot to the theatre and back. The air in the rooms is good, not hot, not cold. Did I write and tell you the heating can be controlled? There's a dial and a fan.

There's electricity in your study, the dining room and Masha's room, we could also light the hall, though that would cost 15 r. a year, i.e. for each lamp. Write and say if that is expensive or not.

And Gorki? How is he? Write and tell me about him. [...]

Your picture is now in a red wood frame – stunning! How I would love to see you, Anton!!! When I think of you, my thoughts run wild and I can't understand them or communicate them to you they are so many and various.

I kiss you, I love my gentle husband, I love your eyes, I love your thoughts. My heart beats faster when I think of our meeting.

Your Knipperkins

Knipper

November 16
Moscow, Morning

Good morning, my dear! [...]

You know, I have all sorts of wild dreams about coming to see you for 2 or 3 days. If they can do two or three of the final performances without me, then I could get away and be back in Moscow on Dec. 25. It may be impracticable but I'll talk to Nemirovich and I think he'll arrange if it's at all possible. I can't recall for the moment when performances usually end. [...]

Judging from your letter it's not warm in your study – is that right? [...]

Your doggie

Chekhov

November 17
Yalta

My darling wife, the rumours you have heard concerning Tolstoi, his health, even his death, are quite without foundation. There has been no noticeable change in his condition and he quite clearly has a long time to live. True, he is weak, but there are no dangerous symptoms at all, except old age ... Don't believe what people tell you. If, God forbid, something should happen, I'll send you a telegram. I will call him 'grandfather' otherwise you might not get it.

Gorki is here, in very good form. He sleeps at the house and has registered this as his official address. A police inspector was here yesterday.

I am writing, working, but, dearest, it is impossible to write in Yalta, quite impossible. Nothing seems interesting away from everyone, and it is cold. I had a letter from Vishnievski. Tell him I will write the play but not before the spring.

The lamp is lit in my study now. It's all right as long as it doesn't reek of oil.

Gorki hasn't changed, still as decent, intelligent, good. There is only one thing wrong with him, or, rather on him – his shirt. I can't get used to it. He looks like a court lackey.[6]

The weather is autumnal, not very good.

Live and be well, light of my life. Thank you for your letters. Don't get ill, be sensible. [...]

Your husband *Antonio*

I am well. Moscow had an astonishingly good effect on me. I don't know whether you or Moscow are responsible, but I am coughing very little.

Knipper

November 18
Moscow, Night

I haven't written to you for just one day and already I feel bored, dearest. It's late but I really wanted to write to you. I sent our address innumerable times and don't understand what happened. Do you get all my letters?

You're sad, I can feel it. My dearest one! I really do understand. We should be together. But everything will turn out right, God willing. And we shall have a wonderful life together.

I am dreaming that in a month I shall see you. If they don't play about with the repertoire. [...]

Today Nemirovich was horrified by the rehearsal of Act 2. Nothing's going right and he's a bag of nerves. [...]

After rehearsal I went to mother's; I haven't seen her for some time. We had lunch and in the evening went to the Viennese operetta. [...] I found it amusing but on the whole I find operetta boring and feeble.

6. The reference is to Gorki's peasant-style shirt, which was often worn by radical intellectuals but which was also the uniform for certain court officers. Even Pushkin was made to wear one.

Tomorrow we are lunching with Ivan. I don't know what I'll do in the evening. Did you get the repertoire? [...]

I'll close now, it's nearly three. Big kisses for my darling poet, I await your kisses.

Your doggie

Chekhov

November 19
Yalta

Good day, dear wife. Today is sunny, calm but cool. [...]

I'm at home, getting bored. Only one consolation – your letters my dearest girl. I'm thinking, why not go abroad? [...]

I'm very glad, sweetheart, that you're happy with the new apartment. And there's electricity? That's very good. [...]

Your *Ant—*

Dr Altschuler is treating Tolstoi. Yesterday he telephoned me to say his patient is feeling well and there's no danger.

Knipper

November 19
Moscow, Night

Oof, Anton mine, I'm absolutely worn out! [...] I went to the Maly Theatre [...] When I was bored with watching and listening, in my thoughts I went to Sevastopol, lived my meeting with you, walked through the town with you, went to the Hotel Kist with you etc...
Or went through Julia, a role in which Stanislavski praises me.
Today we were all in the office and 'the boss' expressed his dissatisfaction that people were not working at home. The minor roles (in Act 2) were not real or three-dimensional. [...]

Your doggie

Chekhov

November 21
Yalta

Dear Knipperkins, my precious, don't be angry if I don't write to you every day. It's matter of circumstance. Every day there's something to prevent me getting on with my life and writing. [...]

Do you want to come down at Christmas? That's a wonderful idea, my clever little love, only ask Nemirovich to let you spend at least three days in Yalta. No less! Leave Moscow on December 20, you'll be in Yalta on the 22nd, you can leave Yalta on the 25th and be back in Moscow on the 27th. My dearest, my dove, get those three days out of these despots. There are no performances from the 22nd and 23rd to the 26th, and on the 20th, 21st and 26th they can put on *The Wild Duck, Enemy of the People, Tsar Fyodor, When We Dead Awake*. They have a huge repertoire for the holiday period. Listen to me, Knipperkins, be a sensible wife. [...]

Gorki is the same as ever, the same good fellow, perhaps even better. He's a great simpleton. He's been living in Yalta, now he's going to Oleiz where he's taken a dacha for the winter. [...]

Your *Antonio*

Knipper

November 21
Moscow, Night

I write to you once more, my dear! How happy you make me with the news of your health – I can't tell you how much. Dearest, dearest, clever Anton! I think you won't be at all bad here. And you'll be able to work. And you won't be alone. But God forbid it should damage your health! You are a 'cure' for me in yourself, you know and understand that.

We've just done *Sisters*. [...]

Nemirovich is an absolute bag of nerves. We had an appalling rehearsal yesterday. [...]

Write, work, dear Anton. I shall shake with excitement when I read something new of yours. I will relish every word, every expression. I kiss you. Do you want to fondle me? I want to see you and kiss you.

Your doggie

Chekhov

November 22
Yalta

I sent you a card with a picture of Tolstoi. Did you get it? He's well, his temperature is normal and there's nothing to be alarmed about except old age, of course.

No letter from you today, my joy. And so I'm low in spirits. [...] The weather is calm, warm and cloudy.

I sent you a photograph – did you get it? What else would you like? [...]

And so, dear girl, in December you'll be in Yalta. For sure! Your arrival would be an absolute blessing for me. This winter has been the most boring of them all, I would go away with pleasure. [...]

How is Nemirovich's play going? Do you like it? [...]

Your *Ant—*

If you don't go to Petersburg during Lent we'll go to Italy. Would you like that?

Knipper

November 22
Moscow, Night

I've just got back from doing *Seagull*. A good performance, very well received and the takings were over a thousand. Happy, sweetheart?

Anton, I feel that you're not happy with my letters, that what I write is boring, monotonous, uninteresting. I really can't write letters, can't convey anything in the least interesting. And life is somehow slipping through our fingers. It's sound and fury, not life. I have the impression of something artificial, and real life passing us by.

Why should that be so, dearest? Why should that be so, my love?

I would so like to talk seriously with you, Anton, but do you know me? Or do you just love me without knowing me? Is that a silly question? You are a real person, Anton, you love and understand life as it is, not as we think it is. And you are terribly funny. I love you. You are unique. I'd love to be with you, just near you, with my head close to your heart, so you could hold me tight and for it to be dark, with the firelight flickering and for it to be quiet all round. And for the heart to be full and calm with a little pain, a touch of sorrow. Do you understand that mood?

I've just remembered your study at the house in Melikhovo, how I used to sit with you, all excited, remember? And how wonderfully the apple-trees and cherry-trees blossomed. How white and bright it all was! How I loved it! I was a little afraid of you then. And that marvellous morning when you saw me off! We will still have a long and good life together. I know it.

I am writing to you in great style by electric light. I'm worried that your house is cold. That's not good. Get them to make up the fire more often so you can be warm and comfortable. There's no one to look after you. I blame myself. Can't you come here? Darling, darling, I will come to you, love you, look after you. I love everything about your picture with Tolstoi. Your dear face is wonderful. I could shower kisses on it. Do they air your rooms. What are they feeding you, tell me. Are you drinking milk? Are your clothes clean and tidy? Everyone asks after you and sends their best wishes. [...]

Your Olya

Knipper

November 23
Moscow, Night

Your letter made sad reading. There was a melancholy about it. You can't bear to be in Yalta, you're thinking of going abroad. Darling. What if you tried to come here! I want that desperately and I'm afraid. For the moment it's warm here, no frost. [...] It's very lonely, comfortless without you, there's no one to think about. I sing a lot. I do exercises as soon as I get up; my voice is becoming flexible. [...] Singing is a great delight to me, only I have to feel that I can make my voice do what I want. I will develop and extend it. [...]

Your Olya

Chekhov

November 24
Yalta

Darling girl, tell Nemirovich to send Gorki Act IV of his play as soon as possible. Tell him it's essential.

There's snow and rain outside. My hands are cold, my study is dark and cold, it's difficult to write, my fingers won't work although the thermometer shows 12 above. The whole winter will be like this! Till the end of April!

Gorki is living in Oleiz, he came to see me; he seems bored. He would work on the play, but there isn't one, Nemirovich hasn't sent it.

They did *Three Sisters* here in Yalta. It was ghastly. The officers looked like policemen and Masha spoke in a wheezy voice. A full house but the audience tore the play completely to pieces.

So, don't ask to come to Sevastopol but to Yalta. Darling, do! I beg you! Nemirovich is an egoist. [...] He ordered you to return August 20 when there was nothing for you to do, and now you'll sit around doing nothing for the whole holidays – and I will break with the theatre and write nothing more for it. [...]

Doggie, let's go to Italy! Let's! Let's go while we have the money and because in two or three years time we won't be able to travel.

I hug you, wife of mine. Sleep sound, God keep you.

Your *Ant—*

Chekhov

November 25
Yalta

[...] I'm working but not on anything important. The weather is foul, the rooms are cold, Moscow is far away and the atmosphere is such that writing seems pointless.

Are you thinking about coming to Yalta for Christmas, doggie? Are you? I think about your coming and staying three days with me daily. [...]

You asked if I've been to see Tolstoi since my return from Moscow? Yes, I have. [...]

Your husband *Antonio*

Knipper

November 25
night, Moscow

I didn't write to you yesterday, darling, because I got back from the [literary] circle at 4 and only got up just before rehearsal today. I'm just back from *Lonely*. I want to see you so much I don't know what to write. Everything seems too trivial and not worth noting. That's stupid. I seem to have spread. Don't be angry with me. I feel a note of sadness in your last few letters. Why suddenly? Has something happened or is it general? Won't you give some more thought to coming to Moscow if the winter is mild? How awful everything is, Anton! I'll be delighted if I am able to come to see you at Christmas. Although Yalta is hardly worth it – I'll waste time on the journey and see less of you. Would it be difficult for you to come to Sevastopol? [...]

Anton, tell me, what is most important in life? I'm in such confusion. There's something I don't understand in life, i.e. something I can't grasp. I try to explain it and do what I must. But I'm terribly weak, fate always has to help me out. [...]

Ever your Doggie

Chekhov

November 27
Yalta

[...] Nemirovich's play will be a success. Don't lose heart. Only it would be a good idea to rehearse *Small People* at the same time as after Christmas you'll have nothing to do but the Nemirovich. Stanislavski seems to be losing heart. He's been spoiled by success and that means anything less than total success is like a knife. [...]

Your *Ant'*

Knipper

My dearest, darling sweetheart, I felt impatience and dissatisfaction in yesterday's letter. I understand and suffer too. I so terribly want everything to be well with you, not sad. Come to Moscow, even if it's only for a month. [...]

In Dreams is bogged down. Yesterday they started work on Act 3, that means I'm free in the daytime. [...]

Things are on the whole difficult at the theatre. I hope to God this mood will soon pass. There's no news about building work. It would be good to take Aumont's theatre, it's a pleasant building on a good spot – don't you think? [...]

I have only one joy now – my singing. I sing every morning. My throat is now fine. [...] I dream of coming to you, darling, I'm filled with excitement already. Will it suddenly be called off?! My only fear is that in Yalta we'll be dragged off to see people, and then other people will come to us, while all I want is to be alone with you from morn till night and night till morn.

Do you understand?

Your doggie

Knipper

Good day my darling, my southern flower. How are you? What's your mood? You weren't teasing when you said you would come to Moscow in January. I live for that, I dream about it. But suddenly you've gone silent about coming. Why? Now you're talking about going abroad. No, darling, you can't do that. You would be so far away from me. When I start writing to you everything seems so pointless, and I get lost and don't write about many trifles which nonetheless fill my letters, and my life. But I think it's the same with you. When what's important is missing, i.e. our life together, the rest seems of little interest. Aren't I right?

I know you pine, you're bored in Yalta and only one thing consoles me, that you're in good health. Darling, write to me more often about the state you're in, don't imagine that it will bore me, as you always say. [...] [I hear] that you're looking well and in good spirits. Is that right? I could feel it from your letters. But I read something else in your most recent letters. Are you well?

Tomorrow there'll be a letter from you. Your doggie is still the same, only getting thinner. I dislike the nights, I go to bed without enthusiasm. I sing in the mornings and then my voice is all right. I never read and that puts me on edge.

I would so like to be carried away by a book. [...]

Chekhov

November 28
Yalta

'What I write is boring, monotonous, uninteresting.' I expect you've forgotten you wrote these words already, little idiot. But I adore your letters! Be boring, be monotonous, only please do it more often and I'll send you a picture.

What have you decided? Are you coming to Yalta for Christmas or not? I need to know for sure.

The house is cold; the stoves are hot but there's no warmth. The usual temperature in my study is +12, rarely +13. We can't light the fire because it hurts my eyes. And it's difficult to work in 12 degrees. I just get angry, although I know that's silly.

What a pleasure it would be to talk to my wife right now, to touch her brow, her shoulders, to laugh with her. Oh, sweetheart, sweetheart! [...]

Your *Ant—*

Knipper

November 28
Moscow, Night

I'm writing just a few words, my dear, so that you can have a letter from me every day. It's very late and I'm extremely tired. [...]

Why two days without a letter from you? That worries me. Your recent letters were sad and suddenly – nothing. That makes me uneasy. Are you healthy? My dearest darling, don't hide anything from me, whatever it is.

Thinking and dreaming about you helps me live, gives me a better view of life. Don't doubt me, believe I love you.

Anton, can you come here to Moscow if I can get free? You could stay here for a month and it would be so much easier for both of us. What do you say? Give me an answer, darling. Your letters haven't been affectionate. [...]

Knipper

November 30
Moscow, Morning

Darling, yesterday had two letters from you simultaneously, I really was beginning to get worried. Thank you, my dear! Only your letters pained me. You're bored, you're in a bad mood, you've grown to hate the theatre because of me, although it brought us together. Sweetheart, it's no good being blue. You are a great man, with a great heart. Come in January. January is an even month, there are no sudden changes, you can live and work here splendidly. I know you don't like flippancy, that's why I am writing this way.

The winter is warm, it thawed the day before yesterday. I live without purpose or pleasure. My mood is so-so; I chat to people.

The apartment is fine but boring without you. You should be living here. [...]

Don't annoy me with dreams of going to Italy. It would be better for you to spend the holidays here and we'll live together. I'm not likely to be released, that was just an idle thought to keep me happy. Although I'll keep reminding them of it. Nemirovich might be willing but it doesn't depend on him. Audiences don't go much to the theatre before the holidays and so we have to put on bread and butter plays. We're now rehearsing Act 3, in which I don't appear. I didn't hear... *Antonio*, darling, we'll be happy, we won't be sour, will we? I keep writing you boring, joyless letters and I don't amuse you very much. That's my mistake, although I'm not happy all the time, I can only cheer myself up for a short while. I kiss you, darling, many times and beg you not to be down.

Your doggie

Chekhov

November 30
Yalta

My dear Knipperkins, my clever wife, I am alive and well, I feel all right today; and the weather is wonderful, sunny, but yesterday there was storm and rain, that shook the trees.

The hotels in Sevastopol are ghastly, slums; if, say, you come to Sevastopol on December 21, then you'll be in Yalta the same day. Do come, dearest, I beseech you! I am so bored, so very bored, I'm not working but just sit around reading the newspapers. Next winter I'll spend in Moscow, whatever happens and whatever the doctors say. [...]

Gorki was here yesterday. He's well and is going to write another play. [...]

Your *Ant—*

Knipper

November 30
Moscow, Night

How are you, Anton? It's a long time since you said you loved me. Say it again in your next letter so I can feel it. I'll answer you the same. I feel you're too lazy to write to your wife. I have the impression you're quite happy saying nothing and just getting letters from me. You never want to tell me anything, you just write out of habit. All I'm interested in is you, your mind, your whole inner world, I want to know what is going on in there or am I being too bold and is entry forbidden? Anton, I'm overcome by a sense of unease, of sadness and despair, I feel that you are growing away from me and that I no longer understand you. What will our life be like in the future!? I so want to kiss your dear face and for you to be in a good humour. [...]

Don't laugh at me or be angry with me, sweetheart. Send me a cheerful letter, if you do write. Shall you come in January? [...] Sleep sound, don't forget...

Your doggie

Knipper

December 1
Moscow, Night

So, you read my letters with interest, dearest? Thank you. My gentle sweetheart! [...] I picture you in every mood, I see every facial expression. I adore remembering you in the mornings, sitting on the bed, after washing, without your vest, with your back to me. You see what wicked thoughts I have, and there are others which are even more wicked but which I won't mention. [...]

Your doggie

Chekhov

December 3
Yalta

Dear doggie, beloved, I had two letters from you today: one typical of you, the other depressed. You write that you haven't had a letter from me for two days. I've only missed one day. I didn't write to you yesterday because I didn't have a letter from you, and everything was dreary and I didn't want to fill you with melancholy. It was one thing after another and today I feel so awful, my head is empty, I feel weak and that's because yesterday they overheated the stove, it was hot and stifling all night. [...] Well, never mind! The weather's fine again today, warm and sunny. They're planting things in the garden. [...]

I love you very, very much. [...]

Your *Ant—*

Chekhov

December 4
Yalta

Good day, my spouse, my sweetheart! You don't like my letters, I know that, and I admire your taste. But what can I do, dearest, if I've been out of sorts these last few days? You will forgive your silly old husband and not be angry.

Your letter dispirited me yesterday: you write that you won't be coming to Yalta for Christmas. I don't know what to do with myself. One doctor says I can go to Moscow, the other, absolutely not, but I can't stay here. I just can't! [...]

Don't be reticent, doggie, write and tell me everything that's in your head, the most trivial details; you can't imagine how precious your letters are to me, how they calm me down. I love you, don't forget that.

I'm going to see Gorki today. Perhaps I'll go and see Tolstoi as well.

Your husband Ant

Aren't there any new plays?

Knipper

December 4
Moscow, Night

Bonjour, mon petit Toto!

Why is it that when a day passes without a letter from you it seems an eternity? [...]

I weighed myself at the baths yesterday *'au naturel'* – 95 pounds, not much, eh? How much do you weigh at present? [...]

It seems to me that when we are going through a bad patch one way of escape is to lose yourself in work, dream, create and enjoy it. [...]

You've been to see Tolstoi again? Why don't you write and tell me all the details, how the meeting went? I only know the fact that you went to see him. That's not enough and I still can't get used to the brevity of your letters. Soon you'll be writing me postcards or simply sending me two words: I'm alive or something of that sort. I'd rather you swore at me, said you weren't happy with your life, that I should be living with you and that you had a stupid wife. I'd agree. Of course I was thoughtless. But I hoped your health would allow you to spend at least part of the winter in Moscow. Don't come then, Anton. Tell me what I should do. [...]

Your doggie

Knipper

December 5
Moscow, Night

Dearest sweetheart, I'm damnably tired. It's one in the morning and I've just got back from rehearsal. [...]

Today I got two letters together and was happy. [...] Tell me, have you been ill? You write 'today I feel all right', does that mean bad? Please look after yourself.

Don't be sad, darling, think how wonderful it will be when we meet! Can you imagine that? [...]

It's warm here, it hasn't gone below –4. A wonderful winter. I was hanging around in wardrobe from 5 o'clock onwards and from 6½ to 12½ I was in rehearsal, I feel quite numb and stupid. [...]

Your doggie

Chekhov

December 6
Yalta

Darling sweetheart, you asked for details – here they are: I've been drinking Ems water for two days, in the mornings. That's no easy matter since I have to get up, put on my shoes, ring and wait, then take off my shoes and go back to bed...You recommended *ol. ricini*: I took some this morning as yesterday I eat pork chops which created quite a storm. [...] It's warm in Yalta right now so I don't suffer. [...]

I went to see Gorki yesterday; his dacha is very well situated, by the sea, but what a hustle and bustle in the house, children, old women. No place for a writer to be. [...]

We'll go abroad, but not to Italy or Nice but to Norway, to the north and from there to Denmark... Yes? [...] Tell your directors I won't let you back to Moscow before September 1, even if they sack you. In August, or the end of August I have wonderful apples. And pears? You've never eaten such pears. Sweetheart, if I were to give up writing and become a gardener, that would be a very good thing, it would put ten years on my life.

What am I to do about my stomach? [...]

Your *Ant*

Chekhov

December 7
Yalta

Little actress dear, why don't you listen to your husband? Why didn't you tell Nemirovich to send the last act of *Small People*? Tell him, sweetheart. What a shame it is, what a misfortune it is that you're not coming to Yalta for Christmas. It seems to be that we'll both be old before we spend many years together. [...]

I haven't been well for the last few days. I took castor oil, I feel emaciated, I'm coughing and not doing anything. Now I'm feeling better, so I'll probably get down to work tomorrow... Loneliness seems to have a bad effect on the stomach. Seriously, darling, when shall we see each other again? Even if you were only to come for one day over the holidays that would be infinitely good. But you know that.

I'm writing this on the 7th in the evening and will post it tomorrow the 8th. You all have a meal for the jubilee – I'm delighted, sweetheart, I compliment you.

You are clever and gentle.

God be with you. I kiss you countless times.

Your *Ant*

Knipper

December 8
Moscow, Morning

I didn't write to you last night because I was tired out, so I am writing this morning. I've just had some coffee, Masha's gone to the school already, she leaves early on Saturdays.

I dreamed about you last night, but I can't remember what. [...] Your last letter was dated the 1st and it's now the 8th and nothing so far. Why is that? Why do you write to me so seldom? That's immoral. [...]

I didn't go to the theatre yesterday. I hear Nemirovich was in bed all day and didn't go to the Act 3 rehearsal. Today, it's Act 1 again and tomorrow we dress-rehearse Act 3. What an endurance! Whether we'll get through, I don't know.

Today is our 500th performance in Moscow. [...]

The day after tomorrow is the anniversary of your trip abroad. Do you remember? How clearly I remember that day! How are you feeling, sweetheart? Why don't you say anything about your health? Don't do that, darling, I beg you, be open with me about everything, I'm a person, you know, not a doll. You offend me by treating me like one. [...]

You'll all be together at Christmas? Will you think of me? I'll either go round visiting friends or sit grumpily at home. I don't know what I'll do. [...]

Your doggie

Knipper

December 8
Moscow, Night

I'm quite drunk, Anton! Forgive your dissolute wife! After the show we gathered in the director's office and had a party. We had pies, caviar, salmon, fruit, wine, champagne and chatter. I laughed a lot. We drank to your health, my darling! It was all very cramped but enjoyable.

Whatever happens in life, I have my Anton. Darling, darling Anton! I don't know where or when we shall see each other. [...]

Your doggie

Knipper

December 9
Moscow, Night

We've just given a triumphant performance of *Uncle Vanya*! Happy? The 62nd time. I had your letter this morning. You write that I don't like your letters – where did you get that idea? Not liking them means there's a note of sadness in them. But I like all your letters. I read them avidly, I'm impatient for them. I don't know how I'll get through the winter if we don't see each other. I shrivel and die without love and affection. If I'm tired, bad-tempered, confused, irritable, it's because I've nowhere of my own, nowhere to rest.

What news of Tolstoi and Gorki? Did you see them on the 4th or not? How is your health? Don't torment me, write and tell me *everything*.

Today we had a dress rehearsal of three acts. Nemirovich seemed pleased. [...] I'm being generally praised. They say it's unlike any of my previous roles. It's good, with foreign chic and fire. We'll see. [...]

It's dreadful, Anton, that I can't come even for a couple of days. I've lost all hope of that. We're going through a difficult time at the theatre, believe me, and the last performance is on the 23rd but there's an evening show and a matinée on the 26th. [...]

Your doggie

Knipper

December 10
Moscow

Today, Anton, I'm being awful, all on edge, shouting at everything, surly – you know? Bless you for your detailed report. But it's wrong of you not to put on slippers, so that you don't have to wear shoes in the morning and you can give orders to bring your Ems water at a certain time to your study. [...]

Your doggie

Knipper

December 11
Moscow

Today I had two front teeth filled, darling! I was in agony when the drill came near the nerve. In a few days I'm having one out. An unpleasant business, but I've so neglected my poor teeth. [...]

Chekhov

December 13
Yalta

Hallo, little actress! I'm better [...] but still weak. I haven't eaten properly for some time. I think I'll be fine in 2–3 days. I'm taking pills and powders.

You write that you were tipsy on the evening of the 8th. Oh, sweetheart, if only you knew how I envy you! I envy your cheerfulness, your brightness, your health, your mood, I envy the fact that you can drink without thinking of spitting blood, etc. I used to be able to get drunk as a lord, as they say. [...]

Your *Anton*

Knipper

December 13
Moscow, Night

Husband mine, writer mine, I kiss you on the lips and give you greetings! Instinct tells me you've not been well. Clever lad to drink Ems water, if you were to drink it all the time then your stomach would be better. [...]

Anton, write a comedy, you must, it would be a revolution because there aren't any Russian comedies. [...]

Your doggie

Knipper

December 14
Moscow

Dearest darling, you've been ill and I wasn't with you. My heart sank today when I got your little letter. Our separation is bearable when I know you're all right, but this is awful! I'm ready to drop everything and rush down to you. I should be at your side, making a decent, comfortable, quiet life for you. And it will happen, my dear. It really pains me to think of you lying there alone and sad... I cried so much today. You're an angel, you know that? I know what you want, what your dreams are, and you say nothing, you suffer and love. [...] Anton, you won't ever blame me for coming into your life, will you? [...]

There's less frost, now it's −10.

Your doggie

1901

Chekhov

December 15
Yalta

Dear doggie, I'm alive, as much as a man on the mend can be. I'm weak and grumpy and doing nothing. [...]

Tolstoi's been ill and living in Yalta with his daughter. Gorki came to see me yesterday. [...]

Your *Ant—*

Knipper

December 15
Moscow, Night

It'll soon be 4, my dearest darling! My visitors have only just gone i.e. the whole Art Th. There's an extraordinary mess in the apartment – they drank, ate, sang, danced, and stayed a long time. I often thought of you, I wasn't in happy mood [...]

I beg you, Anton, don't think of coming to Moscow, look after your health. I feel awful. Be patient until spring and then I'll be with you all the time, and in winter we'll go somewhere to warmer climes and I'll be all yours, I'll look after you and you'll be healthy and at peace. We'll have a little being whom we'll idolize – that's certain, that's what I want. You want that, too, don't you Anton?

The three directors [Stanislavski, Nemirovich, Morozov] were here today. [...] Masha will tell you everything. [...]

Your doggie

Chekhov

December 16
Yalta

Sweetheart, I'm in good health. I've been swamped with visitors who just stayed, there wasn't a moment to write to you, I'm in a rage. [...]

But my health is better, don't worry.

Your *Ant—*

Knipper

December 17
Moscow, Morning

I didn't write to you last night because I had a terrible headache.
After our junkettings I slept for three hours, there was a dress rehearsal in the day and *Sisters* in the evening, which I played in a positive haze; – my head was fit to burst, I drank phenacetin, took Valerian drops the whole time, and mint. Today I slept in until 11, now I'm writing to you then I'll go and have a hot bath, then on to the dress rehearsal of Acts 3 and 4.

Darling, I had two letters I had been desperately waiting for at the same time yesterday. I'm terribly worried about your health. Anton, as soon as the season is over, I shall take you abroad for the whole year and look after you, love you and bore you to death. Yes? I can't live knowing you are far from me and hungry, cold and sad, I just can't. Our lives have to change. This year I'll give up the theatre.

Masha left yesterday. I cried a lot. I'm quite alone. [...] How glad I am you're better now, dearest. [...] I sent you some sweets by Masha. Were they delicious?

Anton, I don't know what to write. Everything seems so trivial. It doesn't matter if I can't think of a present for you, because I know that it's me you need, so the rest is superfluous. If only the winter would go faster! Faster! [...]

Your doggie

Chekhov

December 17
Yalta

Sweetheart, no letter from you today but heaven will forgive you, as I do. My health improves all the time; I put compresses on my right side, take creosote but my temperature is normal and everything's fine. I shall soon be a real man again.

We had visitors yesterday who stayed a long time and I got angry. [...]

Mother is well, but obviously my illness worries her. Masha arrives tomorrow and will take charge of everything. [...]

Your *Ant—*

1901

Knipper

December 18
Moscow, Morning

Hallo, my dearest love! How are you feeling? Today you'll see Masha.

I slept absolutely alone in the house and have just got up and had coffee alone. I'm going to the dentist and then to rehearsal to say my one line in Act 4, I'll have lunch with mother and do *Seagull* in the evening. That's my day. [...]

Your doggie

Chekhov

December 18
Yalta

Dear little actress, I'm alive and well and hope you are the same. [...]

I'm not writing a thing, not doing a thing. I'm putting everything off till next year. You see the kind of lazy-bones you married?

How did Nemirovich's play go? It must have been a roaring success. Moscow audiences love him. I'm thinking of writing a funny play in which the devil goes round as a dragonfly. I don't know if anything will come of it. [...]

Your *Ant—*

Chekhov

December 19
Yalta

Hallo, doggie! Masha arrived yesterday, today she keeps going to the window and breathing the air: life is so good here! I'm in good health, although I still have the compress which I take off on Friday, the day after tomorrow. Apart from that, I do nothing.

Thank you for the sweets, though it's a pity they came from Flei and not Abriskov.[7] Not that Abriskov's are better, but I'm used to them. [...]

7. Two leading makers of sweets in Moscow.

Describe the first night of *In Dreams* to me. I expect it was a roaring success. [...]

Your *Ant—*

Knipper

December 19
night, Moscow

I so want to be with you, Anton! I'm so sad and lonely, it's all so quiet. No one to speak a word to. If only we could live together.

I've just been to the opera to see *Roméo et Juliette.* Utterly boring, silly, not poetic, worthless, ludicrous. I tried to put on a decent face. [...] I'm not fond of opera on the whole and I simply despise ones like this. [...]

The dress rehearsal went well. [...] The costumes are all beautiful but I hate them already and the role, too. Today I received the schedule of performances over the holidays and found I'm only free on three evenings up to January 7. How do you like this? I'm free on the 28th, the 3rd and the 5th. Isn't that wonderful? Oh, I'm so sick of it all! All of it! Where is real life, Anton? [...] Happy the people who go about their little affairs and are content and believe in them. I feel such a nonentity, so weak, so impotent in life. I have the constant impression that I've never done anything in life, I haven't lived. That's because when I was young I vegetated, I didn't see, understand, feel anything of life. And now I'm confused. I just don't know what I should do.

The immensity, the beauty of Life – but all we think about is small change, we understand nothing, everything passes us by, we only feel the profundity, the grandeur of life at rare moments. You're not laughing at me? I most likely express my thoughts badly, I have stopped thinking seriously, I am just living from day to day. In my opinion, fanatics are happier.

I'll stop or I'll bore you. I kiss you, my darling poet. [...]

Olya

Chekhov

December 20
Yalta

Dearest doggie, this is what Nemirovich has just written to me:
'Things seem to be going right with the theatre. Most probably we
shall take Aumont's theatre for 12 years and adapt it to our needs.
I'm going into the whole matter and am spending all my free time
with architects etc.' [...]

I took the compress off today, it was as tiresome as a corset. [...]

Your husband Anton

Knipper

December 20
Moscow, Evening

My darling Anton, how are you? I've just had two letters simultaneously from you. I'm so happy you're feeling well again! [...]
I'm at home alone for the whole evening. The apartment is quiet,
there are only sounds from the outside. [...] Tomorrow evening
[21st] 'we dream' for the first time. [...]

Today I bought a chain for my watch for all of 5 r. and am
passing it off as gold. I'm so-so. I'm sorry you can't see me in my
off-the-shoulder, red frock. The train is in glittering copper-coloured
sequins. The décolleté is fine – beautiful I'm told. You wouldn't
know me. I'm playing the role fast, *à la française*, very lively. I may
be criticized for my boldness, I don't know. [...] X said that I rarely
play a role in a brisk, bold *tempo* but Stanislavski likes it. [...]

Ever your doggie

Knipper

December 22
Moscow, Telegram

Success writing

Knipper

December 22
Moscow

Dear gardener-spouse! You didn't have a letter from me yesterday –
sorry! The reason was my bad behaviour. I won't write at length
now as I am very tired and haven't slept. Yesterday we played *In
Dreams*. To my mind, a mediocre success. [...]

Then quite a large group of us went to the Hermitage [Gardens]
but not the Stanislavskis. We had supper, chatted about ourselves,
didn't feel like breaking up and decided to wait for the papers. We
drank [...] the papers came at 7, we read them aloud till we'd more
or less had enough and started to disperse at 8. Moskvin was a little
drunk, very nice, talkative, and invited himself for morning tea with
[one or two others]. Nemirovich got angry and told us to go home to
rest but they came nonetheless, we drank tea, coffee, had a snack,
talked and laughed and at 10½ I got rid of them and went to bed at
11, but didn't sleep, got up at 3 and went to mama's for lunch and
then on to the theatre.

What do you think of this crazy life? [...]

Your doggie

Chekhov

December 22
Yalta

Sweetheart, I waited all day for a telegram about Nemirovich's play
and – nothing! I suppose that means it was a resounding success and
you all forgot about me.

I keep forgetting to tell you that if you need money, then get it
from Nemirovich, however much you want.

Your *Ant—*

Chekhov

December 23
Yalta

Dear doggie, I still haven't wished you a Happy Christmas! [...]

I got your telegram. I also had one from Nemirovich. What was your performance like? Good? Was it a resounding success? [...] When do you start rehearsing *Small People*? [...]

Sweetheart, I'm healthy, well, more or less, I eat a little, drink a lot and am in good spirits; only one thing is missing – my wife! [...]

Your *An*

Knipper

December 23
Moscow, Night

Dearest Anton, have you recovered? Why don't you write more about your illness, how high your temperature is, how long you were in bed. You're probably grown terribly thin. You don't eat anything. What must we do to make you eat a lot? It pains me to think I can't be with you, to nurse you, change your compresses, feed you and make you feel easy. I can imagine what an awful time you've had! I give you my word, this is the last year things will be like this, dearest! I'll do everything to make your life comfortable, warm, not lonely, you'll see how good it will be with me and how you'll write, work.

I expect in your heart you reproach me with not loving you enough? Is that right? You reproach me with not giving up the theatre – and of not being a real wife to you! I can imagine what your mother thinks! And she's right, she's right! Anton, dearest, forgive me, I'm a frivolous fool but don't think badly of me. You're probably sorry you married me, tell me, don't be afraid to say it openly. I think I'm terribly cruel. Tell me what to do! Won't we really see each other before the spring?! I ask the management to release me so I can come to you, even just for two days, and to adjust the repertoire accordingly. It's all such agony! I can't write about anything else, that is all that's in my head. [...]

At home the rooms are empty and comfortless, I don't want to come back here after the theatre in the evening. No love or affection around me, and I can't live like that. [...]

Your doggie

Chekhov

December 24
Yalta

You see, little actress, I write every day. Today is mother's name-day, tomorrow is Christmas and outside the sun is warm as in summer, all is quiet. I can't go out today because I have two beauty spots. I'll remove them in the evening and tomorrow I may go to see Tolstoi and Gorki. [...]

It would be interesting to know when we shall see each other. During Lent? At Easter-time?

I got your telegram but I still don't know Nemirovich's play went. Write and tell me about it in greater detail. [...]

This summer we'll go abroad, but in 1903, if we're still alive, we'll live in a dacha near Moscow. Yes? Agreet?[8]

Your *Ant*

Knipper

December 25
Moscow, Evening

I rushed home from mother's today, thinking there would be a letter waiting for me! I even felt like sending someone for it during the day, and I get back to find nothing! I so wanted one! You know, I kiss your letters when I get them. Don't laugh. [...] My God, how sad these last few days have been! Terrible. I've been quite lost. Fortunately I'm playing again tomorrow. I don't know what to do with myself when I'm free. I didn't write to you yesterday as I went for the Christmas tree at home and didn't get back till 3, very tired and in a sour mood. [...]

Nemirovich was here yesterday and we talked about the play a great deal. He must be in low spirits but he's reserved and doesn't show it. Everyone hates the play. [...]

Write and tell me what you think about it all. What did you get from the reviews? You could write to him.

8. Chekhov is quoting *Uncle Vanya*, Act 1: a speech by Astrov in which he says: "I have an assistant who never says 'agreed' but 'agreet'."

Sweetheart, how are you feeling? How are you living? God, what a joy it would be to live here in the apartment with you, to live and love each other! But we live only 'in dreams'. We shall wait. [...]

Your doggie

Chekhov

December 26
Yalta

No letter from you today, sweetheart. It must have got stuck in the post. All you need do with letters that come for me is cross out the Moscow address and write – Yalta, then post it; you don't need a stamp. [...]

Will Gorki's play be done this season or not? [...]

Your *Ant—*

Chekhov

December 27
Yalta

So, Knipperkins, you acted well. I'm glad, you clever old thing. If the husband does nothing, then the wife must make mess enough for two. [...]

You were at the restaurant till 8 a.m. Look here, you mustn't ruin your health.

Your husband Anton

Knipper

December 27
Moscow, Night

I didn't write to you yesterday, sweetheart – I was in a foul mood and didn't want to make myself sadder than I was. And you sent me a sort of note, not a letter. You're sick of writing to me, you don't feel anything when you write to me, isn't that right? You're growing out of me a little. I can partly understand that. You'd like to be with me, not filling up sheets of paper.

Yesterday I talked to Nemirovich about releasing me. He thinks he can arrange it for January and free me for a week. Stanislavski spent a long time with me yesterday and I also asked him to help me. The fool consoled me by saying that it was good for me to be on stage and for us to be apart. He told me that before his wife became an actress life was dull, and impossible, void of any interest. The man's a booby! [...]

Nemirovich will shortly be going abroad for three weeks. Tomorrow we read Gorki's play and I expect we'll start rehearsing soon. [...]

I've been at home alone yesterday and today, reading, writing letters, trying to sing but I'm not in the mood. No letter from you again today. My dearest darling, how shall we get through the winter?! Where and when shall we see each other? [...] I'm afraid you're falling out of love with me and that you'll see me as some sort of useless ballast in your life. What kind of useless person am I, sweetheart, tell me, dearest?! [...]

A happy New Year! I kiss you, my dear, my love, my poet. Are you thinking about that comedy?

Your doggie

Knipper

December 28
Moscow

Sweetheart, I had three letters simultaneously from you today, I was so terribly happy, I devoured them. [...] Thank you for writing to me almost every day, I love you for it! With you it's as warm as summer, here it's as warm as winter – it's thawing, everything's slippery.

I got up late today. My greatest pleasure is to lie in bed till almost 12 reading the papers. [...] At one I went to the theatre.

[...] Nemirovich read Gorki's play with a voice full of cold. The reading was frequently interrupted by bursts of laughter. [...]

I had lunch with mama, this evening I was at home. Mother was here, with my aunt and my cousin Lyova and Dorzdova. I played four hands, one piano with my aunt, I sang a little. Nemirovich came for a short while. He's off the day after tomorrow. He looks awful, he's coughing and wheezing, his ear hurts, his head is full of cold.

Lord, when shall we see each other? Do you feel like that when I'm not with you? Good. [...]

Your doggie

Chekhov

December 29
Yalta

You're a goose, sweetheart. Never, while I'm your husband, will I take you away from the theatre, on the contrary, I'm delighted that you have something to do, that you have a goal in life, that you don't talk nonsense, like your husband. I don't write about my health because I'm fine now. My temperature is normal, I eat five eggs a day, drink milk not to mention lunch, which, now that Masha's here, is delicious. Work, sweetheart, don't overdo it and, above all, don't be down. [...]

Masha is cross you haven't written to her. [...]

Dr Altschuler will soon be in Moscow. I suggested he lunch with you. [...]

Are you going to do *Small People*? When? This season or next?

Your *Ant—*

Knipper

December 29
Moscow

Good day once more, my mythical husband! Another day has passed, bringing the moment we are together again nearer. Can you imagine what that moment will be like? I have no idea. And that is why I like it. Suddenly I will be able to take my whole Anton in my arms, I will kiss his head, feel his breathing, his gentleness, I will hear his voice, I will see his charming, wonderful eyes, his sweet smile, his crow lines, his smooth cheek and my Anton will be there beside me, all of him. My God, it is almost unbelievable!

I am alone. I have just got back from doing *Seagull*. [...]

And you, Antoniono, are you working? Make a tiny effort and the time will pass quicker if you write, won't it? You will write something fine, elegant, I can feel it, I mean something very elegant in terms of form. I am very interested because you are now so close to me. Do you understand?

On January 11 we are playing *Uncle Vanya* for the doctors' convention. So, sleep now, darling one, don't say bad things about me, I kiss you [...] my charming husband.

Your doggie

Chekhov

December 30
Yalta

[...] If you see Dr Altschuler, then buy a bag of sweets from Abriskov and get him to bring them. Buy some jam, too.

It's weary without you. Tomorrow I'll go to bed at 9 so as not to see the New Year in. You're not here, that means I don't need anything.

The weather has changed for the worse. Wind, cold, some snow flakes. Winter has evidently begun.

I'll write to Nemirovich. [...]

Your husband *Ant—*

Knipper

December 30
Moscow

A second day and no letter from you, my dearest! I've just come from mother's where I had lunch and now I'm going to play *Lonely People.* [...]

I've just had an invitation from the society of Russian doctors to the opening and closing sessions of the conference. We'll play *Uncle Vanya* for them on January 11.

I'll see the New Year in tomorrow with mother. [...]

Your doggie

Chekhov

December 31
Yalta

Darling wife, I'm well, absolutely well. I eat enough for ten, put on weight, which I haven't done for a long time, my stomach's working well. Don't worry, dearest; word of honour, I'm not lying, I'm telling the truth. [...]

Dr Altschuler isn't coming to Moscow. [...]

No letter from you today! Shameless of you!

The weather's fine again in Yalta. Today I sat in the shade in the garden and breathed the air. [...]

Your *Ant—*

1902

Chekhov

January 2
Yalta

My dear, glorious, incomparable wife, I had a despondent letter from you yesterday but nothing today. You've started to neglect me and have evidently been on a spree because of the holidays. How dour it is without your letters! The day before yesterday I sent a telegram to the Art Theatre, a long one, for the New Year but addressed it to Nemirovich and I fear you never got it, as according to the papers, he's gone abroad. Find out, sweetheart!

Are those two schemers going to let you go at the end of January? [...]

Give Roksanova your role in *Lonely People*, then they'll have a wider repertoire in your absence. On the whole, you're playing far too often, without a rest, that's not good. It's not healthy physically or mentally. You shouldn't play more than 2–3 times a week. [...]

I read that the doctors are going to give you a thank-you lunch. Is that right?

Today I wanted to go into town to have my hair cut and so washed it yesterday but it's cold, no more than three degrees above. I've had to put it off.

Every day as I go to sleep I think of my wife. I think and think. [...]

Your husband *Ant—*

1902

Chekhov

January 2
Yalta

Today two letters came at once, sweetheart. Thank you! And mother had a letter from you. Self-reproach is a mistake, if you're living in Moscow it's just because not of you, but because we both want it. And mother is neither angry or disapproving.

Today I had a haircut. I went to town for the first time since my illness despite the cold (-2) and had my hair and beard trimmed – in case you come. You're very demanding, I must look clean and tidy.

Masha has found a cook. I have to say I'm writing nothing, absolutely nothing. Don't be upset, there's still time. I've already written 11 volumes – joke. When I'm 45 I'll write another 20. Don't be angry, darling wife! I'm not writing but I'm reading so much I'll soon be clever.

Now it's January, and the bad weather is starting, with wind, mud, cold and then February and its storms. A married man without his wife is in a sorry situation during these months. If only you can come at the end of January as you promised!

Gorki's in a dismal mood, he seems unwell. He's coming to stay the night.

Do you feel how much I love you, doggie? Or don't you care? I love you desperately, as you know. [...]

Your husband *Anton*

Knipper

January 3
Moscow

If only you knew how sweet you look in your photograph! Such a wonderfully gentle face! I kissed you. I'm terribly pleased to be seeing Dr Altschuler[9] – it will be like seeing a piece of you. Only why didn't I see him today at the meeting? [...]

9. At the doctors' convention.

I thought of you. You are my dearest sweetheart! Do you love me very much? How are we going to see each other? You should talk to me about that, and I should talk about it to you. It seems to me I will love you even more, I will kneel and look at you and laugh at the happy thoughts that tickle my mind. [...]

We're rehearsing the Gorki again tomorrow. [...]

I'm glad you're eating well. Is Masha angry? Tell her not to be, I write to you every day, at night, I don't see the daylight, I'm busy at the theatre, I've played five evenings running and in the day I'm rehearsing *Small People*. She doesn't write to me either, and she should. She'll be coming soon and will tell me everything, which will be more interesting than writing. [...]

Doggie

I love you, Anton! Love you, love you!!

Knipper

January 4
Moscow

Sweetheart, wonderful husband of mine, guess where I've just been? You give up? To the 'Dresden', room number 35, 'from where Chekhov abducted Knipper', as Vishnievski says. Yes, I was there, having tea after *In Dreams*. [...] I spent the whole time remembering my time there with you, every chair was familiar. [...] I remember coming there late and what I told you and how agitated you were. [...] And how we lingered in the room before the wedding ceremony, I remembered everything we'd lived and talked about within those walls! [...]

Your doggie

Knipper

January 5
Moscow, 4 a.m.

I won't write much today, dearest! It's 4 in the morning, I'm very tired, I've been tense all day, I laugh when I'm with other people, but when I'm alone, I feel like howling. [...]

Altschuler won't be coming, then. [...] I so wanted to see him, hear about you and suddenly, it's not going to happen! Why hasn't he come? [...]

I'm reading the plays of the contemporary Viennese dramatist Hoffmanstahl in German.

Starting tomorrow I shall be playing 7 days without a break and rehearsing *Small People* in the day. You know what that means? [...]

Your doggie

Chekhov

January 5
Yalta

Sweetheart, darling Olya, no letter from you yesterday.

Yalta is snowbound. The devil knows why. Even Masha has lost heart and has stopped saying nice things about the place, she holds her tongue.

Where did Nemirovich go? Nice? What is his address?

We have employed a cook. She seems to be doing well. Grandmother is used to her, that is the main thing.

I dreamed about you last night. But I have no idea when I shall see you in the flesh, it seems a long way off. Because they won't release you until the end of January. Gorki's play and all the rest of it. So, this is my fate.

No, I won't make you unhappy, my good, my extraordinary wife. I love you and would go on loving you even if you beat me with a stick. Still snow and ice outside, nothing new, everything as usual.

I hold you, I kiss you, my dearest, darling wife; don't forget me, don't forget me, don't grow out of me. The roof is dripping, the sound of spring, but if you look out of the window, it is winter. Come to me in dreams, darling heart.

Your husband, Antoine

Did you get the photo of the two blackamoors?

Knipper

January 6
Moscow

What do you mean, you don't get my letters. I rarely miss a day, only sometimes when I'm very tired or go to bed late. I'm so used to talking to you before I go to sleep that I feel ill at ease unless I write to you. [...]

You didn't write and tell me how you passed the New Year. Is it true you were all in bed? I'm glad you're eating a little, my dearest.

Chekhov

January 7
Yalta

My dissolute wife, stay home for just a week and go to bed at the proper time! Go to bed between 3 and 6 in the morning and you'll soon turn into a horrible, skinny old woman. [...]

I'm glad the festivities are over. I may work on something. My health is excellent. I couldn't ask for better. I eat like a horse. Only one thing wrong – my wife isn't here, I'm living like a hermit. [...]

Your *Ant—*

Knipper

January 8
Moscow, Night

[...] Whenever I start writing to you I break off, dreaming of the moment when we shall see each other, dreaming about you, I picture you, I strain my ears to hear your voice, I remember your way of speaking, your shining eyes, everything ... [...]

Are you reading a lot, writing? What? [...] I'm delighted my husband is getting clever. Pity the wife is falling behind.

Anton, you say the weather is beginning to be awful in Yalta. Couldn't you consider coming to Moscow at the end of January? Is there no way? There won't be heavy frosts, you'll be comfortable, you needn't go out in the air, the apartment is big, you can walk and move about it, it's airy. I'm sorry I wrote that. Stop thinking about Moscow, be patient. But what about the spring? [...]

Sometimes I think of you and become very emotional – why is that? Life is so good when I feel your love, when I feel that you are mine. I love it when you caress me even in words in your letters. It warms me, I feel I have a treasure and I haven't yet dug it all up, there is much, much more to come. [...]

Your doggie

Chekhov

January 9
Yalta

Dearest sweetheart, today it's raining, it's cold, it's awful, while the day before yesterday there was a frost which, as the papers put it, went up to –8. I don't go out, I stay in my study. [...] I'm not writing anything, I'm busy with trifles. There were visitors all day yesterday, my head ached, it's still morning and I don't know if there will be any visitors today, but my head isn't aching.

We've had snow. Tomorrow you play *Uncle Vanya* for the doctors, write and tell me how it went and how the doctors behaved etc. [...] As to Altschuler, I wrote to you about that, he's not coming to Moscow. [...]

Our new cook, who seems an excellent woman, fell ill yesterday: we thought it was typhus, then found it was just a fever. She's on her feet again today, taking quinine.

We'll spend May and June in Yalta, but in July we'll go abroad, spend August (second half) in Yalta, September and October in Moscow. I can spend May in Moscow but initially you must come to me in Yalta. [...] How I would love to go somewhere far away with you, Lake Baikal, for instance! It's a wonderful lake; once seen, never forgotten. [...]

Your *Ant—*

Knipper

January 11
Moscow, near Morning

Though it's very late and I've had a very mixed day, I can't go to bed without giving you my news, my dearest, wonderful love! We played *Uncle Vanya* [for the doctors]. The theatre, of course, was

packed, people started arriving at 11. We gave a good performance,
we didn't disgrace ourselves. After Act I, the theatre was presented
with a huge portrait of you, in laurels, in a massive, wonderful frame
with a gold inscription at the bottom (I can't remember the exact
words) and a dark gold laurel branch in one corner – very simple
and elegant. [...] I hear that men wept during the performance and
one woman had hysterics.

After Act III a deputation came back stage and thanked us. They
introduced themselves, took me by the hand and asked me to convey
their respects and best wishes to you. They were all ecstatic. After
the 1st act, [they] read the telegram they had sent you. At the end
there was great applause, shouts of thank you, in fact, absolute
pandemonium. I thought of you the whole time! If only you could
have been here! [...]

After the show we ate at the Hermitage [Gardens]. [...] We had a
splendid meal, laughed a lot and didn't talk about anything serious.
Everyone was very nice. [...] We stayed till 9. [...]

Your doggie

Chekhov

January 11
Yalta

[...] I didn't write to you at the New Year because I didn't see it in,
although I wasn't asleep at 12.

Masha leaves tomorrow and I shall be alone again. She's been
feeding me so I've filled out a lot. And she also keeps everything in
good order.

I'm a little off-colour today. But it's nothing serious; I'll be all
right tomorrow.

How did the show for the doctors go? Did they present anything?
I read in the paper they were going to present my portrait to the
company. What portrait? Where is it?

Ah, darling little actress, when shall we see each other? It's so
deadly dull without you I shall soon be shouting for help. Nothing
interests me in Yalta. [...] I need to live in Moscow with you, I need
to see and observe life, I need to live in Moscow and dream while
I'm there of a trip to the Crimea or abroad. [...]

I drink up to two glasses of milk a day. Masha will tell you all
about me. [...]

How are rehearsals for *Small People* going? Will the play be done? [...]

Your *Ant*

Knipper

January 12
Moscow

Today I played for the seventh time running and now I have two days off i.e. two evenings my dearest, special darling!

I feel sick at heart today, and I feel the division in my life more keenly. I can't live without you, such a life is senseless. I know you need me and that I ought to give up the stage, and I love you to distraction. Forgive me mentioning it again, I know you dislike it, and it's tactless of me to refer to it. Don't be angry with me. You feel what I feel, and I know your each and every thought.

I would be terrible if at some time I saw myself and my life differently, perhaps, from the way I do now. I might feel guilty and not know who I am.

It's so quiet in the apartment! I'm alone. There's just one cold electric lamp burning, no more. Sometimes that calm, unflickering light annoys me. [...]

Your little actress

Chekhov

January 13
Yalta

Dearest sweetheart, if I understand your last letter a little, you won't be coming to Yalta. *In Dreams* is on and you're rehearsing *Small People*. I understand sweetheart and stake no claims. If it can't be, then it can't be.

Masha left yesterday; it's overcast and chilly. I'm well, eating a lot, though I see nothing good in that. [...]

You keep asking me to come to Moscow. Darling, I would have come long ago but they won't let me. Dr. Altschuler won't allow me to go out in overcast weather, although I did today, because I was so bored I could have screamed. [...]

Your *Ant*—

Knipper

January 13
Moscow

I'm absolutely alone at home, dearest. I'm drinking tea, nibbling some sausage and cheese, but not having any vodka. I'm uneasy in my mind. I thought a lot about you and about our lives.

We'll go wherever you like in the summer. [...] Lake Baikal? Let's. Wherever is good for you and your health. Don't worry about me. I'll be with you in Yalta at the beginning of Holy Week and then we'll see.

Are you really unhappy with the letters I write at night? You don't like it when I start thinking about life and complain. You only see me as cheerful and full of the joys of life, don't you? [...]

There's turmoil in my heart, dear Anton. I don't know what I should do. And I feel alone, although there are people everywhere. [...]

Your doggie

Knipper

January 14
Moscow

[...] Write and tell me more about yourself. I don't know what's going on in your head, or where your thoughts are, it's all foreign to me. You obviously have nothing to say to me but still call me your friend. You write about the weather. I can learn what that's like from the papers. If you don't want to write, that's all right, send postcards about the state of your health. Either you and I are close or we're not, and I'm just a woman to you, not a person. Only that's too shameful.

I kiss you, darling.

Your doggie

Chekhov

January 15
Yalta

Dearest, darling Olga, [...] I had a telegram from the doctors, you know about that. Today I heard the birds for the first time this spring. It's warm, sunny, quiet and there's the timid, hesitant chirping of the birds that fly to Russia at the end of March. There was a fire tonight in the white house almost opposite my study window. [...]

Your *Ant—*

Knipper

January 15
Moscow

I'm tired today. I suddenly felt weak during the 3rd act, my nerve went, I was very limp in the 4th act and was all in a sweat from feeling so weak. I'm so unhappy with myself, in such torment when I give a bad performance, I have the feeling I'm not an actress at all, that it's all been blown out of proportion and I'm an absolute nonentity. [...] Why don't I believe in anything?

I think my letters bore you. [...]

I have an awful feeling of being more and more hemmed in. Wherever I turn there's a wall. Life is so vast and we see nothing clearly. [...]

I understood from something Masha said that you've talked to her about the play you're writing. You haven't said a word to me, although you know how important it is to me [...]

Your doggie

Knipper

January 17
Moscow

I won't say anything about my coming down to see you, darling, as I'm expecting Nemirovich. He's being thorough, replacing me where he can, drawing up the schedule and rehearsing with understudies. [...] They may be able to release me at the end of January, perhaps the first week of Lent. At all events we'll see each other before the Petersburg tour. There are two casts for *Small People* and they can replace me in *In Dreams* though I don't see by whom. [...]

What did you do for your birthday today? Did you get any greetings? Why didn't you write and tell me if you were pleased to get the doctors' telegram? [...]

I didn't write to you yesterday because I was tired and had neuralgia in my face and went to bed. [...]

Your Olga

Knipper

January 18
Moscow

No letter from you. Awful. How are you feeling? Forgive me Anton for your being alone and miserable. Don't you get miserable when I'm not there? Tell me, do I mean 'something' to you after all? Would you feel your life was fuller, would you have greater peace of mind if I were there? Forgive me, I know you don't like or understand such questions and think I'm a fool when I talk like this. You're probably very unhappy with my recent letters but I really did write what I felt. [...]

I went to the Morozovs for lunch today with Vishnievski. It was splendid. [...]

The hors d'œuvres were wonderful – fresh cucumbers, fish etc. There were flowers *en masse* on the dining-table. The meal was delicious and I tucked in with great appetite and thought of you. [...] We drank champagne and some vintage red wine. I hear Morozov has an amazing cellar. After lunch we went to the opera – *Boris Godunov* with Chaliapin. [...]

There's a little mouse living in a corner of the big room I've turned into your study. I can see it. I like that. At night, when I'm all alone and writing it scurries about in the corner. At first it frightened me but now I like it. I'm fond of mice. [...]

> Your doggie

Chekhov

> January 20
> Yalta

What a goose you are, my sweetheart! [...] You write that it has all been blown out of proportion that you are a nonentity, that your letters bore me etc. How silly! I didn't write to you about the coming play not because I don't believe in you but because I don't believe in the play. [...]

On January 17, my birthday, I was in a terrible mood, because I felt rotten and the telephone kept ringing with messages and greetings. Not even you and Masha spared me, you sent them, too.

By the way, when is your *Geburtstag*?

You write: don't be sad, we will see each other soon. Meaning? Holy Week? Before? Don't frighten me, my joy. In December you wrote that you would be coming in January and you got me all excited, then you wrote that you would be coming in Holy Week and I told my heart to be still and got a hold of myself and now you are raising another storm on the Black Sea. Why?

[...]

So, my good, my fine, my golden wife, God keep you, be healthy, be happy, think of your husband, in the evening at least as you go to bed. But the main thing – don't be down in the dumps. Your husband isn't a drunk, or a waster, or a lout. I behave like a perfect German husband: I even wear warm underpants.

I hug you 101 times. I kiss my wife endlessly.

> Your Antoine

Knipper

> January 20
> Moscow, Telegram

No letters worried wire me   Olya

Knipper

January 20
Moscow

I've just got back from the theatre and found your two letters after I'd sent a telegram. Forgive me and please don't be angry about it. But it isn't easy for me, stuck here without a letter for three days. [...]

I hate the apartment because there's not a corner in which you might have sat, there are no memories of your being here. Can you understand that, great man? [...]

Your doggie

Chekhov

January 21
Yalta, Telegram

Health fine, greetings to my guard doggie   *Antony*

Chekhov

January 21
Yalta

Dearest little Olga, no letter from you today. Are you angry with me? Or are you generally out of spirits? I had a telegram from you yesterday. Dearest darling, if I were ill I would certainly wire you, don't worry. If I don't say anything about my health it means I'm fine.

What a joy our stupid press is! Something about me or Gorki every day and not a word of truth in it. Revolting. [...]

Gorki has set to work on a new play, as I told you, but Chekhov hasn't. [...]

German *A*

Knipper

January 21
Moscow

Darling, I'm writing to you from my dressing-room, during Act 3.
Electric light, a mirror, the smell of makeup, the air is full of
powder, dust, dirt everywhere. I'm in my wig with curlers in it, all
greasy. You'd laugh at me. [...]

I'm thinking of the spring when we shall be together. I think of
Petersburg with horror. Nemirovich has been there to discuss the
repertoire. I think we should take *Seagull* and open with it. Lilina as
Nina. What do you think? [...]

Anton, don't shout at me because of my recent letters, I wrote
freely, you won't be angry and take them seriously will you? Write
to me about it, sweetheart. Write something about the singing of
birds in spring, write me a tale about birds. You're such a wonderful
man, Anton! I so want to know more about you and love you more.
[...]

The bell for Act 4 has just gone. They're coming to dress me. I'll
finish. [...]

Your good *doggie*

Chekhov

January 23
Yalta

Good little doggie, why have you been so restrained in your endearments, why do your letters seem so unfeeling? Are you angry with
me? What about? Don't hide things, darling, and if you're uneasy in
your mind, then write and tell me. [...]

Your *Ant*

Knipper

January 23
Moscow

Anton, it's awful, three days and not a line from you! Are you angry
with me? Masha says you don't know what to write about. Do you
find correspondence difficult? Really? Is it hard for you to write to

me at the end of the day? I don't know what to think. Have you fallen out of love with me, have you decided I'm just not your wife? Do you really think you have to write facts and events in your letters? – I just feel the need to write to you every day, I like it, I like telling you how I spent my day, what I saw, what I heard and if I had more time during the day I'd write a lot more. Don't you see that?

I didn't write to you yesterday because after *Uncle Vanya* (almost a full house) we all went to a New Year party and I didn't get back until 6 a.m. Sorry, don't be angry. It was very ingenious. You would have loved it. [...] They lit the Christmas tree, the lights were very elegant, and they had built a small platform, a hut, a tea-house, walls with posters of all kinds pasted on, a nomad's tent, there were little barrels in toboggans with refreshments (nuts, gingerbread).

They built a mountainside from the stage (polished boards) and we slid down it. [...] The whole company was there, all the students and everyone had a wonderful time. We drank tea, vodka, ate sandwiches and fruit, that's all. I was very tired but ran about all over the place. [...]

Don't fall out of love with me and don't call me 'guard doggie' in your telegrams.

Your doggie

Knipper

January 24
Moscow

My dearest sweetheart, I got back home late again and won't send you a long letter until tomorrow morning. Don't be angry. Today was a gala – the 50th performance of *Three Sisters*. [...]

Almost a full house. [...]

Your doggie

1902

Chekhov

January 25
Yalta

I won't be writing to you very much now as you'll soon be here.
You're a little German who knows her own mind. You'll turn up on
Monday and leave on Wednesday, or maybe Tuesday ... What a
time I have with you! [...]

I've put up with you enough! I'll have to take you in hand,
threaten you or you won't come at all, or just for half an hour. [...]

Your *Ant*

Knipper

January 25
Moscow

Hallo, dearest! A big kiss. I didn't write to you this morning as I
was copying verses for your worship and now I'm writing at night as
usual.

The long-term future of our theatre is being decided, Anton. [...]

*Early in 1902 the Art Theatre was re-formed as a shareholding
collective. The major shareholder was still Morozov, who nonetheless
lent the poorer members of the company money so that they could buy
shares. Some members of the theatre, notably Meyerhold, were
deliberately excluded, causing much dissension. Chekhov initially
agreed to invest 10,000 roubles but later withdrew because of
Meyerhold's exclusion.*[10]

Chekhov

January 27
Yalta

Dearest sweetheart, I didn't send a wire to 'guard doggie' but 'good
doggie'. It must have been altered at the telegraph office.

Tolstoi is in a very bad way. [...] You'll probably hear of his
death before you get this letter. It's sad, I am full of gloom.

10. See *Moscow Art Theatre Letters.*

Let me know the date and time of your arrival. If you can't come, then never mind, stay home and get on with your own affairs. We'll see each other in Holy Week. I'm in good health. [...]

Your *Ant—*

Knipper

January 28
Moscow

Forgive me, dearest sweetheart for not writing to you yesterday. I felt very tense and it was difficult to write. We were at the Hermitage Theatre from 2 in the afternoon till 10 at night discussing the future of our theatre. Morozov has written to you today, of course much more clearly than I. I'm an utter fool in business matters. [...]

You complain that I'm restrained in my endearments, that I'm angry with you. Don't think like that, darling, I love you and in my mind I whisper sweet names and kiss you and my heart leaps for joy when I think of the moment when we shall be together when I shall hold you to my heart and look into your dear, shining eyes, see your tender smile which has such an effect on me, unsettles me, I'll stroke your soft hair and kiss the back of your head. [...]

Did you eat the sweets? I think they must have been old when they reached you. [...]

Your doggie

Chekhov

January 28
Yalta

[...] Tolstoi is very, very ill. He has pneumonia. So, keep well, my joy. Look after yourself.

1902

Chekhov

January 29
Yalta

[...] You're coming for two days? Is that all? [...] Coming for two days, that's hard. Two days – this is Nemirovich's act of charity, I humbly thank him. If I can stick it out till February, then I can stick it out until the end of Lent, all two days achieves is your being tired out by a journey, my being sick with disappointment and our saying goodbye. No! [...]

Your *Ant—*

Knipper

January 30
night, Moscow

I'm writing to you again and once again in my mind I rush to your side, I'm sitting in your study, in the alcove, I'm settling in with you, listening to you, resting, delighting in the peace and quiet, my heart is full, there's nothing else I need. And I am good for you, I feel that and like feeling it.

I can picture our meeting – I'll be in such a whirl but I know it will be wonderful. I will discover things about you that aren't new but which I never noticed before. We'll look at each other. Who are you, Anton? And do you know who I am? All of me? [...]

Your doggie

Chekhov

January 31
Yalta

[...] Tolstoi was better yesterday. There seems to be hope. [...]

Your German *Ant—*

Knipper

February 1
Moscow, Morning

Everyone's very worried because there's no news of Tolstoi's health, dear Anton! You did promise to wire me if anything happened. Rumour has it that he's dead but I don't believe it. I don't believe the papers could keep quiet if anything had happened. I impatiently await a letter from you today.

You know, earlier this morning I dreamed about you, I was coming to Yalta and you were there at home and had just changed your clothes. Your mother hugged and kissed me endlessly and I cried and rested my head on her shoulder. A crowd of women came and Masha was in her Sunday best. And we were longing to be alone and you ate sweets and (how awful) licked your fingers.

It's the first time I've dreamed about you. [...]

Don't forget your
Doggie

Knipper

February 2
Moscow, Morning

So, darling Anton, I leave Moscow on Friday [...] and will be with you on Saturday. If they put on *Small People* I'll only do the first performance. [...] If they don't, the only thing that upsets me is *Uncle Vanya*. Lilina will play Elena and be the understudy, which means it won't be my role any more. I'm jealous about that part, and that one only, because it didn't come easily, I had a lot of trouble with it and so I prize it. Do you understand that? Of course, I reproach myself for being so weak, one should be above such things, but I just can't do it. I'm not as jealous about *Seagull* or *Sisters* as these roles came to me comparatively easily. There's nothing we can do about it. [...]

Your doggie

Knipper

February 4
Moscow

I've just got back from the theatre and – what joy! – found a letter from you! I'm in a fever – soon I'll be leaving for the south, for you, darling, and I'll rest. Only it will be so hard having to come back again. But still, we won't be apart for long.

[...] Write and tell me in detail what you think about our new association. I'm very worried and I think I shouldn't join because I really don't know whether I shouldn't leave [the theatre] altogether. [...]

Your doggie

Knipper

February 5
Moscow, Night

You've been ill again and have been hiding it from me. Dearest darling, don't hide it from me, it's not good, it means you think I'm just a weak woman, *hors de jeu*, and you're afraid of alarming me. Don't do that, I beg you. In two weeks I'll be on my way, possibly on the 20th instead of the 21st. [...]

What shall I bring you from Moscow? If only you knew how I hate the thought of going to Petersburg, darling! It gives me the shudders to think of it.

Today we didn't do *Three Sisters* because Meyerhold was ill, he writes that his nerves are bad and he's afraid of having a nervous breakdown. [...]

Your doggie

Chekhov

February 6
Yalta

Hallo, darling doggie, Olyusha. I wrote to you about Tolstoi's health and not just once either. It's been very poor. [...]

So, you've decided to come. You've had pity on me. Nemirovich wired me that you are leaving on the 22nd but must be in Petersburg on the 2nd. [...]

Your *Ant—*

Knipper

February 7
Moscow

I'm writing to you during Act 3 of *In Dreams* my dearest darling. Today it became clear I can leave on the 20th and take the steamboat on the Friday. We should have been doing *Lonely People* but it's been replaced by *Dreams*. Raevskaya will take over from me. *Uncle Vanya* won't be on before Petersburg because Lilina is ill. I end with *Sisters* on the 19th and early on the morning of the 20th I'm off. [...]

Antonino, don't come and meet me at the quay-side. It will be better to meet in your study, alone, it will be nicer. Yes? Don't you think? [...]

What's the sea like? Not too stormy right now? [...]

Your doggie

Chekhov

February 9
Yalta

[...] Snowing, cold, nasty. I heard last night on the telephone that Tolstoi is in good health. There was a crisis but his temperature is now normal. [...]

Are you coming soon? I'm waiting, waiting, waiting ... But the weather's atrocious...

Your husband A

Knipper

February 10
Moscow

I've got a terrible headache, dearest, and it's difficult to write, I've just finished *Sisters* and I thought my head would burst. I'm not well today that's why I have a headache. And yesterday I was so worn out I stayed in bed and even when Masha came for a chat I nearly fell asleep sitting in a chair. Everyone's in such a state, everything's so unsettled. [...]

Your doggie

Knipper

February 11
Moscow

[...] Meetings, meetings, talk, talk [about the future of the theatre], but I didn't go to the [shareholders'] meeting yesterday because I had an awful headache. There's another meeting tomorrow. I'm starting to get angry, all I see is the theatre and actors. Life is passing me by. I don't look after my husband, I don't read, I see nothing, I hear nothing; you're quite wrong to say my life is happy and varied. Not at all. [...] I love the theatre but towards the end of the year all this hubbub gets on one's nerves, you're marking time rather than actually do anything. You start asking yourself: what have I got out of this year, what have I learned? And you realize that you've seen nothing of life, that you're more and more blinkered, and that the theatre is largely at fault. Not a nice thought, Anton dearest. [...]

Your doggie

Knipper

February 13
Moscow

Sweetheart, I put the 11th on yesterday's letter – stupid of me. But I was sure today was the 12th.

In a week's time to the very minute I shall be leaving and dreaming of the south and of you. How fast those days will fly! [...]

Masha is well, she's not writing at the moment. The weather has been wonderful – sunny, a breath of spring. Only today is overcast.

Anton, my dear, I don't know what to write. I wanted to sort things out myself, but I can't. That distresses me. I don't know what to do, and I feel absolutely desperate writing to you about this. I have debts on my conscience which I must pay. I didn't know what to do about it. [...] I racked my brains for a long time and finally plucked up the courage to write to you. You can call me all the names you like, I'll understand. I know how people keep you waiting. I'm ashamed to tell you the amount, you'll be horrified. Will you be very angry with me? I owe 7000 r. – is that very terrible? I wanted to pay it off in instalments but that's not possible. If you decide to get me out of my debts to the theatre, so that I can pay off even 500, I'll be so very happy! I'll work it off. You've had 8000 from the theatre. Tell me, would you find it very inconvenient? If you can do it, send me a telegram with just one word: yes; or, if you can't, no.

If only you knew how hard it is to write this to you. I'm regretting it already, only promise me it will be strictly between ourselves. These debts have just piled up over recent years, when I found it difficult to manage. It won't happen again, I am strong-willed in such matters. [...]

Your doggie

Chekhov

February 14
Yalta

Dearest Olya, are you still in Moscow? Sweetheart I want to suggest that if there's a strong wind in Sevastopol and if you hear talk at the station of a storm at sea, then go straight to the coach station and take a barouche, covered, of course, or, better still, a carriage. But only if you absolutely have to; you see, going by sea is so much more pleasant now than going by road, even when the weather's not particularly good.

Chekhov

February 18
Yalta, Telegram

Take as much as you want expecting you.

Knipper

February 22
Sevastopol, Telegram

Coming by road   Olya

Knipper was in Yalta from February 22–28

Knipper

February 28
Simferopol

Darling, I'm in Simferopol and writing to you from there. I was
assured in Yalta I would be late for the train so decided to go
another way. I'm absolutely chilled to the bone. After Lombat it
began to snow, there was snow in Alush and, thereafter, severe frost.
I was swallowed up in a blizzard. The still weather is beautiful, I
don't deny. I'm at the station, it's dark and dreary, I can't get any
tea or anything hot to eat. I'm in the ladies' room with my face
wrapped up. I'm sorry not to have kissed you once again on the
terrace. I thought about it the whole journey. Don't be downcast,
dearest, we shall see each other soon. Still, how wonderful to have
seen each other at all. Write to me very soon. [...]

Your doggie

Chekhov

February 28
Yalta

My dearest wife, my Olya, how was your journey? I'm uneasy in my
mind. Your sore spots and then the bitter weather have ruined my
entire day and I won't feel easy until I get a letter from you. [...]

Come back soon. I can't live without my wife. [...]

Your hermit Antony

Knipper

March 1
between Simferopol and
Kharkov, 12 p.m.

Hallo, dearest! I'm travelling 2nd class, not international class, there weren't any seats. [...] A lady from Yalta is travelling with me. She asked me if I liked Chekhov i.e. the writer. I didn't tell her who I was. Yesterday, before the train left, I felt awful, quite strange. I had a pain in my stomach, nausea, palpitations and I almost passed out. I was very weak. And afraid. Nothing like it has ever happened to me before. I thought I wouldn't be able to travel. It's all right now. I slept. I think of you. [...]

Knipper

March 1
Kharkov

[...] You're sitting in your study but not in an armchair, are you? What are you reading, what are you thinking, my darling? Those 5 days passed as in a dream. [...] It was such a wrench to leave you, I feel I should make a comfortable life for you. You'll end up thinking me an empty hussy. Perhaps you do already. Why didn't I tell you what was in my mind, why?

I'm troubled by the thought that you're pining away, day after day, as in prison, longing for another life and suffering endlessly... When I have such thoughts I feel shabby, worthless, incapable of anything bigger, better in life. I dislike writing this to you when I should be doing, not writing. Well, we'll see.

My travelling companion told me the story of her life. [...]

When I told her about my malaise yesterday she immediately concluded that I was in an 'interesting' condition. I thought so, too. I was very scared and started to take off my jacket, I didn't know what to do, I couldn't make the door of the ladies' room to call for someone, I collapsed and didn't have the strength to get up, my legs and arms wouldn't respond. I was in a cold sweat and bewildered. I thought it was food poisoning. We'll see. [...]

Your doggie

Knipper

March 6
Petersburg

Good morning to my darling!

I got up this morning hale and hearty. Yesterday I was flat out with a headache. I took some phenacetin and wrapped my head in a handkerchief. I had lunch alone at home. By evening my head was better. We played *Three Sisters* but I wasn't good. [...] On the whole a feeble performance, sorry writer. Good reception.

I hated yesterday's show with all my heart and didn't want to see our fans or hear their plaudits. I stayed in my dressing-room. I can't wait for *Uncle Vanya*. How I long to inhabit that play! [...]

Sweetheart, I remember how quiet life was with you, how good it was, how we sat in the armchair and talked. I remember your loving eyes and dear, sweet smile. Do you still remember the Volga? Sometimes I think you don't actually care where you live, do you? [...] Provided you're in a dry place, with a pine forest and you eat well, you're fine. [...]

Your doggie

Knipper

March 7
Petersburg, Morning

Sweetheart, a second day without a letter from you i.e., two days and today's the third. I ought to have a letter from you today.

I got up this morning with a muzzy head, my lips are cracked. It's a grey day, dreadful, thawing, slushy and I'm in a sour mood.

I stayed in all day yesterday [...]

Anton, I haven't the slightest wish to appear on stage. I've turned into an idiot, I don't want to act in anything, what does it mean? Endless performances of *Sisters*. Terribly boring. Samarova was ill so we did *Sisters* again yesterday and again today. My nerves are in shreds. [...]

Are you working, darling, or don't you feel like it? [...] But the main thing is, eat properly to give you strength. [...]

Your doggie

Knipper

March 9
Petersburg

Only 2 letters in 9 days – scandalous!

Chekhov

March 10
Yalta

Olya, my darling wife, hallo! I'm writing to you because I'm bored and idle, but I don't know what to write. My health is exceptionally good today, the best for a long time. I eat very little, my condition is excellent and I explain this by the weather which is sunny and almost warm. If only we could arrange things so that we could live in Moscow! They're trying to find a dacha for us on the Volga. My conditions are: grounds, furniture, no wind, close to a landing-stage, best of all a building so arranged that I can pay court to the local ladies. It would be good to have a little house with you as mistress of it. I would be entirely in your hands and answerable to you. [...]

An

Knipper

March 16
Petersburg

My darling man of gold. [...] Sometimes I hate the theatre and sometimes I love it to distraction. It has given me life, much sorrow, much joy, it gave me you and it has made me a real person. You probably think it's an artificial life, mostly lived in the imagination. Maybe. But life nonetheless. Before I went into the theatre I vegetated, I knew nothing of life, I knew nothing of people and their feelings, I had no life with others and no life of my own. [...]

[After rehearsal] I went to see Lilina and can you guess who I met there?! – Cricket.[11] [...] She asked after you. I asked her how she came to know you. She laughed, 'Have you never heard of Cricket?' [...]

You know, when she talked to me about your early life, I enjoyed it, but it made me painfully jealous, because maybe the better part of your life had nothing to do with me, I only know about it by hearsay. Why didn't we meet when we were different people? [...]

Your doggie

Knipper received rave notices for her performances. The Petersburg impresario, Suvorin, arch rival of the Art Theatre, offered her 1000 roubles a week if she would join his company.

Chekhov

March 17
Yalta

[...] So, soon you'll be a famous actress? Sarah Bernhardt? Will you sack me? Or will you engage me to count your takings? Sweetheart, there's nothing better than sitting under a green birch tree fishing, or wandering through the fields.

I'm eat well, no need to worry. [...]

So *Uncle Vanya* isn't being played? That's very bad! [...]

Your cruel husband A—

I have nothing against your becoming a famous actress and earning 25–40,000 only first make an effort for Pamphil [our future child].

11. The actress Ozarovskaya, whom Chekhov nicknamed 'Cricket'.

Knipper

March 17
Petersburg

My darling, hallo! I kiss you countless times for all your letters.
Every time I come to the theatre I pass the agency where they sell
tickets for the *wagons-lits* and think how I'll soon be buying a
through ticket to Sevastopol. Sweetheart, be a darling and send me
the timetable for the boats after Palm Sunday. I'll leave here on
April 6 and don't think I'll stay long in Moscow but don't know
what to do about the luggage. I have a large trunk with everything I
need for Yalta in it, I won't need winter clothing. If there's a three-
hour stop in Moscow I might be able to transfer it then I'll only need
to spend one day in Moscow to put everything in order. That way
I'll leave on the 9th or 10th. [...]

I'm glad they're trying to find a dacha for us on the Volga. Only,
Anton, if it's out in the wilds it will be difficult to get provisions.
And we need to know if there are all the amenities, utensils, for
cooking for example. We can't carry all that with us. You need all
your creature comforts and a good varied table. [...] Wouldn't you
like Switzerland? Somewhere in the mountains, in wonderful woods,
beside a lake, in a quiet hotel, with good food? I feel you are drawn
to the Russian countryside, that the west doesn't attract you, you
wouldn't feel at home. But you would feel good with me, perhaps. I
will coddle you, pamper you, spoil you, love you. [...] Life in the
Russian countryside will be like camping out.

Knipper

March 22
Petersburg

[...] I'm not going to become a famous actress. [...] I'm not going
to join Suvorin, in fact I'm not going anywhere. The Art Theatre or
nothing!

I, too, like to sit on the river bank and run through the fields, very
much so. [...]

Your doggie

Chekhov

March 23
Yalta

Dearest doggie mine, can't write now. I'm going to the dentist's every day for fillings etc. [...]

Sweetheart, I'm prepared to go to Switzerland only you can't fish there! I really do want to. We need to buy an inexpensive little property near Moscow where I could spend the summer and fish. Only near Moscow we'd have visitors. [...]

Your cruel husband A—

Knipper

March 24
Petersburg

[...] Today's been sunny, sweetheart although it snowed yesterday and there's still a frost. [...] I was very tired after the public dress [of *Small People*], came home, ate, lay down for a while, then went to the hairdressers, got dressed, then Vishnievski came and we went to Kontan's [restaurant] where [a lot of people] had gathered, many of whom I didn't know, women writers in the most awful clothes. [...] I came home late, after 4, slept till 12, got up and sat down to write to you. I'm sick of Petersburg already and its noise and think with joy of breathing the southern, summer air. [...]

Your doggie

Chekhov

March 25
Yalta

Sweetheart, I went to the dentists's today and, do you know, he wasn't in. I'll go again tomorrow, then again the day after tomorrow, and so on for the whole week. [...]

Knipper

March 25
Petersburg

Today's a public holiday, sunny but cold. I can't wait for my trip, dearest, darling man of gold, to see my husband with the holes in his trousers. What are you doing, sweetheart? Are you thinking of your dissolute wife? I'm sick of it here. Tomorrow's opening of *Small People* neither excites me nor gives me any pleasure.

Yesterday I felt bad. Something in the gut. Today I feel rather weak. [...]

Your doggie

Chekhov

March 28
Yalta

Hallo, boozer! Today is overcast. It's trying to rain and has turned cold. I'm still having fillings but it will be over soon. [...]

I need you little German, come soon. [...]

Knipper

March 29
Petersburg

Today I booked a seat in the *wagons-lits*, darling sweetheart. I went to find out how long it was between trains in Moscow and found there was only one upper berth left in the ladies', 2nd class on the 6th, so I grabbed it. [...]

Your doggie

Knipper had a miscarriage that same day.

Knipper

March 31
Petersburg

I haven't written to you for two days, darling Anton. I've had an extraordinary mishap; apparently I did leave Yalta in the hope of giving you Pamphil, but didn't know it. I kept feeling ill and thought it was food poisoning, although I hoped I was pregnant but wasn't sure. [...] They sent for the doctor. It was then I began to realize what the matter was and shed bitter tears. I was so sorry there was no Pamphil. Two doctors came, Ott's assistant and then Ott[12] himself. There were an awful lot of people milling about all day, the women were alarmed.

Stanislavski spent the whole day at Raevskaya's, pacing the corridor. [...] In the evening they took me to the clinic and, at midnight, gave me chloroform. [...] Ott did the operation so there's no need for you to worry. Everyone's been to visit me, I see love and concern all round. [...] I'll be flat on my back for 4 days and won't be doing any more acting; I don't know when they'll let me out, that's the trouble. If I come a few days late, don't worry, everything will be all right. [...] I'm very weak but decided to write to you quite openly. [...] I've been crying again today but on the whole I'm being brave. [...] Are you sorry about Pamphil? [...]

Your failure of a doggie

Chekhov

March 31
Yalta

Dearest heart, I am going to see Tolstoi. The weather is splendid. Are you tired of my letters. Bored? Is it cold?

Was Gorki's play a success? Bravo!

Farewell, my heart! If anything happens, I will wire you, but this is my last letter, unless I write to you again tomorrow.

I am in very good form, I have my last fillings at the dentist tomorrow.

So, farewell wife. We shall be together and none of those miserable hounds will tear us apart until September or October.

12. Dmitri Oskarovich Ott (1855–1929), a leading gynaecologist in Petersburg.

A million kisses.
Was *The Wild Duck* a flop?

Your faithful husband
Antoine

No letter from you today.

Knipper

April 4
Petersburg

Darling heart, I am still in bed, having a very bad time. I desperately
want to be near you, I need your gentleness, your caresses. I have
been having acute pains in the left side of the abdomen, due to an
inflammation of the ovary and it was that, perhaps, which caused the
miscarriage.

I don't know when they'll discharge me. I have to rest thoroughly
because I am going to be shaken about afterwards by three months'
travelling. You'll understand and won't have need to worry. You are
such a good man. There isn't any danger but I have to be careful,
otherwise I could be ill later. Please tell Masha and your mother all
this, and tell Masha I would very much like to write to her but it
isn't easy. I am flat on my back again, I can't sit up and writing tires
me. She will understand and won't be cross with me. I will tell her
everything. I am inundated with flowers. Nothing but warmth and
affection all round me, I am very touched. The company has been
like one big, happy family. The doctor comes every day. The midwife is with me day and night, she is excellent, and young. I talk
about you a lot. I think they will discharge me on Friday. You will
welcome a wife covered in shame. A fine position I have put myself
in! I am so sorry about little Pamphil. You are even nearer to me, a
man of gold.

Your doggie

I just have to tell you about Moskvin's joke about what has happened:
'Our leading actress is in disgrace: to have a child by such a man
and lose it looks like carelessness.' As you can imagine, with an
absolutely straight face.

The whole company is very sad about what's happened.

Knipper

April 5
Petersburg

Dearest, it's so dreary without you, I so want to see you, I so want you to love me, I so want to hold you. I'm lying here, all alone, the company is busy. [...] I'm in less pain today. How I've suffered these last few days, if only you knew! This is the eighth day I've been flat on my back and still no end to it. [...] It all happened so suddenly. [...] I think I'll be leaving on Tuesday if I feel well enough. It drags on so!

You haven't forgotten me, Anton? I need your love.

Your doggie

Chekhov

April 5
Yalta, Telegram

Wire details health

Knipper

April 5
Petersburg, Telegram

Health improving doctor postponing departure. Kisses wire me. doggie

Knipper

April 5
Petersburg

I thought I might be leaving today but I'm still here. [...] lying on my back as much as possible. Don't worry, there's no danger. [...] I would give so much to hold you and weep. I've done a lot of weeping recently. [...]

Your Olya

Knipper

April 7
Petersburg

[...] I have less pain in my left side. [...] I don't eat much, sometimes nothing at all but I'm not off food. They give me caviar. There are flowers every day. [...]

Stanislavski visits me daily, fusses over me as though I were his daughter. Lilina comes, too. [...]

Your doggie

Knipper

April 9
Petersburg

Darling Anton, today I tried sitting up in a chair – my legs felt as though they belonged to someone else, I was very weak but that will soon pass, nothing to worry about. [...]

I've decided to leave on Friday and the doctor has advised me to have a midwife with me as far as Yalta. That will be expensive, but who cares?

Ott wouldn't take a penny for the operation, I have to pay the midwife 3 r. a day but the journey would be awful without her. Do you agree? The doctor has ordered me to be terribly careful for the next six months. [...]

Will you be a dear and ask Masha to prepare my room? [...]

Your Olya

The stay in Yalta proved difficult, although the reasons are by no means clear.[13] The latent tensions between Olga and Masha appear to have surfaced. Olga was in a state of depression and imagined, rightly or wrongly, that Masha and Chekhov's mother were critical of her for losing the baby, mainly due to her late nights and fondness for the high life. This may have been a projection of her own guilt. Her earlier jokey references to herself as a 'dissolute' wife may have begun to ring true. At all events, Chekhov and Knipper left Yalta in mid-May, long before Olga was properly recovered and on their return to Moscow she was

---

13. Chekhov's biographer, J.J. Simmons, and Knipper's biographer, Harvey Pitcher, advance quite different views as to what occurred in Yalta.

ordered three weeks' complete rest. On June 11 she suffered acute stomach pains and peritonitis was diagnosed. Preparations were made for an operation. This proved unnecessary when she made a spontaneous recovery.

Olga's illness placed a severe strain on Anton, who nursed her devotedly despite his own poor health. It was agreed that he should take a holiday in Perm on Savva Morozov's estate. Perm proved hot and dusty and did nothing to improve his condition. Stanislavski then invited them to stay at his family estate in Liubimovka, near Moscow. The pair spent a happy time there until mid-August and it was there that the basic outline of The Cherry Orchard *was begun. Anton then returned to Yalta alone.*

His departure provoked a crisis. The marriage went through the one and only period of serious difficulty it ever experienced. Olga was convinced that she had deliberately been excluded from the invitation to Yalta by Masha. She wrote a 'frank' letter to Masha, setting out her views. Chekhov vigorously denied the accusation although Masha had, in fact, twice written inviting him to go down alone. The entire exchange of letters is full of evasions on Chekhov's part.

Significantly, Knipper makes no mention either of her miscarriage or of the difficulties it provoked in her Memoir.

Chekhov

August 17
Yalta

I'm finally home, dearest. The journey was fine, quiet, but dusty. There were many people I knew on the ferry. They were glad to see me home and asked after you, and rebuked me because you hadn't come; but when I gave Masha your letter, she read it and went very quiet, mother was very sad ... Today they gave me your letter to read, which I did and felt not a little embarrassment. Why are you so cruel to Masha? I give you my word of honour that if mother and Masha asked me home to Yalta it wasn't to come alone but with you. Your letter is extremely unfair but what is written is written, God help us all. I repeat: I give you my word of honour that mother and Masha invited both you and me, never just me, and that they feel warmly and affectionately towards you.

I'll come back to Moscow soon, I can't live here, although it's very good here. I'm not writing a play. [...]

Your A

Knipper

August 22
Liubimovka

[...] You write that I am being cruel to Masha. In what way? I really was very confused when I wrote to her and can't remember what I said. Do you really think I was offended because they didn't invite me to Yalta, only you? That's nonsense. I'm not that petty.

But it was strange of them to expect you to go south, knowing I was in bed. There was a clear disinclination for you to be with me when I was ill. I realize your stay in Moscow did your health no good, particularly when you had a sick wife but these rumours upset me and I wrote and told her so. But it was never my intention to be *cruel*, as you put it. I wouldn't have been so unsubtle as to do that. But that's not the point. If Masha really loved me as she once did, and felt affection for me, she would never have shown you my letter and could scarcely have been aware of the mood I was in when I wrote it. It has been a lesson to me. Henceforth I shall only write formal letters, which can be read by all and misread by none. Whenever Masha wrote me letters which I knew would upset you, I kept quiet about them and didn't involve you, although there were many things should never have happened. You never heard anything about them from me.

Enough of this. [...]

Dear God, had I the power, if I could make an easy, comfortable life for you, if I could change, how happy, how deliriously happy, I would be. Oh, if only I could tell you all that's in my heart. Or perhaps I shouldn't? Should I suffer in silence? But what if I can't, what if I passionately want to talk to you about evertything? I have held myself in check so many times. It seemed to me you were laughing at me, didn't understand me and I was upset and said nothing.

The days are marvellous, bright, sunny, the air is especially pure and I feel an ineffable charm, a gentle sadness that makes my heart ache. I'm not doing anything and don't want to do anything [...]

I've decided to go to Moscow to have my teeth seen to and to be at home. If you need to stay in Yalta and if you feel good there, I beg you to stay there. We'll see what the future brings. Write and tell me when you're coming.

Your doggie

Chekhov

August 22
Yalta

[...] Don't be angry with me, dear wife, don't be angry, dearest. Things aren't really as bad as you think. I'm coming and we'll be together until December then I'll leave and return again in March and thereafter I'll be all yours if you need me. [...]

Your A

Knipper

August 23
Liubimovka

[...] I'm very glad you are enjoying yourself in Yalta. Don't hurry back. Stay in Yalta for the whole autumn, it'll do you good and Dr Altschuler will be happy. Write and tell me what he says. You hear? [...]

Are you getting on with the play? Don't be lazy, sweetheart, ditch everything, write and stick to it. [...]

Chekhov

August 24
Yalta

Sweetheart, it's 3 or 4 days since I had a letter from you. If you don't want to write that's your affair but appoint somebody to keep me informed about your health, please.

A dry, unpleasant wind has been blowing for four days. I'm finally getting used to it and I'm at my desk, writing whatever. [...]

Masha will be coming to Moscow on September 4. We're eating water-melons and melons, there aren't any grapes yet. [...]

You're angry with me, but I have no idea why. Because I left you? But I'd been with you since Easter, without a break, never stirring from your side, and wouldn't have left you had I not had business to attend to, and begun spitting blood.

When are you going back to Moscow? Write and tell me. Have you been to your doctors? What do they say?

Your A

Knipper

August 25
Liubimovka

Two days and no letter from you, dearest! Either you haven't written or it's the post office's fault − I don't know which. But it's dreary with no letters from you. You just don't write about your health. You don't want me to worry, is that it? Think what you like but write and tell me more about yourself so I can have some idea what your life is like in Yalta. You feel uneasy. I can sense it.

It's a clear but cold day. I was out of sorts this morning; I wandered about. People say that without you I wander aimlessly through the garden like Masha in Act 4 of *Three Sisters*. [...]

The garden grows more beautiful, more colourful every day. It's good here. I dream of spending September here with you. [...]

Your doggie

Chekhov

August 27
Yalta

[...] Masha didn't give me your letter. I came across it on the table in mother's room, mechanically picked it up and read it and then realized why Masha was in such low spirits.[14] The letter is terribly blunt and quite unfair. I, of course, understood the mood you were in when you wrote it, and still do. But your last letter [August 22] is a little strange and I just don't know what's going on in your mind, sweetheart. You write [...] 'There's an evident disinclination etc.'

14. This is in flat contradiction to his earlier statement that Masha gave Knipper's letter to him.

On whose part? When they asked me south? But I gave you my word of honour in my letter that I was never invited without you. You must never, never be afraid of anything so unfair. You must be scrupulously fair, the more so since you are a good and understanding person. Forgive me, sweetheart, for these remonstrances, I won't do it again, it frightens me. [...]

Your letters are frosty but nonetheless I'm attached to you, feel tenderly towards you and think of you endlessly. [...]

Your A—

Knipper

August 27
Liubimovka

Another day gone, another day and no letter from you. What does it mean? I really had to stop myself sending you a telegram because I know you hate it and would start swearing. But it's difficult for me, living all alone here, without letters from you. Are you in good health, sweetheart? Are you angry with me, is that why you don't write? Do you dislike me because I complain? Is it restful without me? All sorts of nonsense goes through my head when I don't feel you love me. [...]

Knipper

August 28
Liubimovka

Why didn't you tell me frankly you were leaving and not coming back? I had a premonition. Why didn't you tell me openly you were leaving because you were spitting blood? That means you hid from me. It hurts me that you should treat me like a stranger, or a doll, who musn't be alarmed. I would be calmer, less demonstrative, if you were open with me. It means you think we have lived together long enough. Do we separate? Fine. I don't understand. I simply don't understand. Something must have happened. Although your letters are tender, I tremble when I read them over several times.

How wonderful our life here together was! If only there were one word in your letters to recall this last month! I would be so nice.

You've come to hate my letters. But I can't keep silent. So don't make any preparations because it will be quite impossible for you to come to Moscow in the autumn. I shall have to spend September in Liubimovka. [...]

Dear God, if only I knew you needed me, that I could help you live, that you would be happy – I would be with you always! If you could only give me that assurance! But you are capable of being at my side and not uttering a word. At times I felt superfluous. It seemed to me you only needed me as a pleasant kind of female presence but that my life, as a person, was something quite separate from yours. Tell me I'm wrong, demolish me if it isn't so. Don't think I'm talking nonsense, don't think I'm angry with you if I appear to blame you in any way. You are the only man in the world for me and if I do you an injustice it's unconscious, or because I am sick at heart. You shouldn't blame me, you are strong and I am completely insignificant. You can bear everything in silence, you never feel the need to share anything. [...] How awful it would be, Anton, if everything I wrote were merely to raise a smile and nothing more or if you were, perhaps, to show this letter to Masha, as she showed you mine. [...]

Olya

Chekhov

August 29
Yalta

[...] You write: I'm delighted you're enjoying yourself in Yalta. Who told you that? Why do you ask what Dr Altschuler said? He comes here often. He wanted to sound my heart, insisted on it but I refused. My mood? Splendid. Health? Bad yesterday, all right today. I'm coughing rather more than I did in the north. [...]

Knipper

August 29
Liubimovka

Dearest, darling Anton, I wrote you an awful letter yesterday. Don't blame me, or be angry with me but try to understand. There's no one I can talk to about what I feel in my heart. Please don't end your letters with your usual, 'You're angry with me.' If I were angry I wouldn't write.

I write as I do because I'm burdened by my own weakness of character, my uselessness. I desperately want to be with you but I see you're no better when I'm there. [...]

I feel dreadful. You're fortunate. You are always so balanced, so serene. I have the feeling that separation, feelings, change make no difference to you. Not because you are cold or indifferent by nature but because of something special in you. You attach no importance to the daily round. Does that make you smile? [...]

Have you started the play? [...]

Your Olya

Chekhov

September 1
Yalta

Dearest darling, I've had another strange letter from you. [...] Who told you that I didn't want to come back to Moscow, that I had left for good and wouldn't be back this autumn? I wrote to you in good, clear Russian that I would be arriving in September and would be staying with you until December. Didn't I? You accuse me of not being open but you forget everything I've said or written. [...] You write that you tremble when you read my letters, that we are going to separate, that you don't understand at all ... It seems to me, darling, that neither you nor I is responsible for this mess, but that you've been talking to someone. [...] You write, 'You can be with me and not say a word, you need me as a pleasant kind of female presence, etc.' Dearest sweetheart, you are my wife, understand that once and for all. You are the person nearest and dearest to me, my love knows no end but you describe yourself as a 'pleasant sort of' woman alone and apart from me. Well, God bless you, as you wish.

My health has improved but I'm coughing all the time. No rain, it's hot. Masha leaves on the 4th and will be in Moscow on the 6th. You write that I showed Masha your letter. Thanks for your trust in me. Fortunately, Masha isn't in any way to blame, you'll come to see that, sooner or later. [...]

Your A—

Knipper

September 2
Moscow

Dearest sweetheart, I went to [the doctor's] today and he couldn't believe his eyes, or indeed, as he said, that I could make such a recovery. He was all smiles when he saw me. He examined me and [...] said that I can lead a normal life and do what I like. He was astounded at my bronzed face and said I was a wonderfully healthy woman. Happy? I'll give you a healthy son next year. [...]

However, [the doctor] advises me to leave this apartment. I'm to tell the [proprietor] to end the contract. But apartments are exceptionally dear in Moscow. Nemirovich can't find one, though he's trying. [...]

I'm happy to be seeing Masha. Did she bring the rest of my things? If not, you bring them, sweetheart. [...]

I always have to tell the truth, always. Then I don't get het up, my mind is clear. How is it you haven't seen this side of me before? Don't you have rather stereotyped ideas about women being silly? Forgive me for these remonstrances, I won't do it again. [...]

Your doggie

Chekhov

September 3
Yalta

Olya, my delight, I had your splendid letter [August 29] yesterday, read it and felt calm. Thank you, dearest. Life is so-so. I'll probably leave here on the 20th, unless something happens; I'll come sooner if I can. [...]

Your A—

Knipper

September 5
Moscow

[...] Forgive me for my 'strange letter', please. [...] There's no one who could make me mistrust you. Don't think me so unworthy. I wrote about what worried me; if it was difficult to understand that's because I feel guilty, I feel my life is wrong. [...]

I'll go and meet Masha when she comes. I've put flowers in her room. Please don't think I resent her and don't justify her to me. I'm not a brute and she's not the person to bear a grudge, not by a long way. She's stronger than I. [...]

I'm going to bed, my head is pounding. [...]

Olya

Chekhov

September 6
Yalta

My little crocodile, my very special wife, I'm not coming to Moscow, despite my promise because I had hardly got to Yalta when by bodily barometer plummeted. I began coughing like the devil and completely lost my appetite. I'm not up to writing or travelling. [...]

You see what a tiresome husband you have! I feel a lot easier but there's no rain and won't be. I would come to Moscow but I'm afraid of the journey, I'm afraid spending a whole day in Sevastopol. And don't you come here either. I feel awkward summoning you to this scorching, dusty desert, and there's no need as I shall be in Moscow soon.

If, by any chance, you do come to Yalta then bring my *pince-nez*. [...] Don't bring shirts but woollen underwear.

Your A—

Knipper

September 10
Moscow

[...] The family came to lunch yesterday, including grandma. Nikolai brought me a wonderful little piano, straight from the factory, for 12 r. a month. A pity I can't buy it. They want 200 down and 20 r. a month. It isn't an upright but a baby grand. It looks splendid in the sitting-room, livens it up. [...]

Olya

Knipper

September 18
Moscow

I am terribly tired, my dearest heart, my beloved, my extraordinary man. I have just got back from [a return visit to] Liubimovka. A journey filled with impressions. Nature in autumn, a pale sun, forest here and there. Everything is sad, it withers and fades... I relived my first visit, everything I felt, the whole, happy month. The most wonderful moments were when I went back alone into our little house. My steps had a lonely echo. I went into the bedroom – everything as when I was last in it. Why did I feel so terrible, so oppressed, why this heartache? The summer was so full! The greenery full of sap, the smell of hay, the lime-trees in flower, the church choir, the ringing of the bells ... Everything was harmony and I felt calm and at ease! Will it ever happen again? All the blinds were down on the balcony, hanging disconsolately, only the wind moved them, dragging the metal rings along the ground – the only sound to break the silence. I ran to the little raft to see if Anton was there, I wanted to call him in for tea, but he had gone. I stayed on the raft for a moment, looking at the dark water, cold steel colour and looking at the river banks, I thought of two artists who are remarkably like each other – Chekhov and Levitan. They were the best moments of the day, I adored them. I saw you everywhere, my gentle, sweet, brilliant author. I saw you, fishing rod in hand, I saw you stretched out on the balcony with a newspaper, on the little garden bench during Mass or on the sofa in the bedroom. Don't laugh at me for being sentimental. Or, if it is comic, then you can. I felt very serious about it all.

Stanislavski talked a great deal about you. I went for a walk with Lilina, it was cold – minus 2.

[...]

I kiss you, precious man, I kiss you gently, passionately, tenderly, whichever way you like. Don't be sad, sweetheart. There will be other things in life. Don't be angry and keep loving me.

Your doggie

Chekhov left Moscow on November 27. He and Knipper resumed their normal routine. She kept him informed of the rehearsals for Julius Caesar *and* The Lower Depths. *As Chekhov's health declined, a new note entered her letters. She began more and more to experience feelings of guilt at pursuing her own career at the expense of her 'wifely' duties.*

Knipper

November 27
Moscow

My dearest sweetheart, you've gone again ... I'm alone in the bedroom scribbling. Everything's quiet. You're probably getting close to Orla now, maybe you're there already. There's so much I'd like to say to you, I feel I don't write anything at all clearly, that it's preposterous writing, not saying things. I'd forgotten what it was like. The sight of your wonderful face in the corner of the carriage is etched on my memory. Your beautiful, gentle, refined face, beautiful because of something shining within. I so want to say something very fine, very beautiful, very loving to you. I feel so bad about the moments of disagreeable times I caused you, sweetheart.

I kiss you. How are you? What are you thinking? Have you eaten? You're probably asleep now. It will soon be one. You linger in the bedroom air. I lay down on your pillow and wept. I put my sheets on your bed, I'll sleep there. [...]

I brought the fur coat and boots back from the station, saw the dear dog they brought in my absence. Schnapps we call him. A splendid thoroughbred.

It was difficult to stay at home. There was no rehearsal (*Lower Depths*). After a while I went to see Andreeva. [...]

Your doggie

Chekhov

November 28
Lovozaya

I'm writing this in Lovozaya, ten degrees of frost, sunny. I'm in good health, eating soup and pickled cucumbers. I long for my lady of the house. Dearest sweetheart, write to me about everything, don't be lazy. [...] The train is almost empty. [...]

Your A

Knipper

November 28
Moscow

I just got home to find your card, my dearest and kissed it. You're asleep on the train now. Dreaming about me?

How empty it is without you. I still don't quite realize you're not here. How dreary it is to come home! No one to look tenderly at me, no one to hold me and kiss me. [...] No wonderful husband with gentle eyes. There's an empty bed. No one to give cod-liver oil to. He's in a warm carriage, travelling through frozen fields...

Today we had a rough dress-run of two acts of *Lower Depths*. We showed our make-up and costumes. [...]

My head feels heavy. [...]

Everyone at the theatre is asking after you, I answer endless questions.

The electric light's been off for ages, meaning it's late. I'll finish now. [...]

Knipper

November 29
Moscow

[...] How did you find your mother in Sevastopol? How was your journey? Is the weather really good? I'm terribly happy. Everything is so much easier when the sun is shining. Get used to Arseni being there and looking after you. Write and tell me if it isn't working. Write and tell me everything. But, most important of all, how are you feeling? Are you in good spirits, or do you have that Yalta expression on your face? Don't turn sour, I beg you. No card from you today.

I got to sleep late yesterday, my muscles ached and this morning I was woken by the workmen on the premises. I had coffee and read the papers in bed; at 12 I went to rehearsal. We ran two acts. [...]

I came home on foot. No dashing back in a cab to my dear husband. [...]

Your Olya

Chekhov

November 30
Yalta

My joy, sweetheart, I arrived in Yalta yesterday evening. The journey was fine, very few people in the carriage, four at most. I had tea, soup, ate everything you'd given me on the journey. The further south we got, the colder it became: frost and snow in Sevastopol.

I took the ferry to Yalta, the sea was calm. [...] It's cold in Yalta. I'm sitting at my desk writing to you, my incomparable wife and don't feel warm at all, it's colder here than in Moscow. I expect letters from you from tomorrow onwards. Write to me, sweetheart, I beg you, I'm in the cold here and soon get bored by silence. [...]

Your A

Knipper

November 30
Moscow

A big kiss, sweetheart. You're so far away from me! I had your card from Lozovaya. Thank you, dearest. I bitterly regret not having made you send me a telegram as soon as you got to Yalta. Now I expect a letter!

How did your mother bear the journey? [...]

At 5½ I went with the inevitable Vishnievski to lunch with Stanislavski but there was a telephone call during the meal telling me I had to play in *Small People*. Savitskaya had gone to Tver to the funeral of her teacher whom she adored. He'd become a monk in his final years. She hadn't returned. [...]

Write and tell me when you settle down to work.

Chekhov

December 1
Yalta

My dearest joy, my wife, sweetheart, how are you getting on without me? What are your thoughts and feelings? Everything's fine, I'm healthy, I'm not coughing, I'm sleeping well and eating. [...] Dr Altschuler was here yesterday. He was overjoyed with your present (writing paper) and will doubtless be writing to you. [...] No snow today so far. Sunny. The cranes are calling. In a month or two it will be spring here.

When you get the dog tell me what kind it is. [...]

I get down to writing tomorrow. I'll work from morning to lunchtime and after lunch until evening. I'll send the play in February. I'll hug my wife in March. [...] God bless my baboon. I hug you many times, don't forget your husband.

A

Knipper

December 1
Moscow

Not a line from you today, dearest. How are you? You haven't forgotten me out of levity? Are your rooms tidy? Are you sleeping warmly? I expect you're wrapped in the striped rug you had here, although it's very heavy. Do you like being among your own, familiar things? Do you like sitting at your desk? It was so uncomfortable for you here, I am so very sorry about that. And you, my darling, said nothing, you were so patient. [...]

Your Olya

Chekhov

December 2
Yalta

[...] I had my first letter from you today. Without your letters I'm frozen, in the house as well as in Yalta. [...]

You write that you regret every disagreeable moment you caused me. My dearest, there were no disagreeable moments, we got along fine together, as, God grant, all married people do. [...]

Congratulations on Schnapps. Send him to Yalta, there's no one to bark at here. [...]

Knipper

December 4
Moscow

I don't know what to think, dearest. No letter, not a line from you, about how you are. I don't know what to think. I wait for one every day like an idiot, people all round me ask questions and I don't know what to answer. [...]

I went to Chaliapin's benefit. There wasn't any real enthusiasm. [...]

Knipper

December 5
Moscow, Telegram

No letter, worried, wire.   Olya.

Knipper

December 5
Moscow

Finally, two letters at once, dearest, but I was so worried. [...]

Our dog is wonderful. Masha calls him Tommy but his name is Schnapps. A pedigree. He'll be fine in Yalta.

Chekhov

December 6
Yalta

[...] I've started work on a story. It's cold in my room, no one brushes my coat, someone has removed all the newspapers that came while I was away. But I don't let my spirits droop and look to the future with hope when we shall be together again.

Your envelopes really are awful. Your letters arrive all unstuck. Get rid of these fancy envelopes and buy yourself some simple ones for a few pence.

Chekhov

December 9
Yalta

Your letters are almost cruelly short. [...] You have such a rich and varied life, plenty to write about. Just gladden my heart with long letters once a week. I read them all two or three times over. Remember that, darling. [...]

Chekhov

December 14
Yalta

Darling sweetheart, you poor old thing, doggie, you will have children, the doctors say so. You just have to make a full recovery. Your general health is good, all you need is a husband to be with you for a whole year. So, whatever happens, I will find a way to be at your side, permanently, for a whole year; you will have a little boy, who will break the dishes and pull your dog's tail while you look on in delight.

I washed my hair yesterday and must have caught cold because I can't work today, I have a headache. I went into town for the first time yesterday, it is dead, all you meet are people who look like rats, not one pretty woman, not one decently dressed.

I'll write to you as soon I start on *Cherry Orchard,* doggie. In the meantime, I am working on a story which is not very interesting – not to me, at least; I find it boring.

In Yalta the earth is covered in green grass. It is lovely to behold, when there is no snow.

It is blowing a gale.

It is too cold for Tommy to come to Yalta, perhaps we would find a way of bringing him in one of the carriages, or, perhaps, the dog compartment is heated. If Masha doesn't bring him, maybe Vinokurov-Chigorin, the teacher from Gurzuf, could do so.

The pig you gave me has a torn ear.

Well, light of my life, God be with you, be good, don't be depressed, don't get bored and think of your lawful husband more often. You know, no one in the world would love you as I do, and you have no one but me. You should remember that and take it as read.

I hug you and kiss you a thousand times.

Your A

Write me more details.

Chekhov

December 17
Yalta

[...] It is still blowing a gale, I can't work! The weather is exhausting, all I want to do is lie in bed and eat sweets.

We have broken pipes, so there is no water. They will be repaired. It is raining. Cold. Even in the bedrooms. I miss you terribly. I'm an old man already. I cannot sleep alone, I wake up frequently.

Wonderful girl, my dearest, my joy, my doggie, be well, be happy. God be with you. Don't worry about me, I'm in good health and well fed. I hug you and kiss you.

Your A

1903

Chekhov

January 7
Yalta

Dear little actress doggie, my Tommy, hallo! Things are going well, but what do you think, I have a spot on my left side and the doctor has ordered me to put a compress on it 3 times a day. I have a touch of pleurisy. I'm sleeping splendidly, eating very well, my mood is good and the illness I write about is nothing really. Don't worry, Tommy.

Knipper

January 12
Moscow, Telegram

Wire details health quickly   Olya

Chekhov

January 13
Yalta, Telegram

Everything fine.   Antonio

Knipper

January 15
Moscow

I couldn't get to sleep for ages last night, I was crying, many dark thoughts passed through my mind. I'm ashamed to call myself your wife. What wife? You are alone, sad, forlorn. I know you don't like talking about it but I can't live and bottle everything up. I need to talk to you. I need to say things, even if, sometimes, it means spouting nonsense. – I feel better afterwards. Do you understand? You are quite different from me. You never speak, you give no hint of what is going on in your mind. [....]

Chekhov

> January 15
> Yalta

Dearest Olya, on the morning of the 11th when Masha left, I didn't feel at all well; my chest hurt, I felt sick, my temperature was 38. In the evening it was the same. I slept well, although disturbed by pain. Dr Altschuler came to put on another warm compress (it's enormous). Today my temperature was up to 37. I felt weak, now I'm treating the boil but I was right to wire you that everything was fine. I'll be fully restored to health tomorrow. I'm not hiding anything from you, remember that, and don't trouble yourself with sending me telegrams.

Chekhov

> January 17
> Yalta

Hallo, sweetheart! Do you know what I've been thinking? Do you know what I want to suggest? You won't be angry or surprised? This year, rather than go to a dacha, let's go to Switzerland instead. We'll stay two months. [...] What do you think?

Chekhov

> January 20
> Yalta

I've put all my minor manuscripts and notes in order in the portfolio you sent me, everything is in its proper place. It is very handy.

What have you decided about Switzerland? I think we could take a wonderful trip. We could stop in Vienna, Berlin and elsewhere on the way and go to the theatre. What do you say?

[...]

The sun is shining, today, it is brilliant, but I am staying indoors, Dr Altschuler has forbidden me to go out. I'm happy to say, my temperature's perfectly normal.

My darling, you write that you have pangs of conscience because you are living in Moscow and not here with me in Yalta. But think about it: if you spent the whole of the winter in Yalta with me, your life would be ruined, I would feel bad about it, and things would be no better. I knew I was marrying an actress, I mean, I knew perfectly well when we got married that you would spend your winters in Moscow. I don't feel in the least hurt or neglected, quite the contrary, it seems to me that everything is fine or as it should be, and so, sweetheart, don't have regrets. Be calm, dearest, don't worry, wait and hope. Just hope.

In Yalta four children passed out in the market. [...]

I'm working at the moment, so I don't think I'll write every day. Forgive me in advance.

We are going abroad! We are going away!

Your husband A

Knipper

January 21
Moscow

[...] So we're going to Switzerland? I'm delighted, my dear! Anything you say. We'll live in the mountains, in the pure air, and particularly since you've never been there. Find out all you can about the best places to go, get hold of some maps and work out an itinerary and I'll think about it, too, we'll write to each other about our ideas and then talk about it very soon. Yes, dearest? [...]

Knipper

January 29
Moscow

[...] To which part of Switzerland are we going, the German or the French? I've been to the first but would be happy to go back. We must see Venice, mustn't we? What a wonderful moment it will be when the train draws out and we are alone, just the two of us, we'll be young again, as though we were just married. [...]

Chekhov

February 1–2
Yalta

[...] When we go to Switzerland, I'm not taking anything with me, not a single jacket. I'll buy everything abroad. I'll just take my wife and an empty suitcase. [...]

Chekhov

February 5
Yalta

[...] The temperature in my study has been stuck at 11–12 degrees for days. My man, Arseni can't heat it and outside the weather's cold – rain, snow and the wind hasn't abated. I'm writing 6–7 lines a day, though I do try. [...]

Knipper

February 11
Moscow

[...] Next winter, you're going to do as I say, do you hear? I'll have a frank consultation with the doctors and hope they'll say you can spend next winter near Moscow. If not, we'll have to change our way of life. I can't trust Dr Altschuler alone, he's not enough of an expert. Sitting and pining in that hell-hole, Yalta, can't be doing your health any good. What does your instinct tell you? You're at an age when it can be very effective. [...] I'll never believe you'll be any worse off in a warm house, where you won't be frozen and with good air. Of course, you wouldn't go out in a heavy frost. You could wander round the house or in the glass-covered gallery. Tell me frankly what you think. Sincerely. In my view, living in Moscow itself and going to the theatre would do you no good at all. We must find a place with Masha and your mother near Moscow.

Knipper

March 13
Moscow

[...] I'm in a horrible state. I feel awful about you. What kind of wife am I, when we have to live apart! I dare not call myself your wife. I'm ashamed to look your mother in the face. You can tell her that, and that if I don't write, it is for the same reason.

Since I'm married, I ought to forget my own life and just be a wife. I'm lost, I don't know what to do. I feel like dropping everything and leaving so no one will know who I am.

This isn't just a whim, believe me. The idea keeps nagging at me. Now, I've said it.

I entered my relationship with you, a man like you, very lightly. Since the theatre is my life, I should live alone and bother no one.

Forgive me, darling, I feel awful. I shall get into the train and weep my heart out. I shall be glad to be alone.

Thank Altschuler for his letter. I will write.

Be well, don't think ill of me.

> Olya

Chekhov

March 18
Yalta

Special little heart, you have finally sent me your address and everything is fine. Thank you, my dearest. I received your tearful letter this morning, in which you castigate yourself [...]. I read it, but no address! I was about to ask for a divorce when I got your telegram at midday.

So, I will come to Moscow on Saint Thomas's day. I will be there before you get back from Petersburg, I'll see you again, I'll meet you at home, not the station, when I'm back from the baths and have worked on the play a little, which, by the way, isn't going well. One of the characters is under-developed and that's a stumbling block. But I think it will be clearer by Easter and my problems will be over.

If Masha hasn't left yet, tell her to bring some cooked sausage. You hear? [...]

I'll write again tomorrow. Don't talk nonsense. You're not to blame for not spending the winter with me. Quite the contrary, we are a perfectly respectable husband and wife in not stopping each other from doing what we must. You love the theatre, don't you?... If you didn't, that would be another matter. God be with you. We will see each other soon, I'll take you in my arms and kiss you forty-five times. Be well, little girl.

Your A

Knipper left Moscow for the annual tour to Petersburg.

Knipper

April 9
Petersburg

Darling, don't be angry if I missed a day writing to you. I have been in quite a state, very tired and yesterday I had a cruel headache. [...]

The theatre is very so-so. The auditorium is beautiful, admirably furnished, but the paintings on the ceiling are abominable, really sugary. The boxes are bad, damp. Generally dirty. We hear very strange things in conversations between our stage-hands and the resident staff.

The day after we arrived Yakobson, my doctor, came to see me during lunch, he was very kind. He assured me I had been ill because he had not accompanied me to Yalta. Both he and Dr Strauch are appalled that Altschuler should have recommended me to take hot douches. He is full of praise for Strauch. He told me he was continually pestered in Petersburg because of me. He is a very nice man ... Not a real doctor, I think: he is a pen-pusher.

[...] Your telegram came yesterday. I don't understand why you stopped writing as soon as Masha told you I would not be leaving for Petersburg until the 4th. Why didn't you write direct to the theatre? Almost everyone has their letters addressed there. You were simply too lazy to write, you are sick of it all, aren't you? A little while my darling and we shall see each other. *I'm leaving on the 24th and will be in Moscow on the 25th.* So don't say, later, that I didn't tell you. It's not the first time I've done it. Big kisses.

Your Olya

Knipper

April 11
Petersburg

Not one letter from you! That's more than unkind. I don't know whether to be angry or sad. Didn't you write because you don't know the address? Am I the only individual in Petersburg who can't be found? Well, as you wish. I'm sick of all this endless business over addresses. It's all too stupid and petty.

Chekhov

April 12
Yalta, Telegram

Black Sea sailor healthy, eating a lot arriving 22nd.

Knipper

April 13
Petersburg, Morning

I was about to start my letter with: 12 days and no letter, thank you. Then I got your telegram. I was mollified, but only a little. If you could come directly here. The weather's like summer. [...]

Chekhov

April 15
Yalta

Dear darling, special heart, little idiot thing, it is useless getting worked up over my silence; first, you wrote to me yourself that you were leaving Moscow at the beginning of Holy Week, second, I wrote to you often. And why write, anyway, when we shall be seeing each other soon and I shall pinch your behind and do other such things? I have bought my ticket, I leave on the 22nd and will be in Moscow on the 24th. As soon as I arrive, I'm off to the baths. I'll bring you some sheets.

1903

[...] I don't like your trip to Petersburg at all. I don't feel like writing anything for your theatre mainly because you don't have any old actresses. You'll be stuck playing old women whereas there is another role for you, particularly as you played an older woman in *The Seagull*.

Apart from that, there was a shower yesterday. Spring is fine, only the weather is fresh and dullness reigns.

[...]

I'll write you one more letter, send one more telegram and then – till we meet again! I'm as dark-skinned as an Arab. I'm terribly bronzed. [...]

Your blackamoor

Knipper

April 17
Petersburg, Telegram

Come straight Petersburg on 20th. Weather like summer. Wire me.

Chekhov

April 18
Yalta, Telegram

Coming Moscow 24th. Bought ticket. Don't want come Petersburg. Healthy.

Chekhov went to Moscow but found life in Knipper's new apartment impossible. It was on the second floor and it took him thirty minutes to climb the stairs. He was, as one doctor described him, a physical wreck. After an unsuccessful stay at a friend's estate near Moscow, the couple went to Yalta for the summer. Olga left on September 20. At Chekhov's request, his friend Shaposhnikov accompanied her.

Chekhov

September 20
Yalta

It is all too cruel, sweetheart. I spent the whole of last evening, all last night and all day today waiting for your telegram from Sevastopol and only on Saturday evening did I hear from Shaposhnikov, 'Your wife has left ....' etc. And there was I, thinking the boat had sunk, that you didn't have a ticket etc., etc. It is wrong of you, darling wife. Better not make promises next time.

I feel better today though I'm still not fully on form. Weakness, a bad taste in the mouth, no appetite. I washed myself today, unaided. The water wasn't cold. I feel your absence. If I were not angry with you over the telegram, I could tell you many wonderful things, I'd tell you how much I love my little horsey. Write me all the details about the theatre. I'm so far away from everything I'm beginning to lose heart. It seems to me I have run out as a writer and every sentence I write seems perfectly useless to me.

[...] I forget to take my pills even when I put them right under my nose, but I remember just in time.

I kiss my little wife, my dearest. If my letters seem down, pessimistic, don't worry, darling, it's all nonsense really.

Your A

Knipper

September 22
Moscow, Morning

I'm back in Moscow, my dearest darling. [...]

The apartment is gleaming, everything is spick and span, thanks to Annushka, so it was a pleasure to arrive. I had some coffee, picked some grapes, washed in cold water, dressed and went to the theatre. [...]

1903

Knipper

No letter from you yesterday, I'm worried. Did you get sick of the letters I wrote on the journey, I scribbled them rather. Did you get them all? Oh that Shaposhnikov with his red hair and moustache. How I hated him. He kept sidling up to me and bowing and he took off his hat and crossed himself every time we passed a church, for Chekhov's sake. It was stupid and nonsensical to drink champagne with a total stranger on the sea-shore at sunset. I wanted to be alone and think of everything that had happened recently. [...]

Evening
I had just finished my letter when I discovered yours, which had come by yesterday's post. I was furious with Annushka. When I got home yesterday my first question was: were there any letters? The answer was, no.

My dearest, my man of gold, don't be angry about the telegram. I was writing to you at the station and just had time to jump into the train as the second bell went and begged Shaposhnikov to send you a telegram right away. But he didn't, did he? Please forgive me. I was in such disarray, I wanted so much to write you a letter and not send a telegram. Don't be angry, dearest, don't send sad letters. You are needed as a writer, much needed for peace of mind, for people to understand that there is poetry in the world, true beauty, noble feelings, affectionate human souls, that life is broad and beautiful.

And your lyricism? We need every sentence you write and in the future we shall need you even more. Oh, had I the gift of words I could tell you so much more!! Drive away these futile thoughts. Have pity on people, feel how much they need you. Don't withdraw, give us everything you are capable of from the deep richness of your soul.

Go on writing, love each word, each idea, each soul you elevate and realize people *absolutely need* them.

Nowhere in the world is there a writer like you, don't turn in on yourself.

We are waiting for your plays like manna from heaven.

I'll send the parcel tomorrow. I still can't find the right comb for your mother.

I kiss you, kiss your hands and pray God you may feel well.

Are you getting my letters?

Your Olya

Chekhov

October 12
Yalta

So, horseykins, long may we both be patience itself. The play is finished, truly finished, and tomorrow, or on the morning of the 14th at the latest, I shall send it to Moscow. I'll send you some comments at the same time. Even if changes are needed, they won't be much, I think. The worst thing about the play is that I didn't write it in one go but over a very long period of time and it must drag a little. Well, we'll see.

My health is improving, I don't cough much now and don't run to the lavatory all the time. Meals have got much worse since Masha left, naturally: today, for example, we had mutton for lunch, which I can't eat any more, and so I didn't have a hot meal. I eat very good gruel. I find salt ham difficult to eat. I eat eggs.

My darling, writing the play was so difficult.

Tell Vishnievski to find me a job as a tax collector. I have written a part for him but I feel that after Antony[15] the part written by Anton will seem very rough and ready. But an aristocrat, all the same. Your role is well drawn in Act III and Act I but not much more than a sketch in the other acts. But again, it doesn't matter, I don't lose heart. [...]

Well, little chicklet, don't complain about me. God be with you. I love you and will go on loving you. I might even beat you, Kisses.

Your A

Chekhov

October 30
Yalta

[...] Life is dull, I can't work. The weather is overcast, it's cold, the stove stinks out all the rooms...

15. Vishnievski played Mark Antony in *Julius Caesar.*

It looks as though I rushed to finish the play for nothing. I could have spent another month on it.

What torture it is to cut the nails on your right hand! I feel generally terrible without my wife.

I'm getting used to your dressing gown. It is Yalta that I can't get used to. While the weather was good, I thought everything was all right but now I can see everything is all wrong.

Did you get the chrysanthemums? How were they? If they were all right, I'll send you some more.

I kiss my little cockroach. Be happy.

Your A

Chekhov

October 14
Yalta

[...] I sent for Altschuler as I was sick of having the runs. He ordered me to eat up to eight eggs a day and minced ham. [...] Being without you is like being without hands. I'm on a desert island. [...]

Your A

Knipper, *Memoir*

Chekhov longed for Moscow the whole time. He wanted to be closer to life, feel it, be part of it, he wanted to see people although they occasionally annoyed him by their conversation, but he could not live without them. All he liked about Yalta initially was building the house, planting the garden, making a life for himself and later got used to it, even though he called it his 'hot Siberia'. He longed for Moscow the whole time, to be among actors, go to rehearsals, talk, joke, see plays. But he was cut off from Moscow life at the very moment when it was at its most interesting. It was only in the winter of 1903–4 that the doctors allowed him to come to the capital and what delight he took in a real snowy, Moscow winter and in going to rehearsals, he was as happy as a schoolboy in his new coat and fur hat.

Chekhov

November 12
Yalta

[...] It will be difficult for me to get up to the 3rd or 4th floor, especially in a heavy coat. Why don't you change apartments? Well, never mind, I'll stay at home in Moscow. I'll only go to the baths and to your theatre.

Knipper

November 16
Moscow

[...] I can't change apartments until March (contract). We'll have to look for the kind of apartment we need and like in July or August. The present apartment was a matter of pure chance. We took it because it was better than the one we had, not because it suits us. I'll get a lift for you. [...]

Your Olya

Chekhov

November 27
Yalta

[...] You and other people really must understand that I feel much, much worse in Yalta. The sea was calm but now it's stormy, waves as high as the sky and such rain. The weather's so bad no one can get in or get out.

I'll come by sleeping car. Don't bring my coat to the train, it will be cold. I'll put it on in the station.

What a skinflint you've become. Soon you'll be putting used stamps on your letters. Why don't you wire me? [...] I'll give you ten roubles, just don't be mean, wire me, stop being stingy.

Chekhov

November 29
Yalta

Horseykins, I still don't know what to do or think. There's a resolute reluctance to ask me to come to Moscow, or don't they want me to come?[16] You should tell me bluntly the reason, so I won't waste time and can go abroad. If you knew how wearisome it is with the rain hammering on the roof, how I want to see my wife. Do I have a wife? Where is she? [...]

Knipper

November 29
Moscow, Telegram

Frosty. Talk to Altschuler and come. Wire me. Kisses

Chekhov

November 30
Yalta, Telegram

Coming Tuesday [December 2]

Knipper

December 1
Moscow, Telegram

Don't leave train. Dress up warmly.

16. To attend rehearsals of *The Cherry Orchard*.

1904

Knipper, *Memoir*

That winter we looked for a plot of land with a house near Moscow so that in the future Chekhov could spend the winter near his beloved Moscow (nobody imagined the end was so near). And so, on one sunny February day we went to Tsaritsyno to look at a small estate which it had been suggested we buy. On the way back (not that we missed the train, there was none) we had to go about thirty-five miles by road. Despite the very heavy frost, Chekhov revelled at the sight of the white plain mourning in the sun and the sound of the runners in the tightly packed snow. It was as though fate, in his last year, had decided to spoil him a little and give him all the joys he longed for: Moscow, winter, the production of *The Cherry Orchard* and the people he loved... Work on *The Cherry Orchard* was, I would say, sheer torture. There was no understanding between the directors and the author. But all's well that ends well and after the trials and tribulations that surrounded its birth we performed *The Cherry Orchard* on January 17 1904, Chekhov's birthday.

Chekhov stayed in Moscow until February 1904. When he left for Yalta he took Knipper's dachshund, Schnapps with him.

As his condition deteriorated, Chekhov became more and more irritable, his reactions more and more unreasonable. This extended to all areas. He had quarrelled with his friend, the critic, Efros, over a mistake for which he himself was actually responsible.[17] Having in the past dissuaded Knipper from sending telegrams, he accused her more and more frequently of being mean and even complained about the quality of the ink she used.

17. See *Moscow Art Theatre Letters.*

Chekhov

February 17
Sevastopol

Hallo, my wonderful horseykins! I'm on the boat which leaves in three hours. I had a good journey. I'm with Schnapps. He seems to feel at home and is being very nice. He behaved just as he does at home on the train, barked at the ticket inspectors and had a great time. He's cheered me up, now he's on the deck resting against my legs. He's obviously forgotten about Moscow, which is good. Now, sweetheart, horseykins, I'll expect a letter from you. I can't live without your letters, you know that. Either write every day or divorce me. There's no middle way. [...] Write more fully. Don't be stingy with the ink. [...]

I can hear Schnapps barking at someone down below. I'll go and see. [...]

Your A

Chekhov

February 20
Yalta

Darling horseykins, it's wearisome, cold, dull without you and you spoiled me so I was afraid I would have forgotten how to undress myself at night and dress myself in the morning. The bed is hard, cold, the rooms are cold, zero outside, boredom, nor a breath of spring. [...] I spend my time dealing with last year's mail,[18] and old newspapers, my sole occupation for the present.

Schnapps is either deaf or dumb. He simply won't go out. He jumps about with the other dogs and insists on spending the night in mother's room. He's very happy but dim. [...]

I have no wife, she's in Moscow, I'm living like a monk. [...] I'm cleaning my teeth. I'll go to the baths in May when I come to Moscow. In the meantime I'll plant corn on my body – at least I'll make some money. [...]

---

18. Chekhov filed all his letters in chronological order.

Chekhov

February 27
Yalta

[...] The sun hasn't shown its face once since I've been in Yalta i.e. since February 17. It's terribly humid, the skies are grey and I stay in my room.

[...] Have you had any thoughts about the summer? Where we'll stay? I'd like something not far from Moscow, not far from the station so that we can get there without a carriage, without benefactors and admirers. Think about the dacha, sweetheart. [...] I have such happy memories of our trip to Tsaritsyno and back. [...]

Your A

Chekhov

February 28
Yalta

Sweetheart, if you go to Tsaritsyno again, take Ivan and Masha with you and take a good look at everything and come to a decision. [...]

Your A

Chekhov

March 1
Yalta

[...] If we can buy the dacha then it would be a good idea to move all the furniture you don't need out of your apartment. Masha could go there. And her cook. It's spring and the fine weather is starting. There are rooks, probably, migrant birds.

Tell Masha that mother calls Schnapps, Schwartz. He either runs round the garden or sleeps downstairs near the warm ovens and whimpers. [...]

Your A

Chekhov

March 3
Yalta

[...] If you decide to buy Tsaritsyno then have a water-closet installed, immediately. We need one, like the one in Yalta. Run the pipes through the courtyard then downwards, dig a hole the size of a large pan and cement it, put wooden planks over it, then put a lid of equal size on it and buy a pump, as in Yalta, so that the fluid flows onto the garden.

Got it? Only you must do it right away. In the autumn I'll construct a bathroom. But then, all this is dreams, dreams! [...]

Your A

Knipper

March ?
Moscow

Today I looked at two apartments and like them both. One is on Leontievski Lane, rather high but with a lift, light with a wonderful view over Moscow with two WCs, roomy and for the same price as our present home. The other is near Korsh's theatre, giving onto the courtyard, on the first floor but 32 steps all the same. No lift and costs 1350 roubles. [...] What do you think? I would opt for Leontievski Lane. It's an excellent spot. Korsh lives there and praises it. Chaliapin lives there, too. The lift is very good and works day and night, there's also the telephone under the stairs. [...]

Chekhov

March 6
Yalta

Aren't you ashamed, my little sperm whale, to write in such dreadful ink! You won't believe it, but, word of honour, I had to tear the letter from the envelope, they were so stuck together. And Masha's letters are the same, all stuck together. [...] Take the apartment in Leontievski Lane it's near to everything. I'll come for two or three days before you go to Petersburg [on tour].

Chekhov

March 8
Yalta

Sweetheart, another letter all stuck together from you today, I had to tear the plan of the apartment from the letter. Where did you get such poisonous ink? [...]

A lift will be fine, but the trouble is, with luck like mine, they're always out of order. Whenever I try them, they're being repaired. [...]

Your A

Chekhov

March 10
Yalta

Dear horseykins, you haven't wired me about your health. That's dreadful and stupid! Your postcard distressed me and here I'm now with all sorts of thoughts in my head. [...]

Do we have to forget about Tsaritsyno? [...]

Your A

Chekhov

March 12
Yalta

[...] You haven't a good word to say about Tsaritsyno. i.e., you talk about fever but I stick up for it. If the owner maintains that there's no fever where her dacha is then you should take her word for it. [...] And if we should fall ill with fever then Moscow's close by and there's no fever in winter. The main thing is you can walk to the station and there are frequent trains. [...]

A

1904

Knipper

March 14
Moscow

You blame me for not wiring you about my health, dearest, but why? It was only a cold, nothing more, why frighten you with telegrams? [...]

Chekhov

March 26
Yalta

[...] Today I heard you were going to divorce me. Is that true? Who will beat you? Who will you sleep with in the summer? Think about it first!

I'm working but not with much success. The trouble is the war[19] and in the last few days, upset bowels. People are unlikely to read because of the war. [...]

A

After the end of the Moscow season Knipper, went on tour to Petersburg as usual.

Chekhov

April 4
Yalta

Hallo, darling horseykins! I had two telegrams from Nemirovich about the success you all had in Petersburg and how the audience treated you like a first class actress. I've known for a long time that you are a great, a genuine artist, I value you highly, only, please, don't catch cold, don't tire yourself out, sleep properly. [...]

Today is Sunday, I took some powder – heroin – and I feel pleasantly calm. [...]

19. The Russo-Japanese war in which the Russians fared so disastrously. The sense of national humiliation was very deep.

I think you've fallen out of love with me. Is that true? Admit it. I love you as before and am even considering coming to see you in Petersburg. [...]

Your A

Knipper

April 5
Petersburg

[...] You've stopped talking about Tsaritsyno. Obviously you've had thoughts or Masha has been talking to you. You and Masha had better decide then, because the council isn't getting anywhere and my contribution is no use whatsoever; and you're just split down the middle and don't know who to listen to.

Chekhov

April 7
Yalta

[...] I'm alive and sort of well, apart from my upset stomach which has been going on for a week and will drive me out of Yalta earlier than I had intended. My bowels are in a general mess, they won't settle down. [...]

Your A

Chekhov

April 10
Yalta

My darling linnet, you're angry with me, you complain but truly it's not my fault. I don't remember ever talking to Masha about Tsaritsyno, I know nothing about it at all: I met Martunov, whom you talked to me about, but he has only lived in Tsaritsyino in the winter, he can only say what it is like in summer from hearsay. Besides, I don't know why, I didn't take to him. [...] To be frank, I thought you were going to deal with this business of the dacha, not me. Because in matters like that I'm worse than useless.

[...]

The weather's warm, but it's cool in the shade and the evenings are chilly. I walk listlessly because, I don't know why, I'm short of breath. [...]

I can't wait to see you, my joy. Living without you I'm less than nothing. The day is ended, thank God, no thoughts, no desires, just a game of patience and much walking up and down. I haven't been to the baths for a long time, six years, I think. I read all the papers, and it is that which has made me gloomy.

Please write as soon as you get to Petersburg. Don't forget me: think occasionally of the man you once married. I scratch your little shoulder, your little back, your little neck and kiss my little heart.

Your less than nothing

Chekhov

April 15
Yalta

[...] The fast trains have started running, so I'll leave for Moscow by the morning train, my joy. I'll come as soon as possible, i.e. May 1 as I can't stay here: indigestion, actors, audiences, the telephone and God knows what.

How are the takings? Good? I can imagine how exhausted you must be. I sit here, dreaming of fishing and wonder what I'll do with all the fish I've caught, only all I'll catch is one gudgeon with a death-wish. [...]

Chekhov

April 17
Yalta

[...] We have to make up our minds about the dacha in Tsaritsyno. It's damp, that's true, but very near Moscow, easy of access and you'll feel at home there, not like a visitor. We'll have to make your room as fine and comfortable as we can so you'll fall in love with it. [...] It's cool here in Yalta, and raining. My stomach is upset, too, and there's nothing I can do to stop it, medicine or diet. [...] I'm so short of breath!

Knipper

April 17
Petersburg

[...] You know what I suggest? Give up the Moscow apartment and take the house in Tsaritsyno for a year: it's going dirt cheap. We could probably get it for about 700 r. a year. What do you say? We could buy it. We could, it's going. Come and talk about it. I'm only afraid it's already been taken for the summer.

Chekhov

April 20
Yalta

Darling doggie, I had a letter from Sobolevski, the editor of the *Russian Bulletin* about the dacha. '[It] is in the best part of Tsaritsyno and has been built so as to make a comfortable residence the whole year round. If you want to move in, financial gain is the least of their concerns.' Further on he writes that they caught a fifty-kilo sturgeon in the local pond some years ago. I'll write to Sobolevski today to tell him you are arriving in Moscow on May 1 and that you will meet Madame Ezuchevski [the proprietor] on the 2nd or the 3rd and, in all probability, will settle matters with her. We will go there on the 5th.

I'll write one or two more letters then the machine stops. I'll leave Yalta with the greatest of pleasure: it is tedious here, there is no spring and I don't feel well. I ran to the lavatory at least five times yesterday, although I didn't eat anything out of the ordinary, I'm on a diet, plus the cough. Now I'm having my teeth seen to. [...] Life is very dull without my wife but I'm afraid to take a mistress. If, as you say, my letters aren't reaching you properly, yours are all over the place. I get them two at a time. Obviously they – my letters – are being held somewhere and read. Well, since it has to be! ...

You ask me: what is life? That is like asking: what is a carrot? A carrot is a carrot and that's all there is to it.

[...]

Be well, don't pine, don't be sad, soon you will see your husband.
[...]

Your A

Chekhov

April 22
Yalta

Sweetheart, I'm writing my last letter to you and then if need be, I'll send telegrams. I was off-colour yesterday but feel better today. All I'm eating is eggs and soup. It's raining, the weather's damp and cold. Still, today, despite the rain and being ill, I went to the dentist. [...]

Knipper, *Memoir*

In the late spring, at the end of April 1904, Chekhov came to Moscow from Yalta, fell ill and had to stay in bed, which was rare. Chekhov bore all his ills with courage, never gave in, but fought his illness. Three weeks he lay in bed in Moscow, suffering from great pain in all his muscles, especially in his legs (he suffered from diarrhoea). Doctor Taube, who was treating him, suggested that he should go to Badenweiler, a clinic for chest diseases in the Black Forest. Chekhov could stay in a hotel, or a private apartment as he would not hear of a sanatorium – that seemed to him to be the end of everything.

In early June, we went to Berlin where we stayed for a few days so we could consult a famous professor, Dr Ewald, who could do no more than stand up, shrug his shoulders, say farewell and depart. I'll never forget Chekhov's gentle, bewildered smile. It made a striking impression. In Berlin Chekhov met Iollis[20] for the first time, talked to him a long time and found him a sympathetic companion. His visit did something to alleviate the gloomy impression left by the doctor's visit.

In Badenweiler, Chekhov seemed at first to improve, he would walk round the house – he was very breathless, from slight emphysema; we went for a drive almost every day. Our doctor, Dr Schwörer was a kind person and a friend. Obviously he knew that Chekhov's state of health was critical but he treated him with exceptional gentleness, care and affection. And Chekhov who usually hated doctor's visits, so much so that our doctor at home, Dr Altschuler always had to find some pretext or other to hide the real reason for his visits –

20. A Russian newspaper correspondent.

as I say, Chekhov always received Schwörer without a murmur, while he, on his side, often made it seem like a friendly visit. Three weeks into our stay we changed quarters twice. There were a lot of smart people at the Hotel 'Römerbad' and we moved to the bottom floor of a private villa so that Chekhov could go out by himself and sit in the morning sun. He would wait impatiently for the postman bringing letters and newspapers. He was very worked up by the progress of the war with Japan. We then moved to the Hotel 'Sommer' and a very sunny room. He started to feel warmer, better, had lunch and dinner downstairs every day at our own table. He spent a long time in the garden, or sat on his balcony watching the small-town life of Badenweiler with great interest. Three days before his death he said he wanted a white flannel suit and jokingly accused me of dressing my husband badly. When I told him one could not buy a suit here, like a schoolboy he asked me to go to the nearest town of Freiburg and order a good one to measure. The trip took the whole day so that he was alone and as usual went down to lunch and dinner. Just as I got back he was coming out of the dining-room evidently pleased at his own independence and was delighted when I told him his suit would be ready in three days.

The weather turned hot. The next morning [30th], as he was going down the corridor he became very breathless, came back to our room, very anxious, and asked to change rooms for something with windows facing north and in two hours we were in our new room, on the top floor, with a fine view over the mountains and the forest.

The penultimate night was dreadful. It was hot and storm followed storm. It was stifling. In the night Chekhov asked me to open the door to the balcony and the window but it was uncanny opening it because there was a thick white mist as high as our floor and it filled the room with its fantastic, ever-changing shapes the whole night. The electric light was off as it hurt Chekhov's eyes, there was only one candle-end burning and I was terrified it would not last till dawn and the clouds of mist stole everywhere and it was particularly eerie when the candle died and then sprang to life again ... I took a book and pretended to read so that Chekhov wouldn't know I hadn't slept and had been keeping watch when he woke up. 'What are you reading?' he asked as he came round. One of his books was open at *A Strange Story*. I told him what it was. He smiled and said, weakly 'Little idiot, who takes their husband's books away with them?' and once again lapsed into oblivion. When I put ice on his heart, he pushed it away weakly and murmured indistinctly: 'An empty heart needs no ice.'

I waited impatiently for morning and for Dr Schwörer to come. I felt I would go to pieces if I had to go through another night like that. Chekhov was better, even took some gruel and asked us to put him in the armchair by the window.

At dusk I went to the chemists for oxygen and Anton told me to go for a swim in the pool, to take a walk in the park and get some air as I had not been out of the room for days. When I returned and saw his gentle smiling face and felt calmer, as though the worst was over after that terrible night. I missed the gong for dinner because we were talking but a servant brought me up something to eat and then Anton began to make up a story about an expensive health spa where a group of overweight, rich English and Americans gathered after an exhausting day of all kinds of sporting activities, greedily looking forward to a copious meal only to discover – horror of horrors! – the chef has run off, he described the effect this disaster would have on all these pampered, overweight people. Anton told the story so wonderfully I laughed with all my heart. He asked me to remove his pillows, lay down and as usual said with a smile: 'You see, I'm better today, I'm not so short of breath.'

About one, he woke up. He was in pain which made it difficult to lie down, he felt sick with pain, he was 'in torment' and for the first time in his life asked for a doctor... It was eerie. But the feeling that something positive had to be done and quickly made me gather all my strength. I woke up Lev Rabenek, a Russian student living in the hotel and asked him to go for the doctor.

Dr Schwörer came and gently, caringly started to say something, cradling Anton in his arms. Anton sat up unusually straight and said loudly and clearly (although he knew almost no German): *Ich sterbe.*[21] The doctor calmed him, took a syringe, gave him an injection of camphor, and ordered champagne. Anton took a full glass, examined it, smiled at me and said: 'It's a long time since I drank champagne.' He drained it, lay quietly on his left side and I just had time to run to him and lean across the bed, and call to him, but he had stopped breathing and was sleeping peacefully as a child...

21. I am dying.

Widow

After Chekhov's death, Olga Knipper kept a diary for some two months, consisting of imaginary letters to him.

August 19

At last I am able to write to you, Anton, my dear, my sweet, so near and yet so far! I don't know where you are now. I've been waiting a long time for the day when I could write to you. Today, I went to Moscow and visited your grave ... How splendid it is, if you only knew. After the arid south everything here seems so lush, so scented, so fragrant, it smells of earth and fresh grass, the trees make such a gentle sound. I can't believe you are not among the living! I need desperately to write to you, to tell you everything I have been through since your final illness and that moment when your heart stopped beating, your poor, sick, worn-out heart.

Now that I am actually writing to you, it seems strange but I have a quite irrational desire to do so. And as I write to you, I feel you are alive, out there somewhere, waiting for a letter. Dearest darling, my sweet love, let me speak some words of tenderness, let me stroke your soft, silky hair and look into your dear, shining, loving eyes.

If only I knew whether you felt you were going to die. I think you did, vaguely perhaps, but you did. On June 29, when you were feeling very ill, you told me to get Iollos to send the last of our money from Berlin and to write to him to do it in my name. I wasn't comfortable about it but you were adamant. Then you told me to write to Masha and I did so immediately. We parted on bad terms in May, when she left; but I gave my word to write to her every day and so I did but then stopped. Did you know the way things were between us? Jealousy, pure and simple. We love each other very much but she felt I was taking everything away from her – her home, you – and was behaving like some sacrificial victim. At first I tried to explain, talked a great deal, did all I could to convince her, begged her; if only you knew how many tears I shed! But nothing was of any avail and in the end I gave up. If only she knew how often we talked [on our honeymoon] in Aksionov, remember, about her not feeling left out in the cold. In Yalta, I never behaved as though it were my house, or had any inclination to, but always considered it *her* home, and so I was very hurt to hear her say that she had no home, no place to call her own, no garden. Dear God, why did it all have to turn out this way? [...] It didn't work from the very first day. If my hopes had been fulfilled, I would probably have given up the theatre ... But I felt right away that I wouldn't have a full life there, in complete harmony. Oh how I tried those six weeks in Yalta! But it was all so complicated, like some church ritual.

August 20

Darling. I have just come back from seeing your brother, Ivan. I upset him by telling him about your last days but I felt it was good for him, even if it was distressing. And I could talk about everything, about you for ever, about Badenweiler, about something great, grand that occurred in that rich, emerald-green town in the Black Forest.

Do you remember how we loved our carriage rides, our 'Rundreise', as we called them? You were so affectionate, I understood you so well at times like that. Do you remember how you would discreetly take my hand and squeeze it, and when I asked if you were all right, you would say nothing, just nod and give me a smile for an answer. With what reverence I sometimes kissed your hand! You would hold my hand for a long time and so we drove through a fragrant pine wood. Your favourite spot was a lush, green glade, filled with sunlight. A stream babbled splendidly along a ditch and you kept telling the driver to drive more quietly, taking delight in a large expanse of fruit trees that stood in the open and weren't fenced in, and no one took or stole a single cherry or pear. You recalled our own, poor Russia... Do you remember the charming mill, so low it was completely hidden in the thick greenery and only the water sparkled on the wheel? How you liked the comfortable, clean villages and little gardens with the regulation rows of white lilies, rose bushes and kitchen gardens! And with what pain you said: 'Dearest, when will our peasant farmers live in little houses like these!'

Dearest, dearest one, where are you now?

For a time in Yalta, I could feel you everywhere, in the air, the grass, the murmuring of the wind. When I was out walking, it seemed your light transparent figure was walking with me, stick in hand, sometimes close to, sometimes far away, leaving no trace on the ground, in a bluish mountain haze. And now I feel your head next to my cheek.

August 24

It's so long since I wrote to you, my dear. I've been so shattered by the evening that I haven't even been able to pick up a pen.

[...] On Sunday morning I went to the Novodevichi cemetery. My heart beats with joy so each time the monastery turrets come into view. As though I were going to meet you and you were waiting for me. I wept so on your grave! I could have spent hours on my knees, burying my head in the earth, in the green grass on the mound in which you lie...My own one, where are you?

Today I finally plucked up courage and went to the theatre. I got as far as the office and burst into tears. Meeting friends was difficult. I sat and listened to a rehearsal of *Les Aveugles*[1] – watched rather than listened. [...] Luzhski tried to bring me out of myself by telling funny stories. It seemed strange to me that they should all be talking and walking in the same old way.

The family lunched with me, Vanya and Sonya. There was heated, wild talk about the war but I just couldn't listen. It caused you such pain, my own one. How often we read the German papers and how hard it was for me to translate the cruel things that were written about Russia, when I knew how hurtful it would be to you. This horror must come to an end quickly. But when it will end, no one knows.

In the evening there was a discussion about *Ivanov*. Nemirovich made a few introductory remarks and then talked about the individual characters.

Yesterday I went back to the monastery with Kostya. I'd like to go every day. Yesterday I bought a bench and had it sent to the graveside so I can sit there.

Yesterday, at mother's, I met Rabenek, the student who was with me all the time at Badenweiler. He's a splendid young man.

August 27

I haven't written to you for two days, my heart, but it seems like an eternity.

I went to the rehearsal of *Ivanov*. The atmosphere is very sour, they're all idiots, no one is coming alive. Times, of course, are

1. One of Chekhov's last recommendations to the Art Theatre was to stage Maeterlinck.

difficult. Your death, the war, oh this terrible war. Is Uncle Sasha still alive?

I am terribly alone, my dearest one.

I live my life as though you were coming to me once more, looking at me with your wonderful, shining eyes, stroking me, calling me your doggie ... My darling, where are you?

I have turned your study into my sitting-room, it's terribly cosy. Masha will go into our large bedroom and my bedroom will be what was Masha's study. She's a horror, she rarely writes to me although she promised she would every day, I keep my word and write to her often.

I was at your grave at dusk today, at 7. It was quiet, lovely, the only sound was the birds flitting from tree to tree and you could hear the steps of the monks hurrying past and see their shadowy figures. There are ever-burning icon-lamps all round. There is one on your grave and it seems to warm my heart. I wept and kissed the grass on your grave. The bench is here now and I can sit. In imagination I went back to Badenweiler and tried once more to understand what happened. Dearest, I should tell you everything but, for the moment, I can't ...

When I saw the student [Rabenek] I relived through every moment of that dreadful night painfully. I even heard the crunch of his feet on the gravel in the middle of that amazing, majestic, terrible night, when he ran to fetch the doctor.

But there is no death.

Of that later ...

The staging of Act I of *Ivanov* is ready. [...]

August 30

Days pass, nights pass with scarcely any difference between them. Another mass of wonderful roses and gladioli from Krasni, again anonymously. These flowers touch me.

My dearest heart of gold, I wrote to you and I feel we are only momentarily parted. Masha arrives on the 2nd.

How depressing, how inexpressibly difficult the time in Yalta was. I just kept to your rooms, I was upset and went through and arranged your things. Everything is where it should be. Mother lit the lamp in your bedroom. That was what I wanted. In the evenings I could wander through your darkened study and the light from your lamp would glimmer through the fretted door. I waited for you, every evening I waited to see you in your place. I even spoke to you out loud and my voice was lost in the room. In the morning, Masha and I went shopping as usual. I was in no hurry to get back home... There was no one waiting for me to begin his morning wash, no one awaiting my return in bed with his sly face, cocking a snook or two at me. It was the same every morning. It was all so happy, I kissed you, caressed you, so you would feel the freshness of the sea and the charm of an early morning swim with me. How grand you looked, lying there. I admired you and you talked nonsense and made me laugh.

The garden is in a sorry state this summer, everything has withered. Not a drop of rain or water. Arseni, the lazy bones has gone, and now Onufri has made the garden look decent. He dug a ditch round every tree and they have been watered.

Today we finally had a telegram from Uncle Sasha, saying that he's alive and 'kicking'. I have just come from mother's where I found Uncle Sasha's landlords (Officer Gretman and his wife). They are very fond of him and talked a great deal about him. The telegram came from Mukden.

Yesterday I saw a run-through of Maeterlinck's *Les Aveugles*. It doesn't exactly take your breath away at the moment but it's interesting [...]

September 11

Dearest darling sweetheart, it's so long since we had a chat. I've been so unkempt, so overwrought you wouldn't have liked me at all. I feel as though I am on my knees before you, leaning my head against your breast, hearing your heart, and you are tenderly stroking me. Anton, where are you? Are we really never to see each other again? It cannot be. Our life together was just starting and suddenly it came to an end, abruptly, for ever. How glorious our life was together! You always used to say one could live so well 'as married people'. I believe that so blindly, I shall live with you a long, long time ... A few days before your death, we were talking and dreaming of the little girl we should have had. I was so sick at heart there was no child to leave behind. We talked a great deal about it. My child would have been two in November if disaster hadn't struck. Why did it happen? The child would have won me over, I know. How you would have loved it! Just think!

The theatre, the theatre ... I don't know whether to love it or wish it to hell. It is so delightfully muddled. Now it's all I have left in life. These last three years have been one long struggle for me. I have lived in a constant state of self-reproach. That's why I was so anxious, nervy and couldn't settle anywhere, curl up in my nest. I acted against my own conscience. Still, who knows – if I had given up the theatre...

Knipper survived Chekhov by some fifty-five years. She never remarried.